INTRODUCTION

MATTHEW McLENDON

Garbage, trash, waste, detritus, junk, refuse, crap, rubbish, cast-off, debris, scrap, dross, spam—

these are but a few of the words commonly used to describe that which has been discarded, or is no longer useful.

Each of those words carries its own connotations and slang uses. Garbage is bulky, weighty, smelly; it is a heterogeneous miasma of the organic and inorganic. Trash, on the other hand, is something completely different. It is light, more homogeneous—possibly paper, or leaves; it is not necessarily repugnant in the way that garbage tends to be. Neither trash nor garbage is as offensive, as *abject* to use Julia Kristeva's term, as waste. Waste is human—more specifically, it is the residue of the human, what is left behind in the sewers for rats and other unsavory, and preferably unmentionable, denizens of the putrid.

This very casual word play only hints at the multi-valiancy of a word, or group of words, used to name, isolate, and describe what may be argued as, after death, the greatest commonality of the human experience—our production of garbage, of leftovers. We are, and always have been to varying degrees, surrounded by what we have discarded—now more so than ever. Yet, what is trash? Is the maxim that one man's trash is another man's treasure true? In her survey of trash and its uses in predominately European art of the twentieth century, Gillian Whitely points out that "attempts to define trash lead back to a fundamental link to systems of value which are time and place specific. There is no material which is intrinsically trash. Indeed, it is a social and culturally constructed concept—the word, like its physical manifestation, is in a continually shifting state of conceptual, symbolic, and material flux."[1] So, the unwanted email that clogs our inboxes today, pejoratively known as "spam," would have been valued in those first heady days, when as new email users we longed for the dulcet tones of "you've got mail." On a more serious note, Whitely is right in highlighting the temporal aspect of what we consider garbage. The museums of the world are populated with the discarded shards, bowls, decorations, and tools of antiquity. Their rubbish becomes our archaeology, transformed and elevated through the patina of time.

The exhibition that accompanies this catalogue presents work by contemporary artists who regularly employ cast-off or discarded materials. Keeping in mind the above discussion of the cultural and temporal specificity of these notions, the artists presented, except for one notable exception (the Ghanaian-born, Nigerian-based artist El Anatsui), are working in the United States. Their work is truly contemporary, as it was created within the last few years or, in the case of

previous spread: El Anatsui, *Alter Ego*, 2012

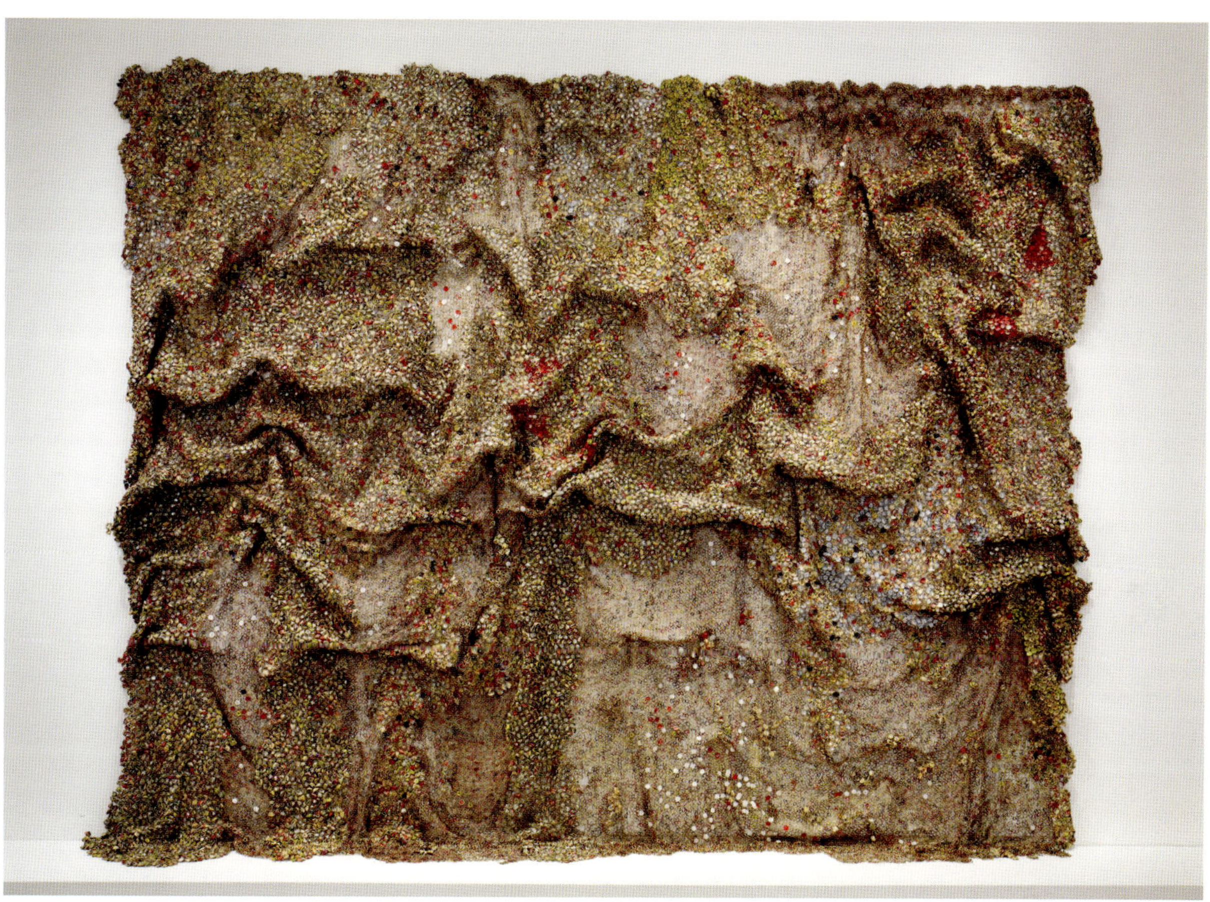

Jill Sigman, specifically for the exhibition. This is in no way intended as an exhaustive overview of artists who have or are currently working in this manner. Rather, this is intended as an entrée into an important contemporary practice with roots in some of the most vanguard artistic ruptures of the last century.

El Anatsui is included in this exhibition for two reasons. The first is that a viewing of his work a number of years ago was the catalyst for my interest in this subject. On a rainy day in New York I took refuge in the Metropolitan Museum of Art hoping to wait out the weather. It was a particularly rare moment in that I was not visiting the museum with an agenda. I was not there to meet a colleague, or see a specific exhibition. I was afforded that all-too-rare experience (for everyone, including, strangely, curators) of looking at art without a deadline. After wandering the galleries I rounded a corner and was confronted with El Anatsui's magisterial work *Dusasa II*. It measures some twenty-four feet wide and nineteen feet tall, yet, because of its material—thousands of discarded bottle caps and liquor bottle seals meticulously woven together with copper wire—it appears ethereal, diaphanous, almost as though the air itself has been painted

El Anatsui, *Dusasa II*, 2007

what is a profoundly important movement within contemporary practice. This exhibition and catalogue will, I hope, help to focus attention on this issue.

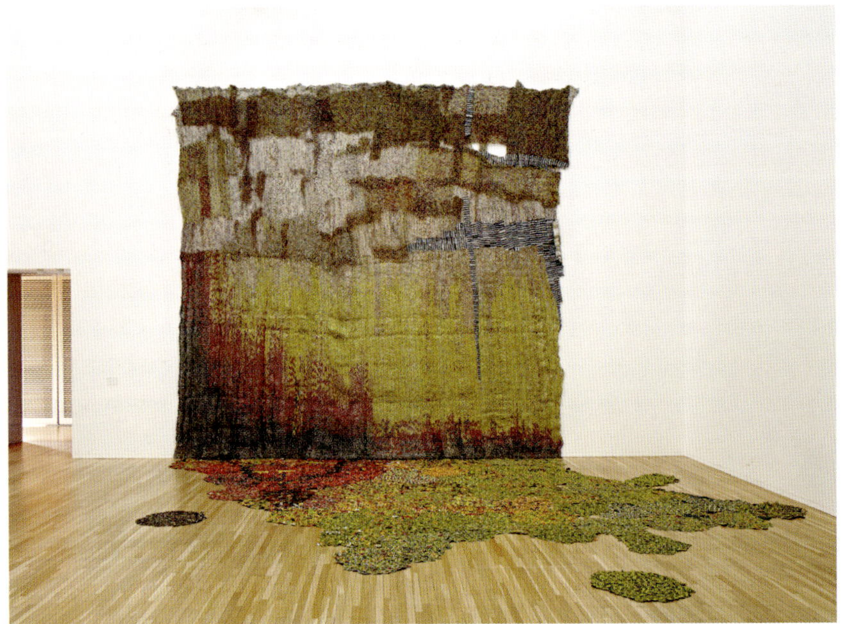

I include this personal story about my encounter with El Anatsui's work because it highlights some of the key issues explored in the exhibition and this catalogue. *Dusasa II*, according to the Met's website can be translated as a "communal patchwork made by a team of townspeople." Much of the work included here has some aspect of the communal, usually in the gathering of materials. The source material for the works is discarded and, more importantly, transformed so that in some cases, such as the work of Aurora Robson, those items are no longer identifiable. The title for the exhibition, *Re:Purposed,* resulted from a debate with students in two seminars that I taught; in the beginning, the working title was simply "Garbage." Frankly, I had Dada-fueled dreams of hanging banners on the pink Italianate palace façade of The Ringling with that title in an act of schoolboy provocation. However, my students, rightly so, were vehement in their opinions that even though "garbage art," or "trash art," had precedent in the literature, those terms were inaccurate taxonomies that bordered on derisive. The one word that was used repeatedly in these classes, and the only one that seemed to adequately convey the process of creating art from detritus, was "repurposed." This has proven to be a wise choice, as the artists themselves repeatedly used the word when discussing their practice and it differentiates the process from two other terms in frequent use, recycle and upcycle, both heavily laden with environmental connotations.

and sculpted. I stood there in awe, as I am sure most visitors who are lucky enough to see this work do. The transformation of the lowly, the disregarded—the bottle cap—into a work of such significance, transfixed me. I began to learn more about El Anatsui's work and his engagement with postcolonial discourse through the use of soda or liquor bottles, which for him symbolize European colonization of Africa and the continuing European influence on that continent. His work is also included because, through several notable exhibitions in this country, most importantly the exhibition of monumental works at the Akron Art Museum and the Brooklyn Museum, El Anatsui typifies the global contemporary artist, one whose practice may be rooted in a specific location, but whose influence and reception is global. Trash, after all, is a global experience.[2] El Anatsui's work led me to look at a number of other contemporary artists working with garbage. While there was no shortage of material to view and artists to meet, I was immediately challenged by a dearth of scholarly material on

El Anatsui, *Garden Wall*, 2011

FROM DUCHAMP TO GARBAGE: A SHORT DISCUSSION ON THE ANTECEDENTS OF THIS PRACTICE

The exhibition also grew out of a desire to engage with a small but important subcollection within The Ringling: Marcel Duchamp's four 1964 edition Readymades. The use of garbage—the quotidian products that we dispose of—as an artistic medium surely has its origins in Duchamp's rupture of Western art history when in 1913 he joined an ordinary bicycle wheel with a stool and produced his first Readymade sculpture. If we take Duchamp at his word, the 1913 "discovery" was for him just a distraction at the time, the significance of which would not become apparent until two years later after he left Europe for America. Beyond this, Duchamp insisted on the necessity of "indifference" in the selection of the Readymade. In his conversation with Pierre Cabanne he stated: "It's very difficult to choose an object, because, at the end of fifteen days, you begin to like it or to hate it. You have to approach something with an indifference, as if you had no aesthetic emotion. The choice of Readymades is always based on visual indifference and, at the same time, on the total absence of good or bad taste."[3] Much later, when speaking of the intended effect of the Readymades, he said, "The main point is disorientation for the spectator . . . according to the observer's imagination, he can go into any field or any form of imagination and association of ideas he wants, depending on his own reactions."[4] The Readymade, through the juxtaposition and recontextualization of the everyday object, then, was to serve as a catalyst for imagination; an object free from strictures of aesthetic theory or choice, and, most importantly for Duchamp, from taste. The Readymade, however, was almost always a single object, and while it certainly broke ground for the artists featured here, the critical bridge between them and Duchamp can be found in the work of mid-twentieth-century Assemblagists.

In 1961, William C. Seitz, the recently appointed associate curator at The Museum of Modern Art, New York, mounted what would be both a controversial and groundbreaking exhibition: *The Art of Assemblage.*[5] Aiming to be encyclopedic in scope with more than 250 works, though with notable exclusions, Seitz presented art that was for him an extension of the other great rupture in Western art of the modern period—collage. The majority of the exhibition consisted of contemporary work, yet many important Dada, Surrealist, and Futurist precursors were included to enable a discussion of lineage. Duchamp was represented in the exhibition (and corresponding symposium) with thirteen works, many of which are now considered his most famous. In choosing the word "assemblage" to describe the works exhibited, Seitz hoped for a "designation not only more embracing, but also more indicative of the mediating principles which they demonstrate." He then identified two commonalities of the vast majority of the works selected: "1) They are predominately *assembled* rather than painted, drawn, modeled, or carved. 2) Entirely, or in part, their constituent elements are preformed natural or manufactured materials, objects, or fragments not intended as art materials."[6]

Throughout his catalogue, Seitz stressed the genealogical links between the early twentieth-century European avant-garde and assemblage while noting, "although in its structure assemblage is like abstract painting and constructivist sculpture, it diverges sharply from these traditions not only because its raw elements are associationally "charged," preformed, and often precisely identifiable (nails, photographs, old letters, weathered wood, automobile parts, leaves, doll's eyes, stones, or whatever), but also because its ultimate configurations are so often less predetermined."[7] The recognizability of the constituent elements is one of the

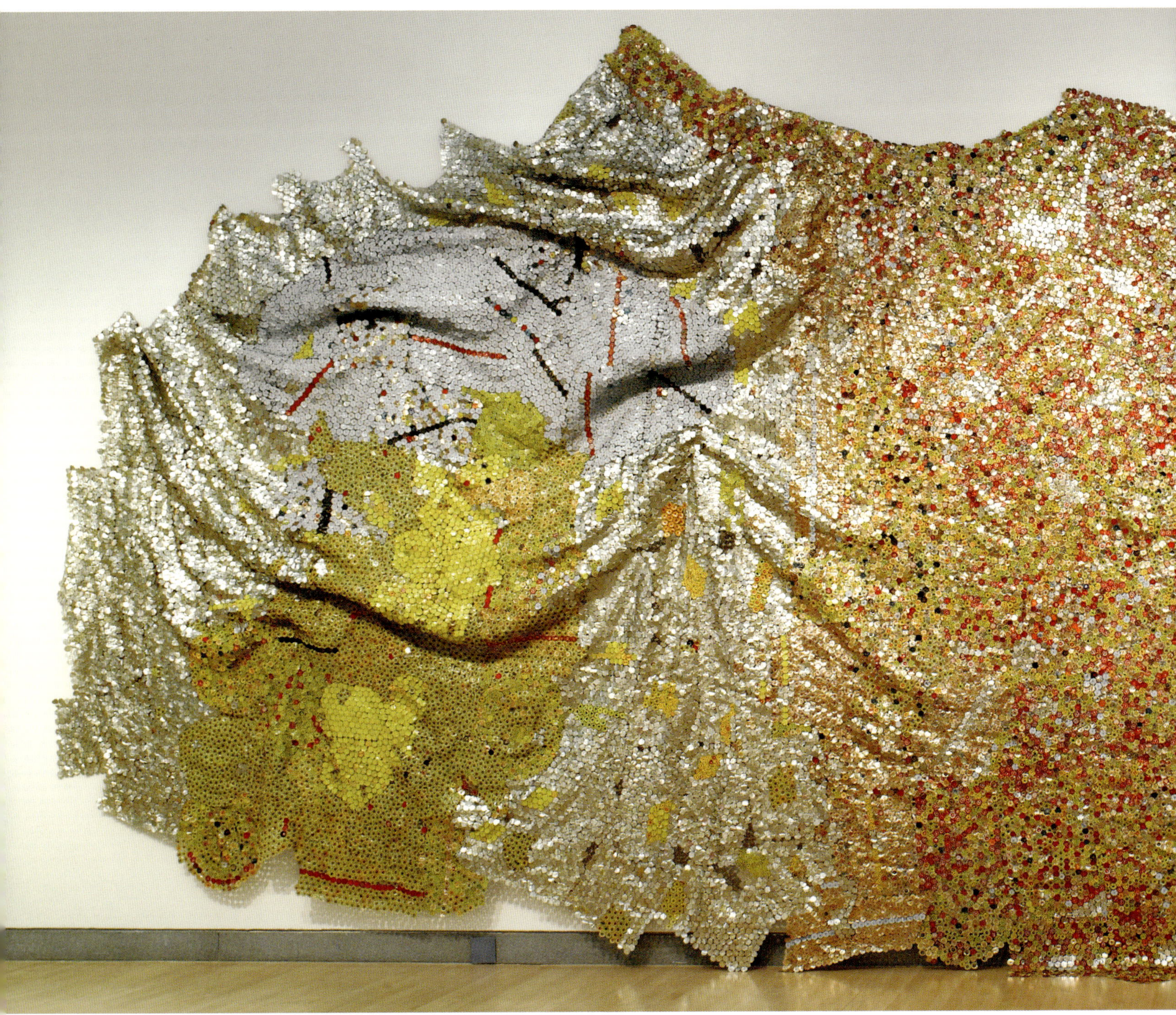

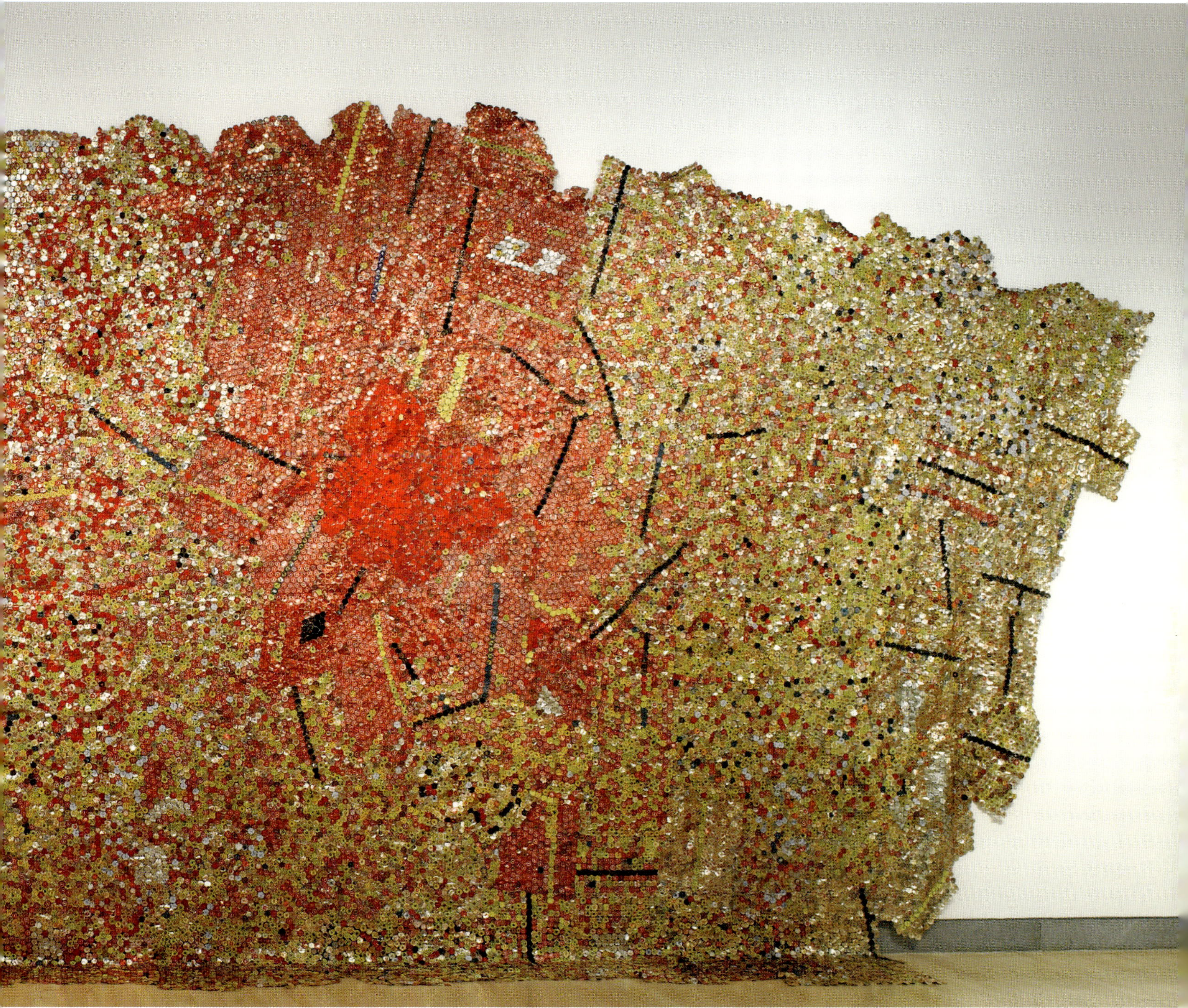

El Anatsui, *Gravity and Grace*, 2010

main criteria Seitz used in the selection of his checklist.[8] Further, he stressed the importance of the juxtaposition of these objects within the work.

The "precisely identifiable" quality of the assembled objects is one of the main connections between mid-century assemblage and artists who work with garbage today. The work of Nick Cave, Jill Sigman, Mac Premo, Vanessa German, Matt Eskuche, Daniel Rozin, and Emily Noelle Lambert to a lesser degree, all rely on the recognizability of the media. El Anatsui, Aurora Robson, and Alyce Santoro each transform their source material until it is almost unrecognizable. This tension between the recognizable and the unrecognizable is one of the important aspects of a contemporary practice that is a continuation and elaboration of Assemblagist heritage. Each of these artists, to varying degrees, experiments with a recontextualization of materials that allows for one of the most "associationally charged" artistic resources—garbage—to be repurposed and recategorized into any number of denotative slippages. Seitz linked assemblage to poetry—in particular Beat poetry—for this very reason. It is not simply that these artists are using found objects, but specifically and intentionally that they are employing the lowest of those items—those that have been discarded. That concept opens up the practice to a wide assortment of socio-political and institutional critiques that are perhaps more pressing in 2015 than they were in 1961. Arguing for a broadening of the canon through a "polycentric aesthetics," Ella Shohat and Robert Stam look to the reclamation of garbage as the "strategic redemption of the marginal," and see it as a way of linking marginalized, often non-Western practice to the history of the European avant-garde in a provocative and, ultimately, encompassing dialogue.[9]

In selecting the word "assemblage," Seitz also privileges the act of making over the object.[10] Anna Dezeuze and others link assemblage to *bricolage,* an act that Claude Lévi-Strauss most famously theorized in 1962. In his anthropological study *The Savage Mind*, Lévi-Strauss uses the image of the *bricoleur* as an example of pre-scientific, or mythical, thought based on direct observation, as opposed to the "scientist" and scientific thought, which sought to explain the imperceptible and is therefore abstract. In short, "the scientist [creates] events (changing the world) by means of structures and the 'bricoleur' [creates] structures by means and events."[11] For Lévi-Strauss the *bricoleur* "'speaks' not only *with* things . . . but also through the medium of things."[12] Dezeuze then extends the act of *bricolage* to argue that "assemblage presented itself as the privileged expression of a new consumer subject whose every identity was defined through an increasingly accelerated cycle of acquisition and disposal of objects."[13] In this way, assemblage is read as critique of consumerism embodied in the notion, and more importantly the act, of the *bricoleur*, the repurposing of waste. Manufacture through labor is upended by creation through the collection of that which has been deemed worthless. Here, we come full circle back to Duchamp and perhaps the most destabilizing criticism inherent in the Readymade—the disassociation of value from labor.

In the creation of the Readymade, Duchamp not only ruptured the canonical dialectic of high and low art but he also forfeited one of the cornerstones of what had been used to judge high art, intense labor over time. As much as it was an extension of the radicalism of collage, assemblage was also a backlash against hierarchical modes of postwar art, namely abstract painting. Coming to prominence in the postwar economic and consumer boom, the use of found objects as the literal building blocks of elaborate constructions was a perfect "temporalization of the object" in order to critique a late-capitalist society.[14] Value was created not from the manufactured, but from the waste of the manufactured. Assemblage of the 1960s short-circuited the value system just as its inheritors do today. Yet, artists who repurpose the discarded do so knowingly in this long shadow and are therefore able to incorporate this critique inherent to the material while extending it in numerous other directions as well, three of which will be outlined here.

IDENTITY, INDEX, AND ENVIRONMENT

While the incorporation of junk into a work of art carries with it the implicit rupture of labor creating value as outlined above, the artists presented here may be viewed as predominately engaged with the broader discourses of identity, index, and environment. For the purposes of this brief introduction each artist will be discussed within the parameters of one of those contexts. However, like the practice of *bricolage*, each ultimately crosses barriers or falls into the spaces between.

IDENTITY:
NICK CAVE, EL ANATSUI, VANESSA GERMAN, AND DANIEL ROZIN

How better to define an individual or culture than by that which is discarded? In the creation of his *Soundsuits*, Nick Cave develops a new skin, a new identity—one that is relieved of the cultural associations of race, class, and gender. As an African American gay man, Cave has spoken of being doubly discarded by society. Therefore, the *Soundsuits* enable the wearer to step out of a prejudicial environment and into a creative act of persona making. In her "power figures," Vanessa German elevates the forgotten lives of her neighborhood by ennobling the seemingly insignificant objects they have left behind. The items become literal stand-ins for linking her works to centuries-old metaphysical practice. As the only self-taught artist in the exhibition, she also opens an important space for a consideration of those who have come up outside the academy. El Anatsui may also be seen as a bridge figure. Trained in Africa by European teachers, his use of the discarded calls attention to a vital post-colonial discourse, one that continues to play out across the countries of Africa and other formerly colonized lands that, arguably, remain colonized in cultural ways. His bottle caps and liquor bottle seals simultaneously reference the past and present identities. In *Trash Mirror #3*, Daniel Rozin uses garbage as a mirror, literally. The viewer is embodied in the discarded, and the participatory nature of the work underscores the active construction of identity.

INDEX:
MAC PREMO, ALYCE SANTORO, AND EMILY NOELLE LAMBERT

Index closely follows the idea of identity. The indexical nature of garbage is self-evident. It presents a record of both the individual and the larger society. The notion of "object biography" becomes a critical method through which to explore this work. Coming from archaeology, object biography allows that, just like people, objects accumulate meaning through time and changing circumstances.[15] In Mac Premo's *The Dumpster Project* it is a particularly personal index. The works comprising his cabinet of curiosities come from Premo's former studio. Some are personal mementos; others are discarded elements that were collected. All were about to become garbage before Premo decided to create this work. Alyce Santoro's sound collages, which combine the personal with the universal, are literally woven into her sonic fabric. These "philosoprops" of time and place are made archival in the discarded audiotape that is now considered obsolete.

While Emily Noelle Lambert's "found form" sculpture may not at first appear indexical, each constituent piece recalls a story and a place for the artist. Through the recombination of elements in the "soup" of her studio, Lambert's practice mirrors the very nature of the material that has been part of any number of combinations and juxtapositions over time.

ENVIRONMENT: AURORA ROBSON, JILL SIGMAN, AND MATT ESKUCHE

Environmental issues are perhaps the first things that come to mind in a time when garbage has been rehabilitated, and freegans and eco-warriors maintain their own spheres of cool. Each of these artists, however, approaches notions of the environment obliquely. Aurora Robson used her childhood nightmares as the source material for the sculptures and installations for which she is best known. The PET (polyethylene terephthalate) plastic bottles with which she constructs these works are transformed to such a degree that they are unrecognizable, producing a tension between contemporary practice and Seitz's definition of assemblage practice.[16] While the detrimental environmental impact of plastics is an important aspect to the overall nature of her work, Robson is quick to point out that it is art first; the environmental message is a byproduct. Choreographer Jill Sigman explores notions of sustainability and community through her *Hut Project* series of installations and performances.[17] Created as "outposts" of discussion, the huts, which feature location-specific detritus, operate in a liminal space between dance, performance art, community organization, and environmental activism. Following in a tradition of artists such as Claes Oldenberg and Jud Nelson, Matt Eskuche's glass sculptures approach an unparalleled mimesis. In his *White Trash* series,

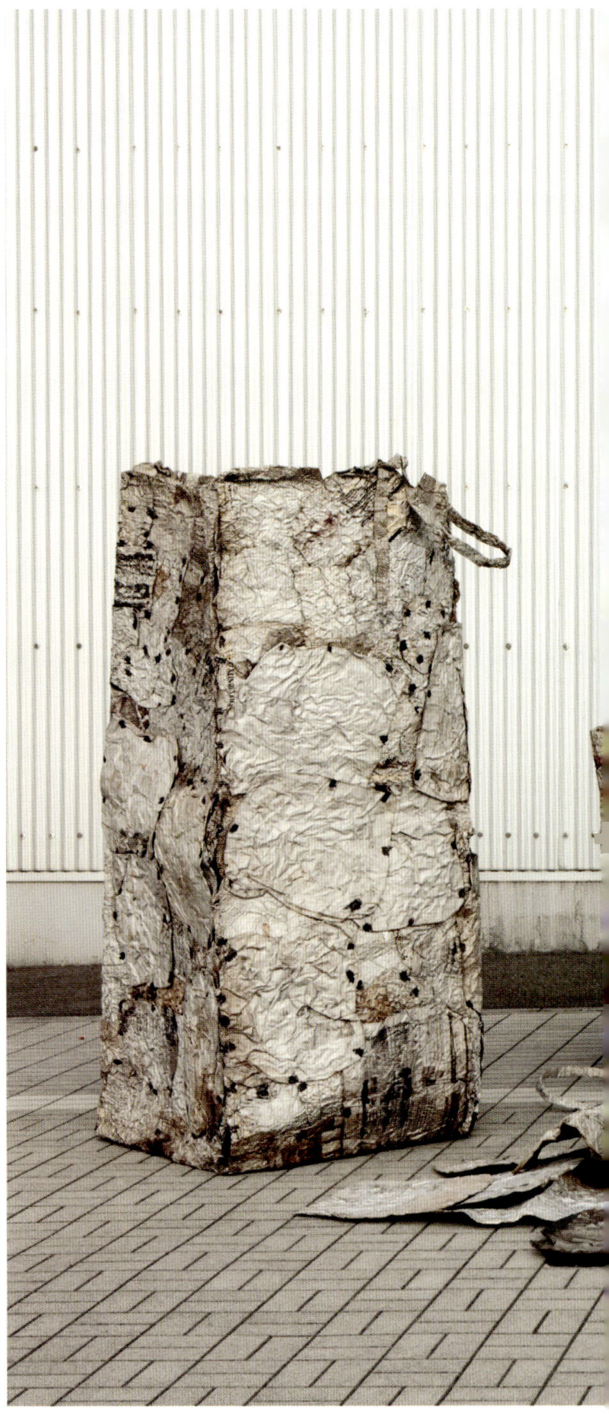

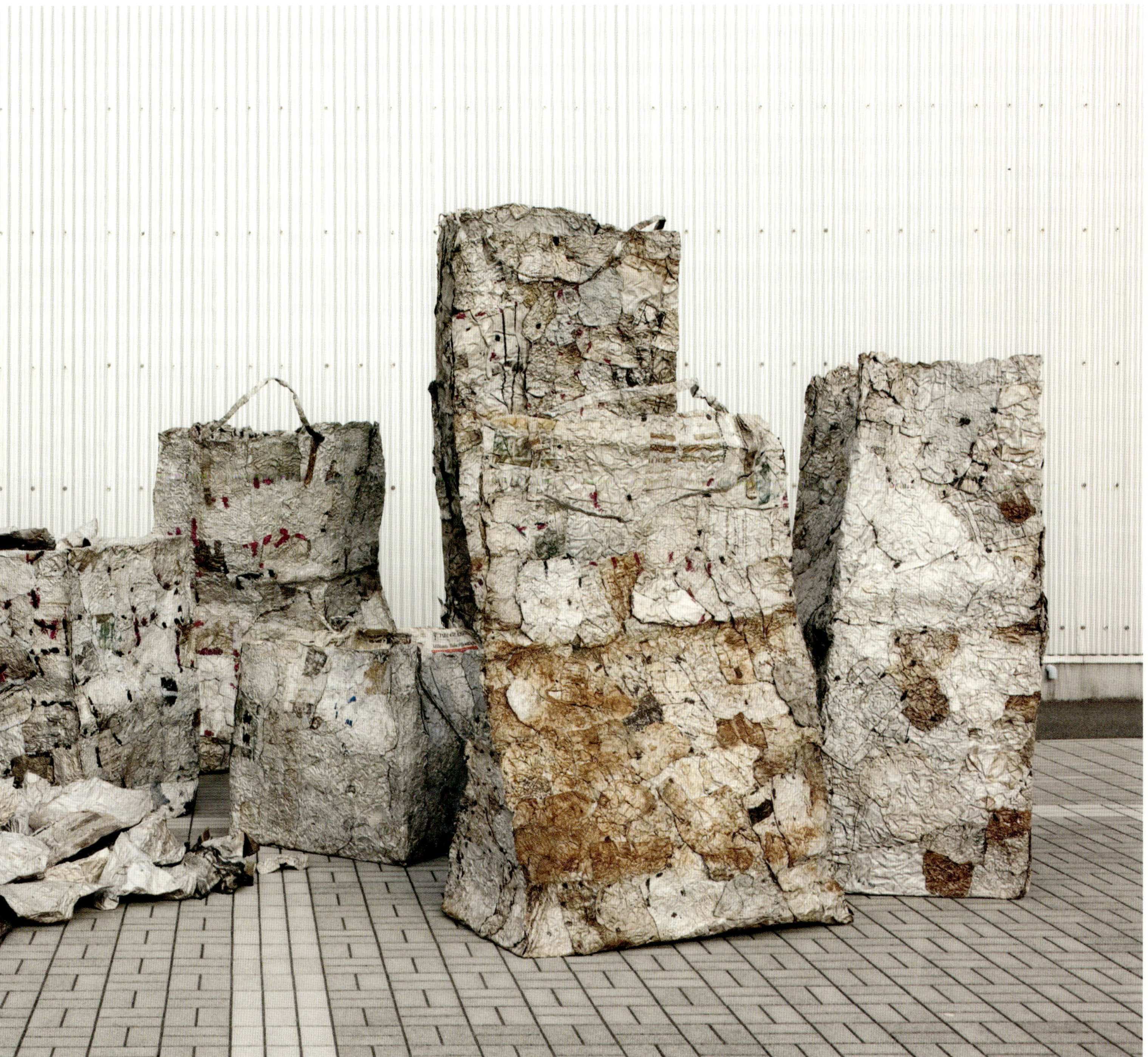

El Anatsui, *Waste Paper Bags*, 2004–10

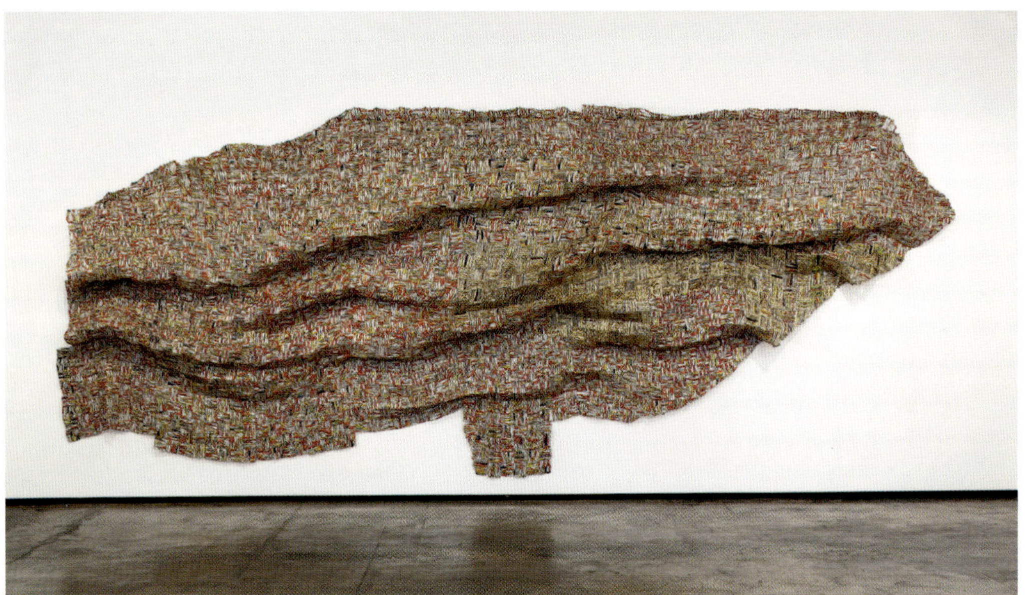

Eskuche executes what might be viewed as a pessimistic act of nihilism, the creation of the simulacra of garbage. His perfectly rendered water bottles, coffee cups, and beer cans force the viewer to consider a late-capitalist society in which manufacturing and consumerism are so hyperbolic that we are faced with such abundance and now have the substitute for refuse.

As stated above, while the artists in this catalogue have been grouped in discreet categories, they, like the objects themselves, *combine*, *juxtapose*, and *bricolage* these discourses within the works, echoing the material history of the constituent parts. Jill Sigman certainly should be discussed in terms of the index, and Mac Premo is definitely constructing an identity, et cetera. These broad categories of identity, index, and environment demonstrate that they are, in fact, intersecting methods of approaching a contemporary experience built upon obsolescence and impermanence. It seems almost facile to remark that garbage is all around us. At best, societies use it as a rallying point for environmental action, at worst, it is completely ignored, pushed further and further away in both time and geography. In some ways, garbage is the most intangible of concrete realities because of its ubiquity. It is so great, it is unfathomable. Yet, we discard in ever greater quantities and forms. Thirty years ago the virtual garbage of spam was unknown, but now it clogs the arteries of the of the cyber realm just as printed junk mail clogs our postal system. We "unfriend" people in social media, discarding them with an unparalleled nonchalance. We delete memories with the stroke of a key. "Trash TV" and "trash reading" are celebrated forms of mental recreation. All serve to further the divide, both physically and mentally, between us and our waste. It is either out of sight, out of mind, or it is "virtual" and therefore not "real." The artists presented in this exhibition and catalogue force us to confront our relationship with garbage, each to very different ends. They reclaim the agency of those "associationally charged" objects, repurposing them into potent reminders of how easily we create, consume, and discard.

El Anatsui, *Anonymous Creature*, 2009

A NOTE ON THE CATALOGUE

While this text accompanies an exhibition of the same name, it is intended to stand alone. Nine of the artists represented in the exhibition were interviewed at length about their practice as it relates to the use of discarded material. The images throughout are representative of each artist's oeuvre and are not necessarily images of work in the exhibition. Owing to the radically different temporal realities of the publishing and gallery worlds, it is difficult to establish checklists of working (hopefully selling) artists. In the case of Jill Sigman, *Hut #10* will be created specifically for the exhibition.

NOTES

1 Gillian Whitely, *Junk and the Politics of Trash* (London and New York: I. B. Tauris, 2011), 24.

2 *Gravity and Grace: Monumental works by El Anatsui*. Brooklyn Museum, February 8 – August 18, 2013. The exhibition was organized by the Akron Art Museum.

3 Pierre Cabanne, *Dialogues with Marcel Duchamp* (London: Da Capo Press, 1979), 48.

4 "The Art of Assemblage: A Symposium (1961)," in *Studies in Modern Art no. 2: Essays on Assemblage*, ed. John Elderfield (New York: The Museum of Modern Art, 1992), 144.

5 An edited version of the exhibition would travel to The Dallas Museum for Contemporary Arts and the San Francisco Museum of Art.

6 William C. Seitz, *The Art of Assemblage* (New York: The Museum of Modern Art, 1961), 6.

7 Seitz, 25.

8 Anna Dezeuze, "Assemblage, Bricolage, and the Practice of Everyday Life," *Art Journal*, Vol. 67, No. 1 (Spring, 2008): 31–37.

9 Ella Shohat and Robert Stam, "Narrativizing Visual Culture: Towards a Polycentric Aesthetics," in *The Visual Culture Reader*, ed. Nicholas Mirzoeff, 2d ed. (London and New York: Routledge, 2001), 53.

10 A criticism, as Anna Dezeuze points out, that was made by Helen Franc, editorial consultant to the director of MoMA.

11 Claude Lévi-Strauss, *The Savage Mind* (London : Weidenfeld and Nicolson, Ltd., 1966; reprint, Chicago: University of Chicago Press, 1968), 22 (page citations are to the reprint edition).

12 Lévi-Strauss, 21.

13 Dezeuze, 32.

14 Ibid.

15 Chris Gosden and Yvonne Marshall. "The Cultural Biography of Objects," *The World of Archaeology* 31, no. 2 (1999): 169.

Purposed

Re:

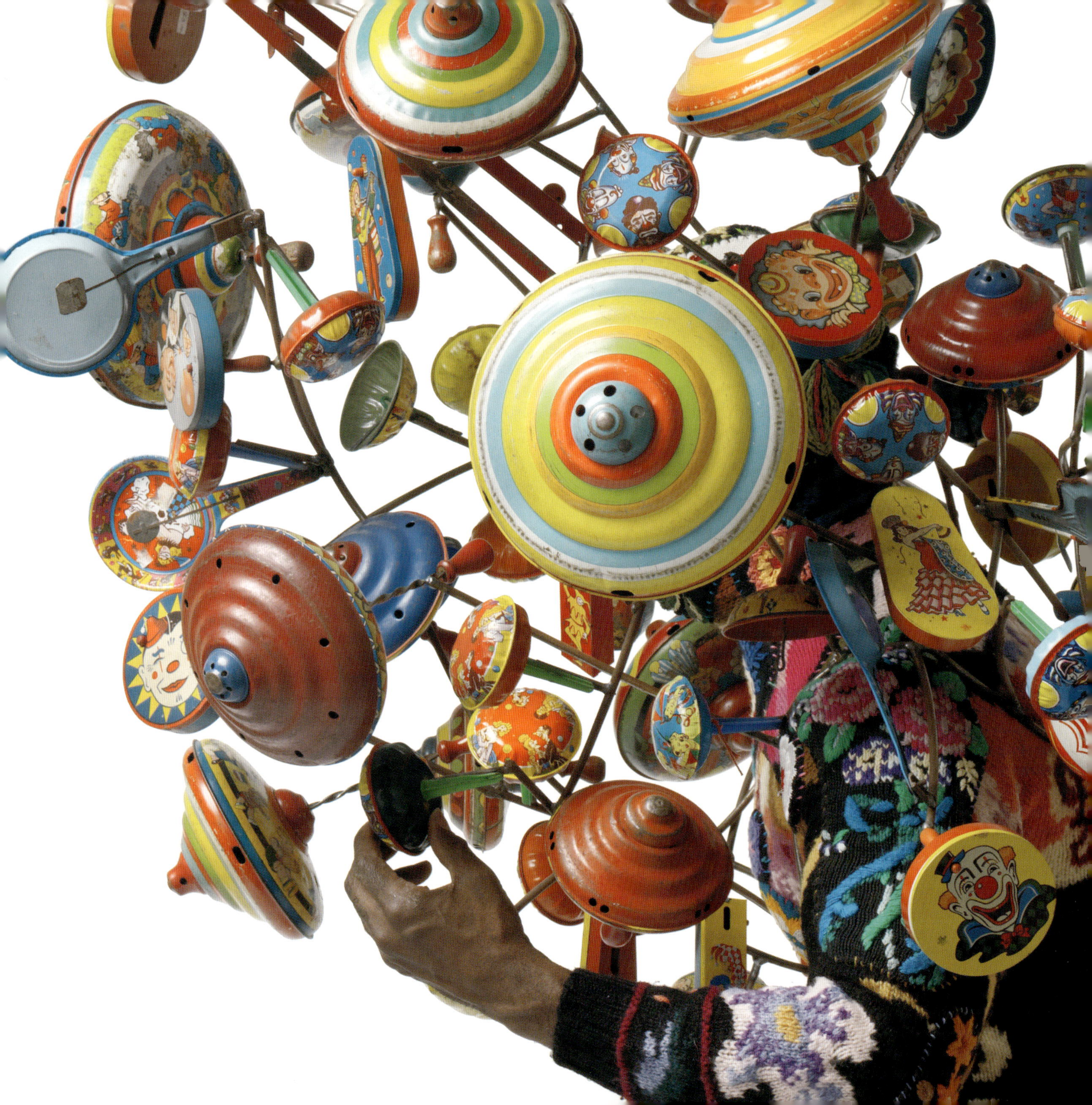

Nick Cave (b. 1959) is best known for his Soundsuits, *hybrid constructions that are part sculpture, part costume, and part performance art. Constructed from a wide array of discarded objects found in flea markets and antique shops, the* Soundsuits *provide an alternate skin through which new personas can be constructed that are free from the biases of race, class, and gender. Having trained in dance at the Alvin Ailey American Dance Theater, Cave is uniquely poised to explore movement and sound when wearing the* Soundsuits. *Based in Chicago, he is the chair of the Department of Fashion and Design at the School of the Art Institute of Chicago.*

Nick Cave

MATTHEW McLENDON **Let's start with the basics. You've said in interviews that you can walk out of your front door and find your material. Have you always been collecting, even as a child?**

NICK CAVE I think I've always been a collector. Actually, I think as a kid I was making things and I would tend to always incorporate things that I would find. I would go out into the woods and find a particular rock or type of branch or rock to incorporate in what I was making. So, I was always on this search for materials in my surroundings, for ways to embellish and help express these ideas.

MM **What types of things were you making as a child? Were you starting with fashions and textiles?**

NC I was starting more or less with textiles or wall hangings, things of that sort. That then led to articles of clothing or repurposing a pair of shoes. I really started to migrate into these areas of interest, then that led to doing installation. It's not like I'm not familiar with this kind of approaching and building an object or space. It has always been there.

MM **You use the term "searching," looking for things in your surroundings. Was anyone else in your family doing that?**

NC Yes, my older brother Jack was as well. I think coming from a family of seven siblings—all boys, all one year apart—I think that also this whole idea of hand-me-downs for me, when an article of clothing was handed down to me, I was always re-approaching that object, redesigning it. Feeling that I needed to create my own identity or marking on the garment. So I think that also has played into my way of thinking and making. Coming from a lower-middle-class family, it was about invention, it was about being able to make things based on what's in front of you. I didn't have the means to go out and buy materials, so I think that whole process has been critical—innovation as a way of thinking and making.

MM **And constructing you as both the individual and the artist as you matured.**

Soundsuit (detail), 2008

NC Exactly.

MM It's telling that you talk about going out and looking for branches and stones in your surroundings because, of course, the first *Soundsuit* you created in reaction to the events surrounding Rodney King was made of branches.

NC Weird that it was twigs, yes, totally.

MM Yes, this was a return in a sense. Has the process of collection remained largely the same? Are you still the primary collector?

NC Oh yes, definitely. And the reason why is that it is just not as easy as you think it is. You can't just send somebody out and gather up some things. I collect based on an impulse. I collect objects that have multiple readings so that I know when I am interested in using something, I know that I can shift its meaning by applying it in a particular way. It's always about this impulse; it's always about this multiple reading. It's based on immediate reaction. People have sent stuff; some of it has worked, most of it has not. So it's not random, any kind of surplus. It's me, moving through a space and being affected by it.

MM Let me clarify. Are you thinking about each *Soundsuit* individually, or are you seeing objects out in the world and thinking "I might be able to use that in the future"?

NC Occasionally I think of it in terms of the future, and when I do, it's because that object has to be so amazing. But what I do is find something and I'm not really sure how I'm going to use it. I just know it has the equivalent information that it needs in order for me to know it's a "go." The object is then moved around the body until I locate it.

MM Are you constructing the *Soundsuits* on a mannequin?

NC No, they are constructed flat. I look at it as though we're building a cloth, that we're building a dimensional cloth. I never look at it in terms of "*Soundsuit*." And, I'm not sure what it's going to be because I don't sketch anything. It is purely me moving this object around and then I start thinking about form.

MM Is there a typical place that you find material? Are you going to flea markets, to garage sales? Do you have particular locations you like to look for objects, or is it really just as you move through the world?

NC As I really move through the world. And, how I move through the world is really the critical thing here. For example, we will jump on a plane and fly to Seattle, and then we will rent a van and we'll drive across the country and Google antique malls, then based on the route, these are the avenues we explore. It's either an antique mall, sometimes a flea market, or a mom-and-pop antique store. I do thrift stores locally, and that's really for some of the surplus that I use on a regular basis. So this is what we tend to do, because I'm interested in other parts of the country. What is there that is not in this area?

MM Do you then think of some of the *Soundsuits* as "regional"?

NC I thought about that once, but then I thought I really didn't want to pin it down as opposed to looking at and gathering resources that provide us a broader range of readings. It's not about where it was found, as opposed to memories, for example.

MM Yes, that leads me to what I am particularly interested in with the *Soundsuits*—the biographical or narrative associations with the objects. The object biography mingles with your biography before coming into contact with the viewer's biography. How do you think about this? Do you think about this?

NC Let's use, for example, the ceramic bird figurines. I started collecting that object only because I was thinking a lot about my grandparents. That object was a kind of symbolic memory bank for me. It was what was considered an art object in the home, and it was precious, it

Soundsuit, 1998

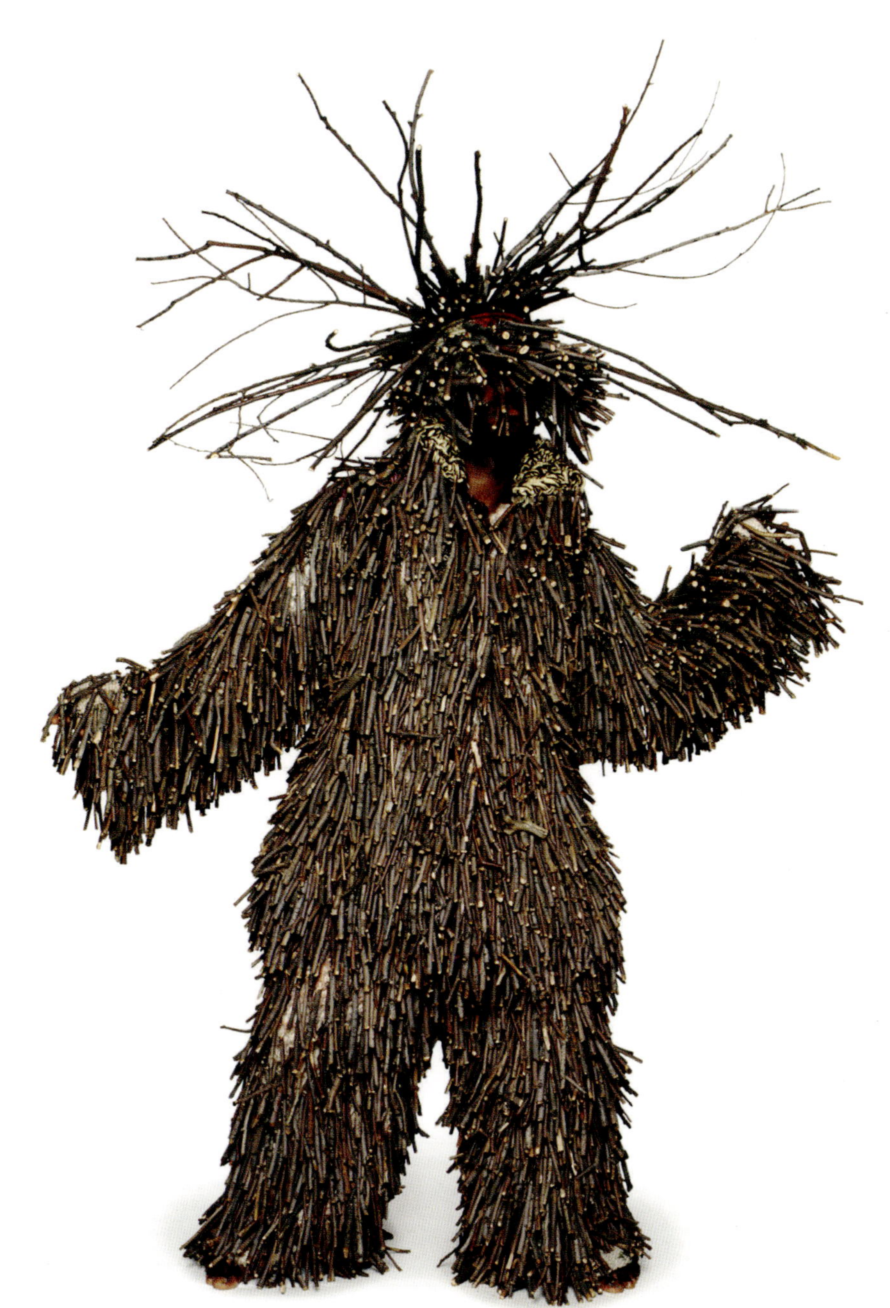

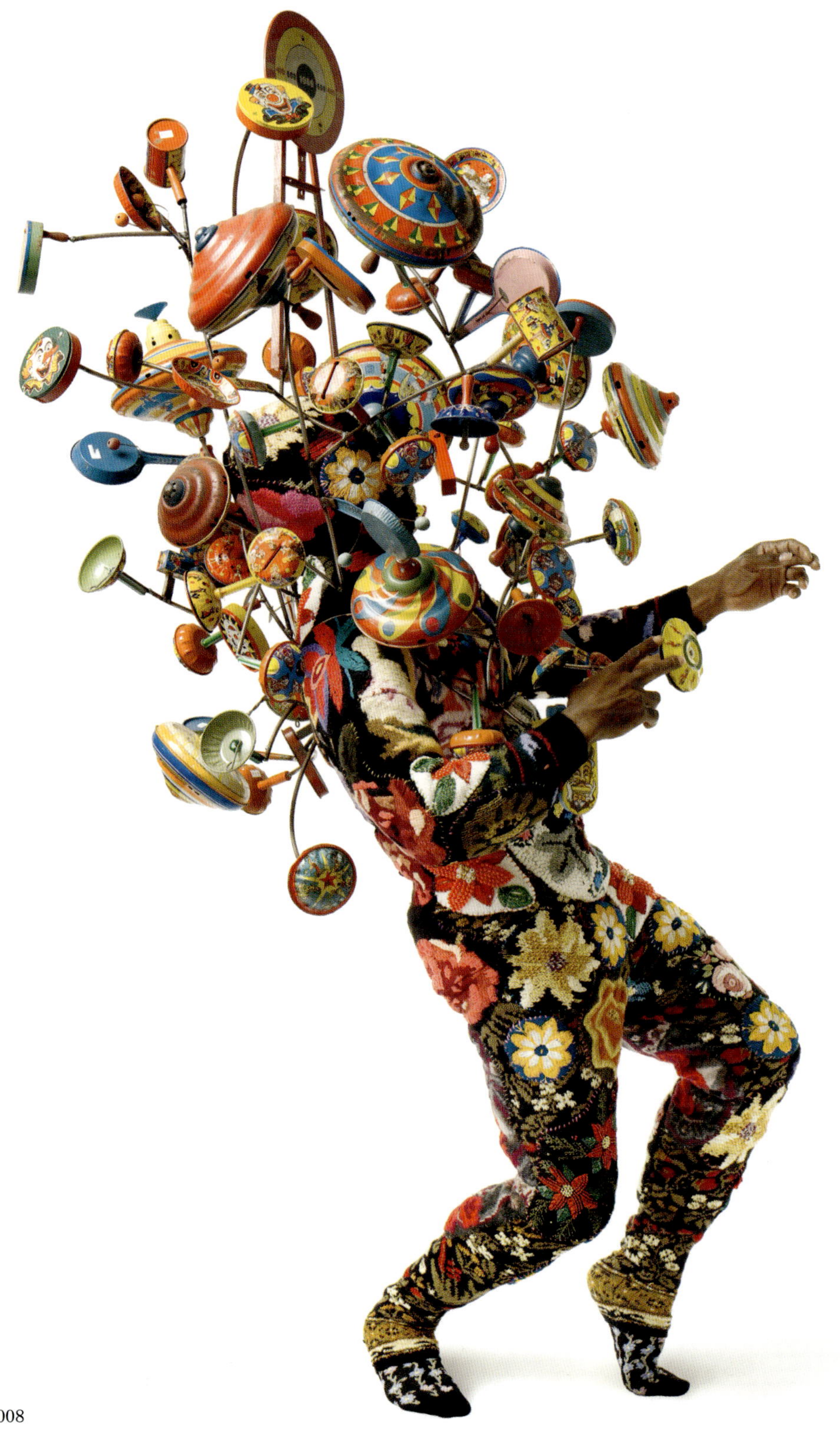

Soundsuit, 2008

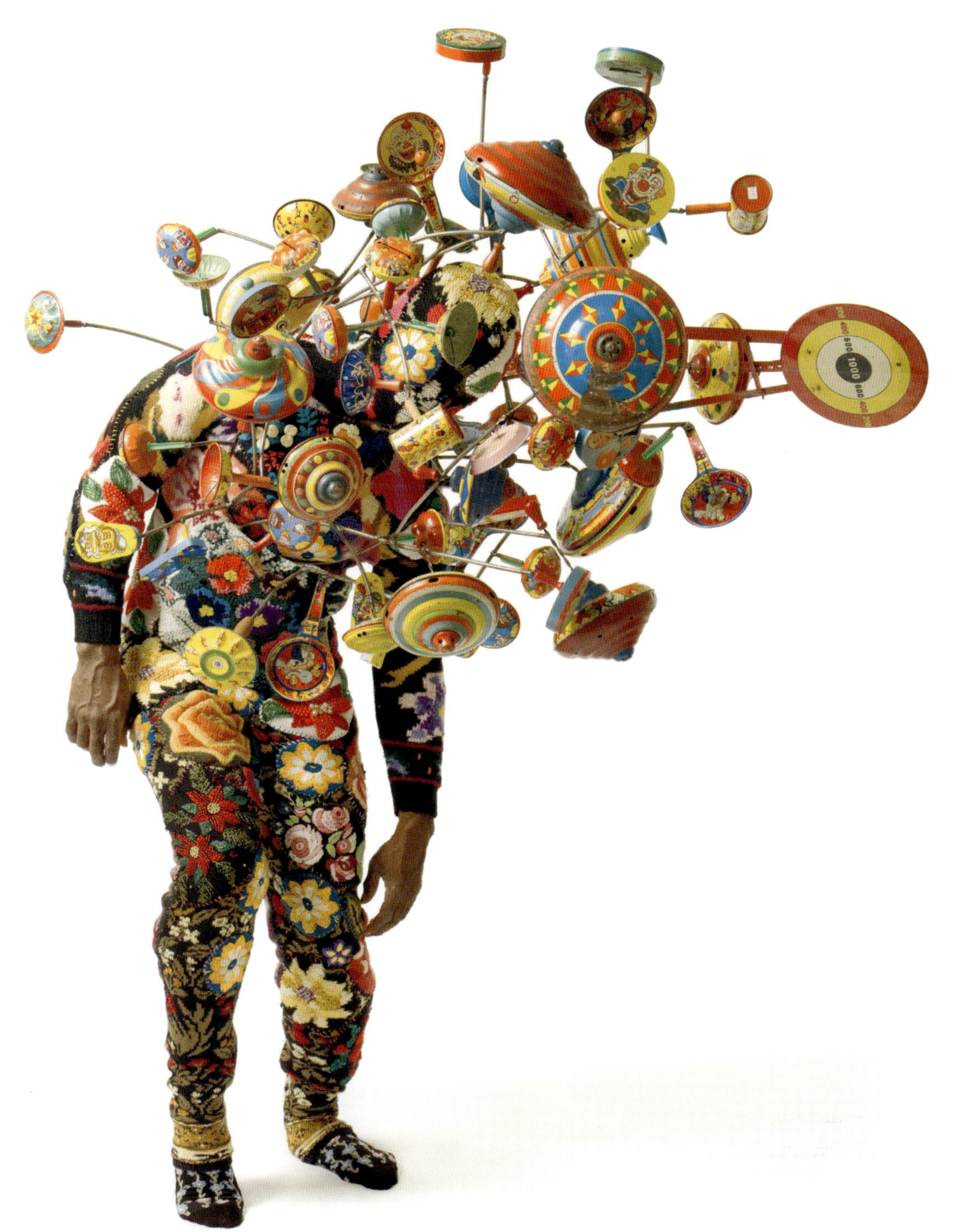
1000

was protected by the china cabinet. I could be a voyeur, looking at it through the glass but never touching it. It became this sacred moment for me that when I started to incorporate it into the work, it moved me into looking at high art and low art, what was forbidden for me in grad school. This idea that this object was not considered an art object, but as a child growing up it was a decorative art object in the home. So, this was an amazing object for me to implement into the work, and then I realized it was an object we all can connect to and it brings us to a place that is rather extraordinary. We all go to that place of grandparents, childhood memories that tie us into a sense of security and home.

MM **Well, you talk about having an affinity for objects with multiple meanings, but what you've just described is a very concrete meaning. Where does the ambiguity come in? Where does specificity fall away and take on a different meaning?**

NC I think where it falls away and takes on a different meaning is that I am now honoring that object. I want the object to be accepted in this new formality. It is now being reconsidered as building part of this sculptural monument. So, it becomes not only the figurine but it's also now put onto the body in this tree of life figuration.

MM **Is the tree of life something you think about?**

NC Part of making that particular *Soundsuit* brought me to look at the family tree and history in that way.

MM **What types of memories, other than the obvious associations, do you think the *Soundsuits* constructed out of toys bring to mind?**

NC It's so funny. I had seen these toys forever, of course, and had never been interested. Then, the toys brought to mind this idea of the one-man band concept. Then I started to think about, as a visual artist, other associations—the taskmaster, this shaman or one who wears many hats, and then navigating through the world—multiple things. So, it became about that, and then I started to look at the history of pop culture, particularly cartoons. I was looking at Batman, and then looking at when you hit someone in the head it goes "BANG" through text. So I looked at that as a sensation, the "BIG BANG" of sound and motion. Also, this is what my head feels like, this vortex of ideas forming and generating in this cosmic space. It became about this world of ideas and transmitting energy within that space. Also, again, it's about location. This is about the head, a place where we can play with these things. Then, I started to move in it and it made this amazing sound, this orchestrated instrument that became adornment that surrounded the body. When I'm thinking about things, it's this mass or intersection of thought, and then, what does that manifest into.

MM **Manifest through the performance?**

NC Yes, through the performance, through it as a sculptural form, through the ideas of creating something that is somewhat bigger than life—that is fantastical. How do you create the fantastical through form?

MM **And then, certainly, as you look at these tin toys bought for pennies, they are incredible design.**

NC Oh sure, and then you're looking at it from a graphic point of view, which then led me to look for doilies and hot pads, then to bring that to the body. Then take this three-dimensional surface and then taking it to a two-dimensional plane, looking at the doily as a medallion. Then, it's honoring this domestic craft that is no longer in existence. We're not makers like that anymore.

MM **So you are seeing it as a process of transformation?**

NC It's about paying attention. It's like when anyone repurposes or finds a discarded object and reclaims it. At that moment you are giving a new birth, a rebirth of the object.

MM **Transformation of the object, and then transformation of the wearer. I'm interested in your thoughts on the relationship between the object and the wearer. You've spoken at length about creating the "skin," the new persona, hiding or masking the features of the wearer. Do you see the objects of the *Soundsuit*, or the *Soundsuit* itself, as being completely dominant over the viewer?**

NC Oh, totally. That's the whole idea of hiding gender, race, and class—that you're now forced to look without judgment. I think that, for me, I'm interested in looking at my work in a socially conscious way. It allows me to consider how I can move through this world in an objective way.

MM **How do you mean?**

NC How can I remain open to respond to something? We always want to find a similarity to try and understand something. How do we come to a form or an object with new consideration, a new meaning?

MM **And by donning the *Soundsuit*, that becomes a personal experience?**

NC Yes, and then how do you as a human being surrender to this transition? It's amazing how difficult it can be for a lot of people when I move into this performance arena. There are a lot of requirements when one starts this collaboration with the *Soundsuit*. How can you be open to this transformative work? It's an opportunity to liberate. Once you are disguised, that is the moment you can become something other.

MM **Sure, and that goes to the whole history of Carnivale or Mardi Gras. You've talked about the Mardi Gras Indians as influences, as well as certain African tribal customs.**

NC Yes, and my thing is, how do you come at that kind of experience with conviction as the performer? When you're in a *Soundsuit*, it all depends on your willingness to surrender and to conceive this other being. I can

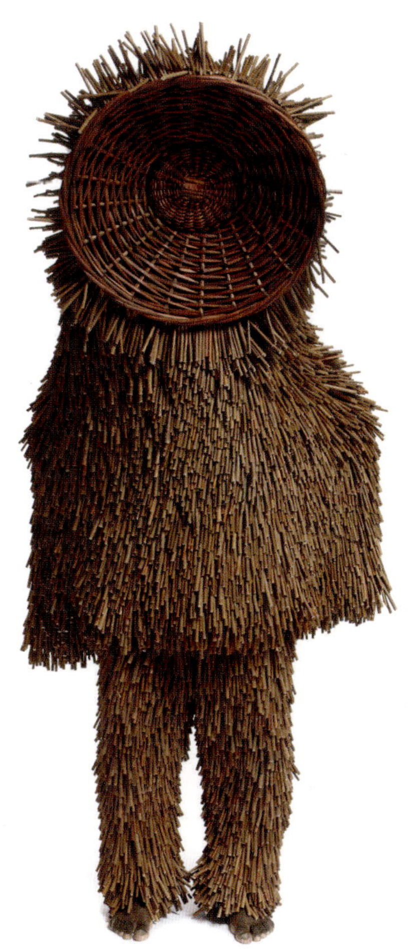

Soundsuit, 2012

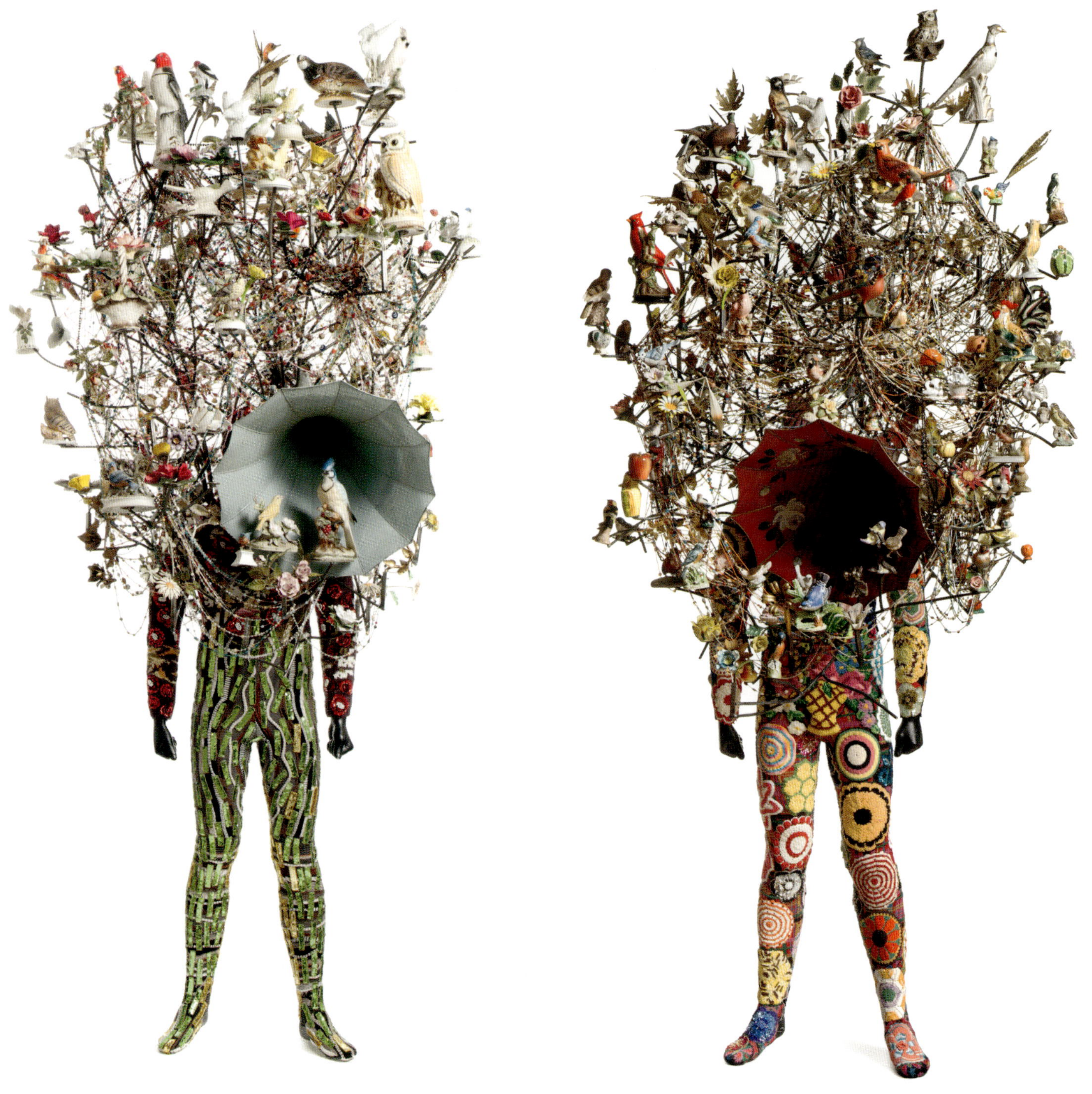

Soundsuit, 2011

Soundsuit, 2013

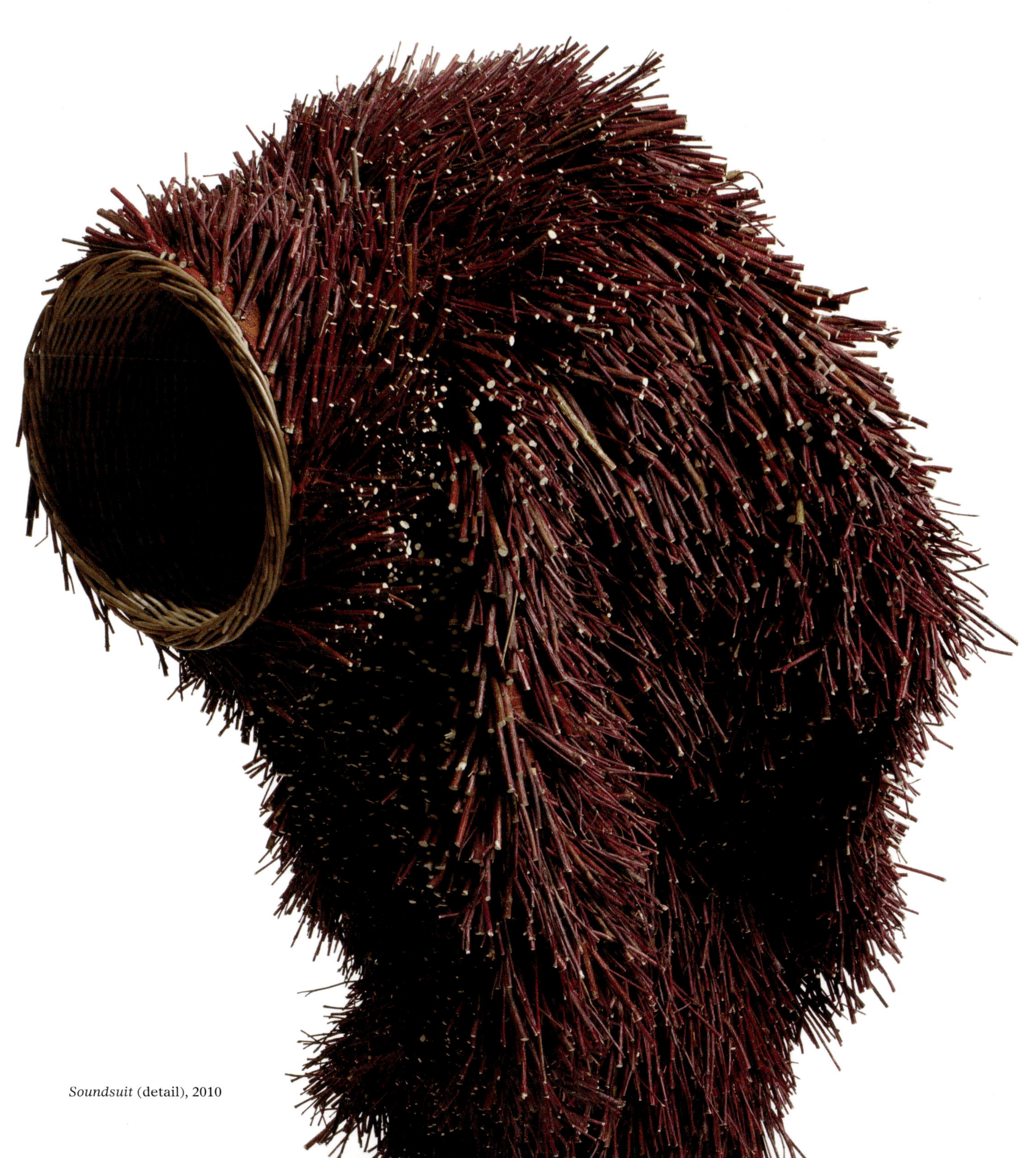

Soundsuit (detail), 2010

completely forget that you are there, the person that I know, and that comes through a willingness to step in, too. It's a true collaboration.

MM **When you are creating the suits are you thinking about sound at all, or is that a surprise at the end?**

NC I'm never thinking about sound. I don't think about a lot of things because I don't want any of that to hinder the process of building. So, when I put something on and then start to move in it, that is when I have the realization, "Oh, okay, this is the sound this makes," or "Okay, this is what this feels like, or this is what this looks like." There may be restriction in terms of movement. This is the extent of the posturing I can do in this. So what does that mean? It's not about dance, it's about movement.

MM **And what's the difference for you between dance and movement?**

NC To me, I think dance really falls under a structure. Movement, I think, is more fluid; it's more structured under the improvisational.

MM **Would you say dance is more artificial whereas movement is what we do in the everyday? You're using ordinary, everyday objects to create these fabrics, this *Soundsuit*, so the movement falls into this everyday-ness?**

NC Exactly. So I'm more into the authentic—the authentic, everyday movement.

MM **But often, the viewer's interaction with the *Soundsuits* is static; they are presented on mannequins in the museum or gallery. They are meant to be moved in as a collaborative performance, but in the museum they are sculpture. Is that a compromise—is that a necessary compromise? Or, is that just another life?**

NC It's just another life. For me, it's like when I was doing research and going to the Museum of Natural History. I'm reading about all these objects and I'm thinking who wore them and what is their purpose. I'm thinking, it's interesting how these are taken out of context and I am forced to look at these as an artifact. So, I start thinking about things in terms of stasis versus function and then purpose. That's part of the whole negotiating of my playing field. How do I want to play with my work in the context of art? I want to work between sculpture, installation, performance, and video.

MM **How are the videos informing the work now?**

NC The most recent ones are really about the sound. The sound in the video is the sound that the actual object makes. It's providing the heartbeat of the *Soundsuit*.

MM **Are you finding that you prefer to display the *Soundsuits* and the videos together so that the viewer has both experiences?**

NC Well, not necessarily. Sometimes I like it to be—when it's a sculpture—accessible to the mind. For you, as the viewer, to imagine what it would be like to be in it—what it would be like moving. What would it sound like? I want to make you work, to keep that imaginary space in your head in dialogue with the sculpture. And then, sometimes, I like it just being a video, because that again allows you to think, "God, I want to touch that surface!" "I'd love to be able to view that up close!" It allows me to reposition myself and the work, keeping the viewer active. Then you could be in the same *Soundsuit* as I would be in and you are going to come at it differently than I am going to come at it. So, I don't think the work ever is completed.

MM **It's always transforming.**

NC Right, I think it goes back to these objects and materials; this surplus that is discarded in the world and then reclaimed. It's then going to go back out there into the world. This whole idea of regurgitating form and material is going to continue being part of our existence. It is always interesting to think about the object's responsibility in the world.

Soundsuit, 2013

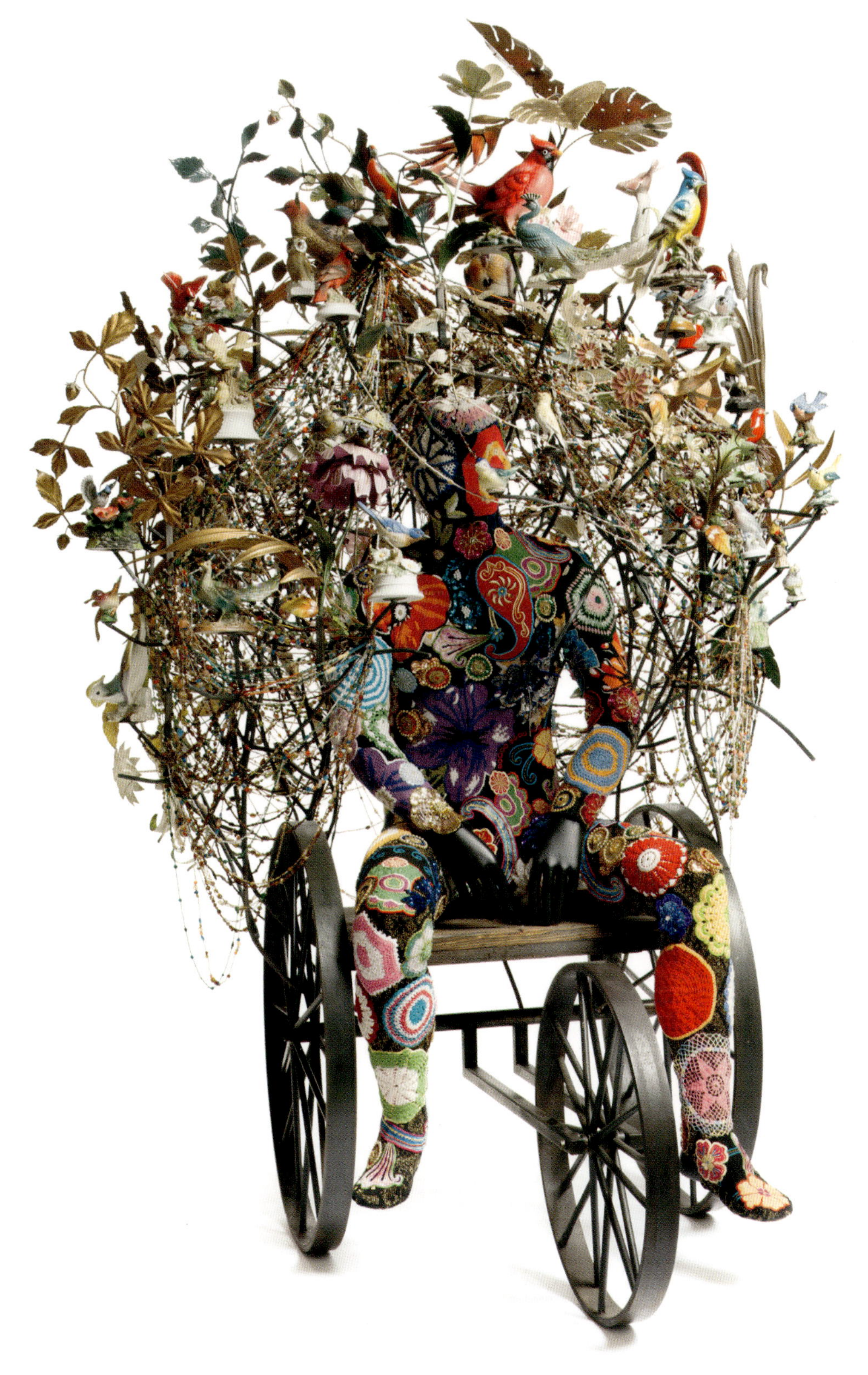

MM **What is the *Soundsuit*'s responsibility in the world? I love that phrase.**

NC I'm interested in creating and using my work as a vehicle for change. The *Soundsuit*'s responsibility is that I have to be able to walk away from it, and it has to be able to sustain itself in the world. I think it has this social commentary that is integrated within the work. We could talk about the abundance of surplus and discarded waste—that's one thing to talk about. Then we can break it down and dissect it and talk about hierarchies. I first have to decide how I am going to lead you into the work. What is the device that is going to do that? Then once I have you, you have to decide how you are going to approach it. There is this level of seduction through material, through adornment, through embellishment. I think within the work there is this very political undertone—looking at gender, as a gay male. I'm interested in reaching a broader community. I have to think, "What is the face of that and not be offensive?" But I can still talk about the flamboyance.

MM **Yes, and I think in this climate, that is a transgressive act—trying to reach across boundaries to a broader community is transgressive.**

NC I think so, and I think we have to think about our purpose, our duty, our contribution.

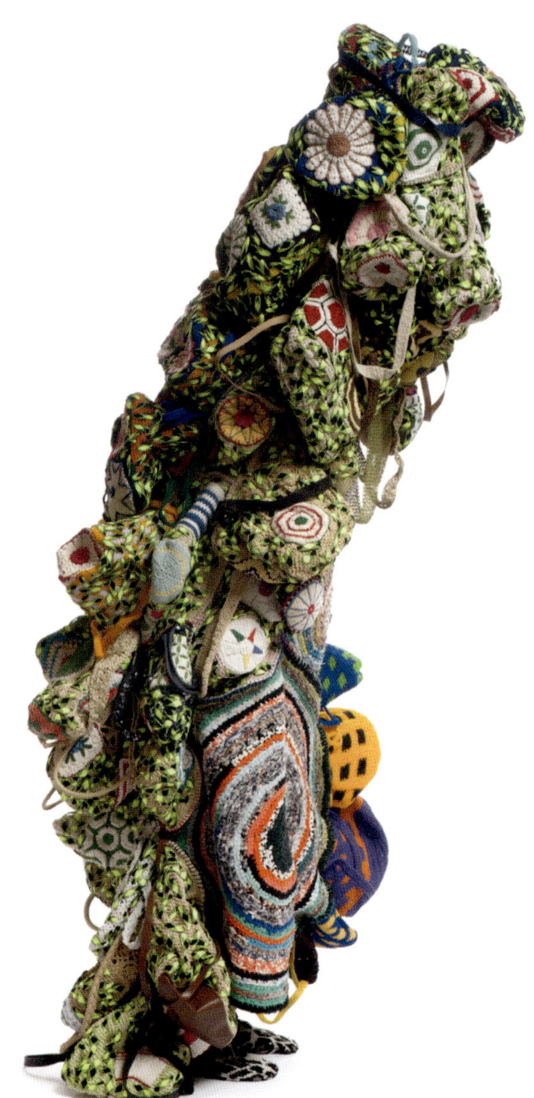

Soundsuit, 2013

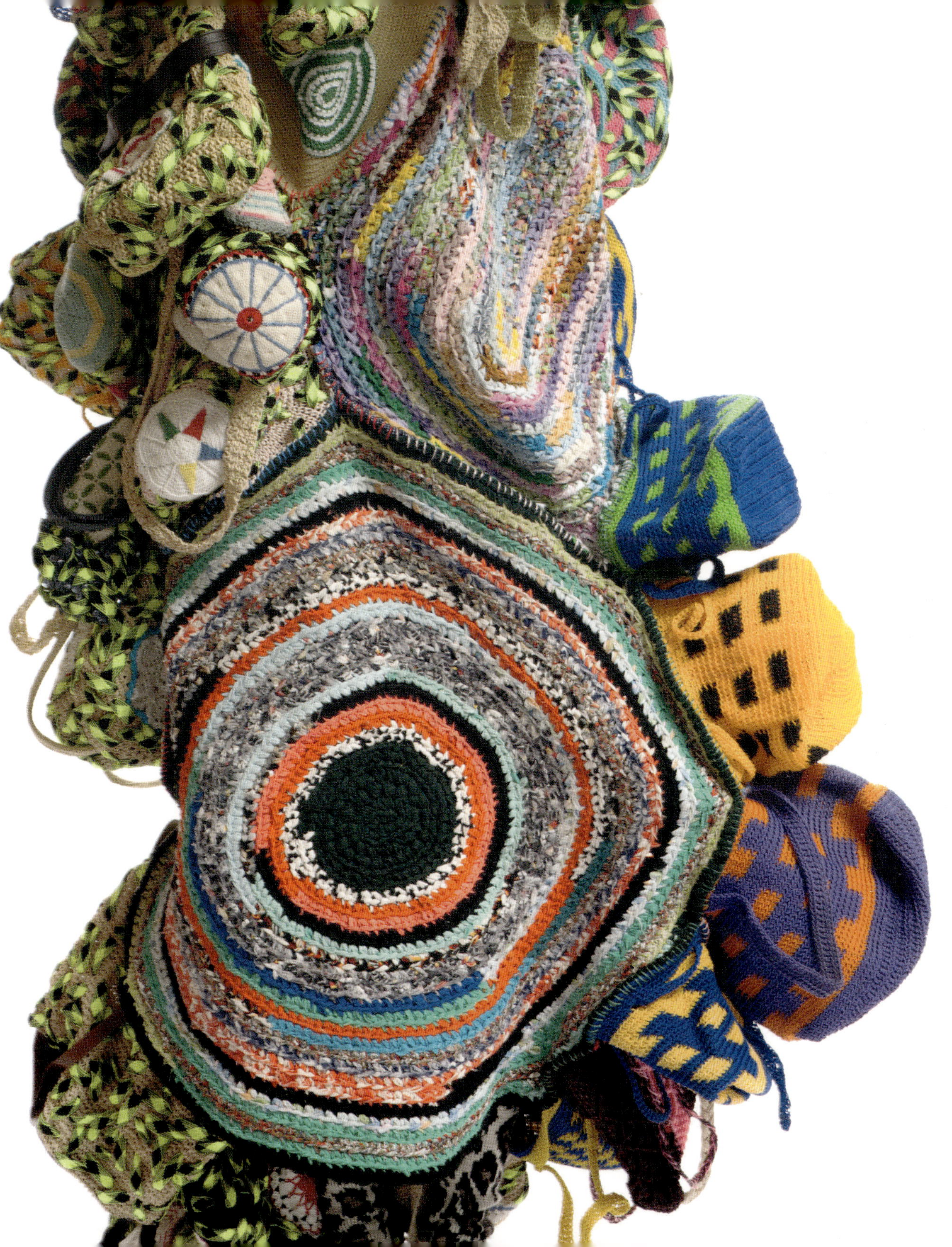

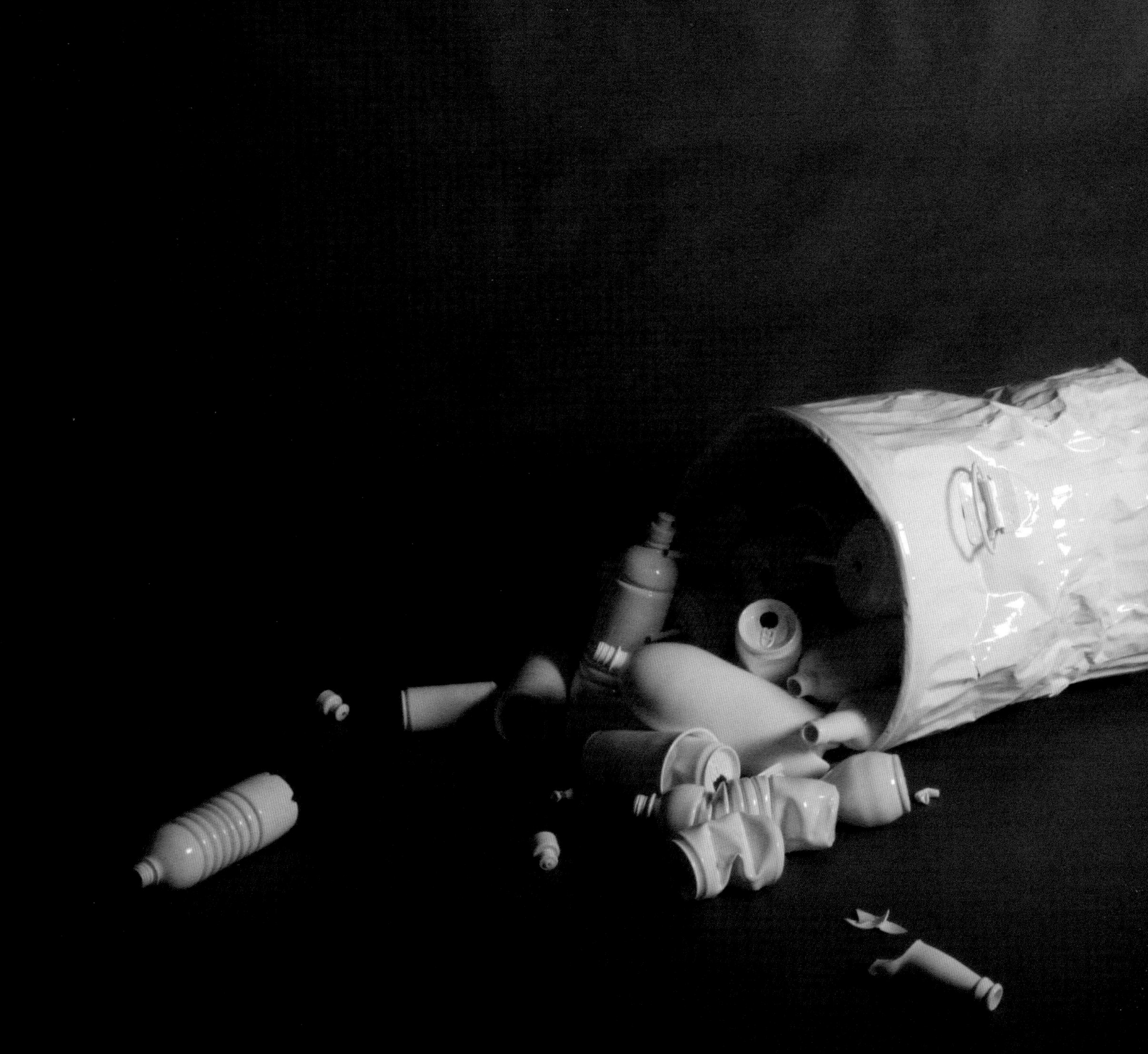

Creating hyper-realistic simulations of plastic bottles and cartons in glass, Matt Eskuche (b.1972) forces his audience to consider a culture so overcome with consumption that it allows a space for the simulation of waste. After studying metalsmithing and practicing as a bench jeweler for several years, he began flameworking in 1998. He has demonstrated multiple times at the International Flameworking Conference and the Glass Art Society Conference, and since 2005 he has traveled to Australia, Japan, Turkey, and Bulgaria to demonstrate and teach. Eskuche's work is in numerous private and public collections, including those of the Lampwork Glass Museum in Kobe, Japan; the Philadelphia Museum of Art; and the Museum of Arts and Design, New York.

Matt Eskuche

MATTHEW McLENDON **How did you decide that you wanted to start simulating consumer waste in glass?**

MATT ESKUCHE It wasn't so much a conceptual idea at first as it was an interest in mimicking. When you're working in glass, you can mimic things quite realistically. There was this crushed can one day, and I was interested in making that. It didn't really strike me as anything outside of trying to reach the form itself in the beginning. But, then it expanded from there once I held that first one in my hand. It was pretty intriguing; it was the form that struck me as being the most important thing at that point.

MM **So, you are mimicking the mass-produced in the handmade. Is that where the interest is now?**

ME Not at first, again, it was form, and then it followed several tangents through the years. I am interested in the time, energy, and effort that goes into craft. So, then it became very interesting to me watching people's reactions as they came to understand that I was spending all of this time to make something that [in its original form] nobody cares about at all. So, I have this secret interest in making something that takes a long time but that, when you see it, you associate with something that is made in a split-second by a machine that no one cares about.

MM **What are some of the typical reactions when someone sees your trash glass?**

ME It's a huge range. When I first made the work, I had a couple of good opportunities when I was first showing it and people didn't know what to expect. The initial reactions are a look of confusion and then you see their minds calculating what's actually in front of them. Once they realize it's not what they first thought it was, then it is a very wide range. And, quite often, people actually think it is garbage. You get that "Oh, I can't believe artists these days. They just paint trash white and call it art!" I'd actually like to do that someday; it would be a lot easier [*laughs*]. It would be fitting right into the history of Warhol or Duchamp. Then you have the people who

Apocalyptic Permafrost, 2012

are intensely interested in the technique once they realize it's not trash.

MM **How do you go about collecting the forms that you want to recreate in glass?**

ME Well, it is tied to the technical aspects; what I'm excited to make. There are certain types of trash that would be very difficult for me to make using my usual methods. I do everything freehand and do not use any molds. If I wanted to make a square juice box, I can get away with a crumpled up juice box, but to make a perfect square juice box, I can't really do that. I would have to use a mold, and that is not the process I am interested in. So the technical puts a limit on it to some degree. Conceptually, though, it is the corporation that makes the object and its effect on the environment. That works into my thought process, to my interests.

MM **So, it began formally, but as the project has progressed you are now interested in consumer and environmental issues. When did that shift occur?**

ME It came in through my reaction, and the reaction of others, to those original forms. You can create a perfume bottle, and it's pretty and blue, but it doesn't continue on from there. These forms, because of their origins, take you to other realizations. I was thinking of where I was at as a consumer in a capitalist society surrounded by manufacturing, and tons of products, and advertising and corporations, tax subsidies, all of these things that happen. So I was realizing where I was, what my role in this was. I started thinking about what it would mean not to create waste or not to use a plastic bottle again. The work opened up these questions more clearly and quickly for me. I was thinking about my impact.

MM **Do you not use any plastic in your daily life now?**

ME I'm pretty good with some things. I have a cup or a bottle with me when I go to a coffee shop. When I'm in a grocery store, I have a backpack. But, then I drink a lot of beer and wine and sparkling water in glass bottles. So that is the raw material of the material that I use. So, I'm not on a commune or anything, but I try to make a pretty good effort.

MM **When did you do the first works in the trash series?**

ME I started in 2005. I'm usually not good with dates, but I was spending time with my grandfather in my hometown, Milwaukee, and so I know for sure when it began. No one in my family is a practicing artist, per se, but as I look at them, I know they could be. My father is an engineer and is incredibly skilled with materials, and my brother is an architect and also skilled with materials. We all have this dexterity, but they took a different route.

MM **And you started out in metalwork, right?**

ME I did. I started out in metalsmithing in high school. My father and brother had both done some. I liked it because I could make a design and then make an object from that design.

MM **How did you move from metal into glass?**

ME Even in high school, I took an in-depth course at the Worcester Center for Craft and in that course you were exposed to wood, fiber, ceramics, glass, photography, et cetera. Through that I was beginning to work with glass. Then I lived in Colorado for a bit, and a guy owed me a little money so I told him if he showed me some things with glass, we'd be even. I was intrigued because in metal it's a very lengthy process to plan how it's going to come together and make the object. In glass, you are creating so quickly.

MM **How do you feel your trash series has evolved over the decade?**

ME Well, it has been on the wane for me the last couple of years. When the economy tanked, it really affected my sales; they were in a high enough price range to really hit

opposite: *Brittany Before Noon*, 2008

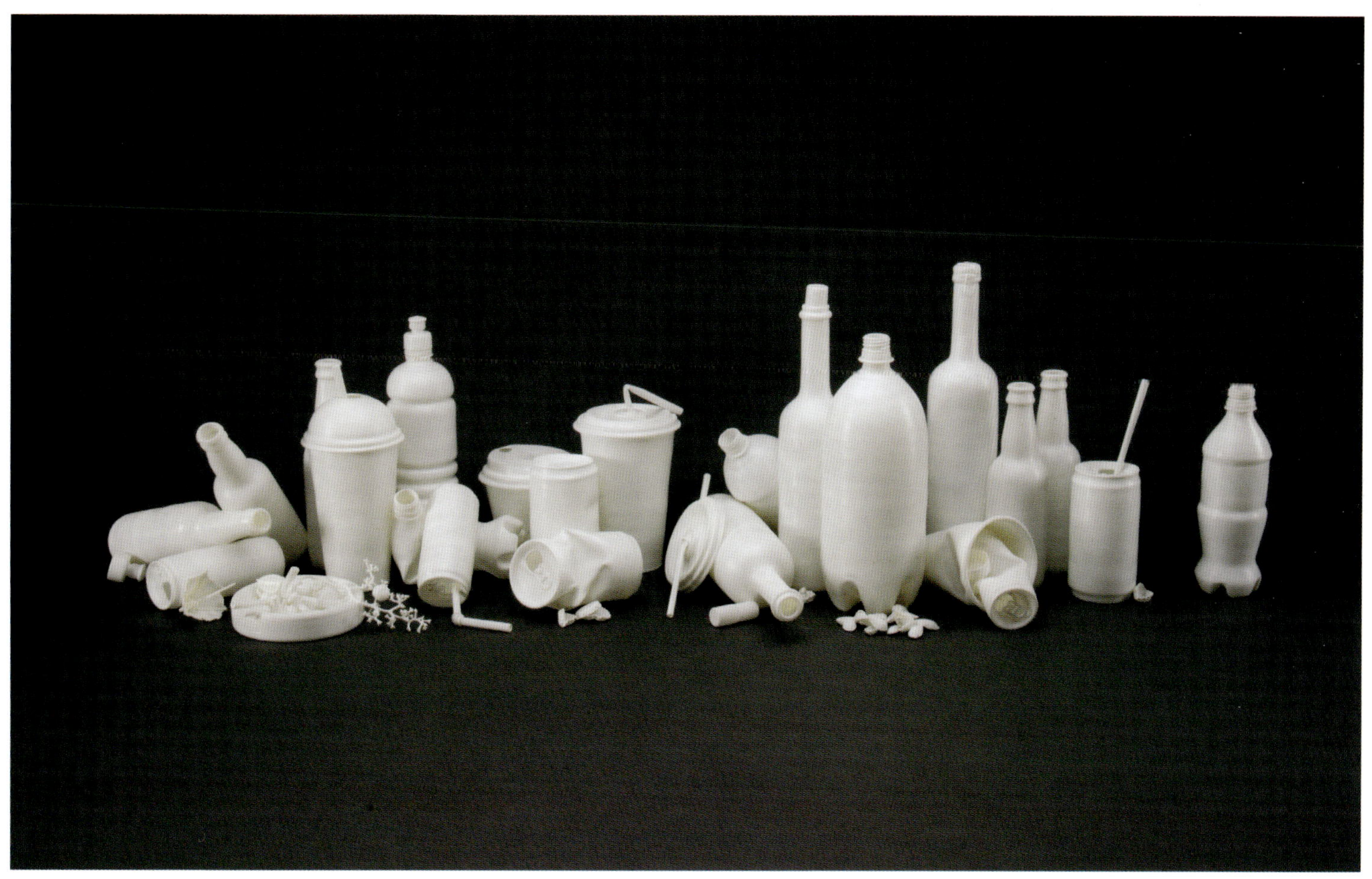

following spread: *White Trash*, 2007

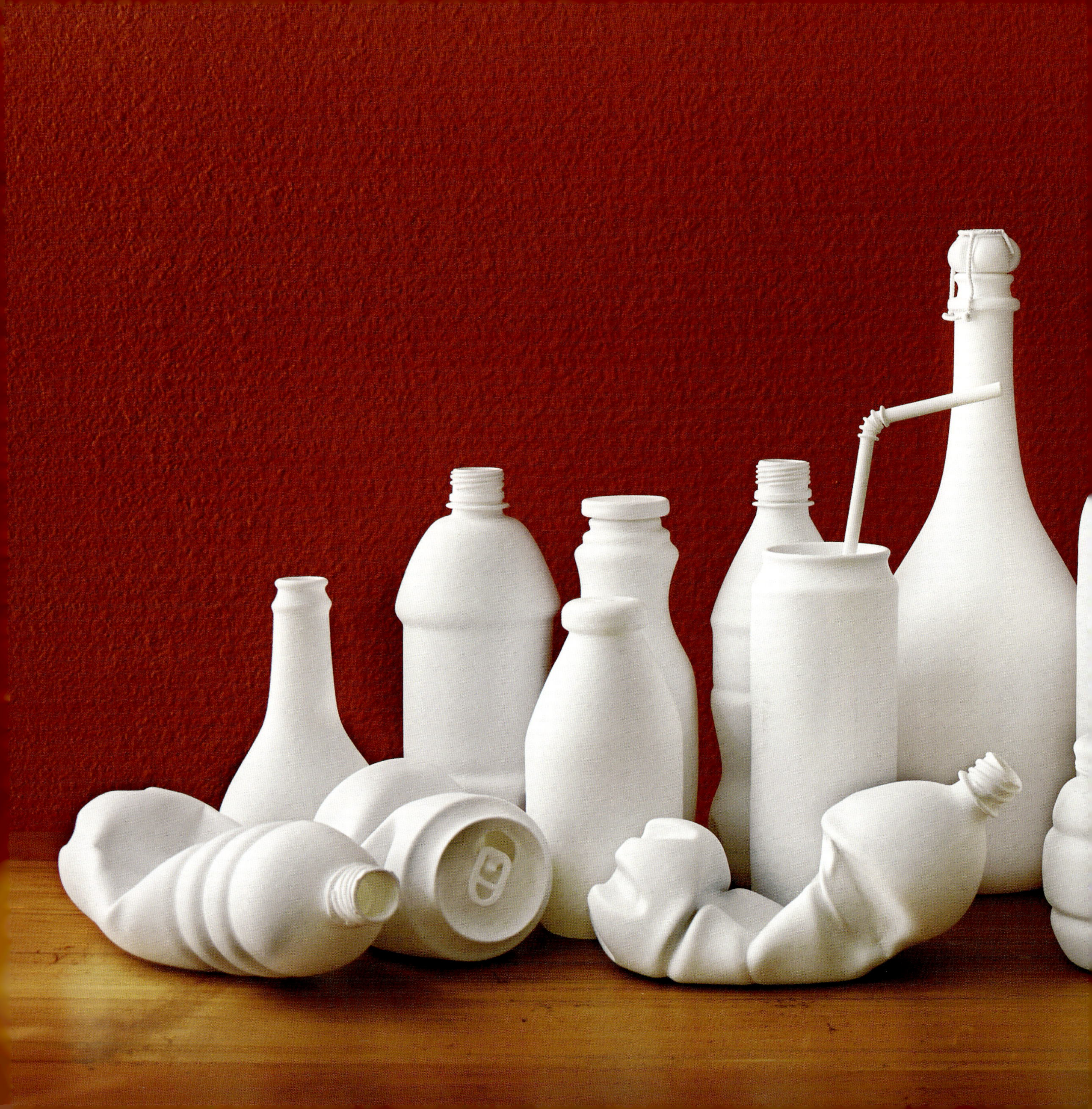

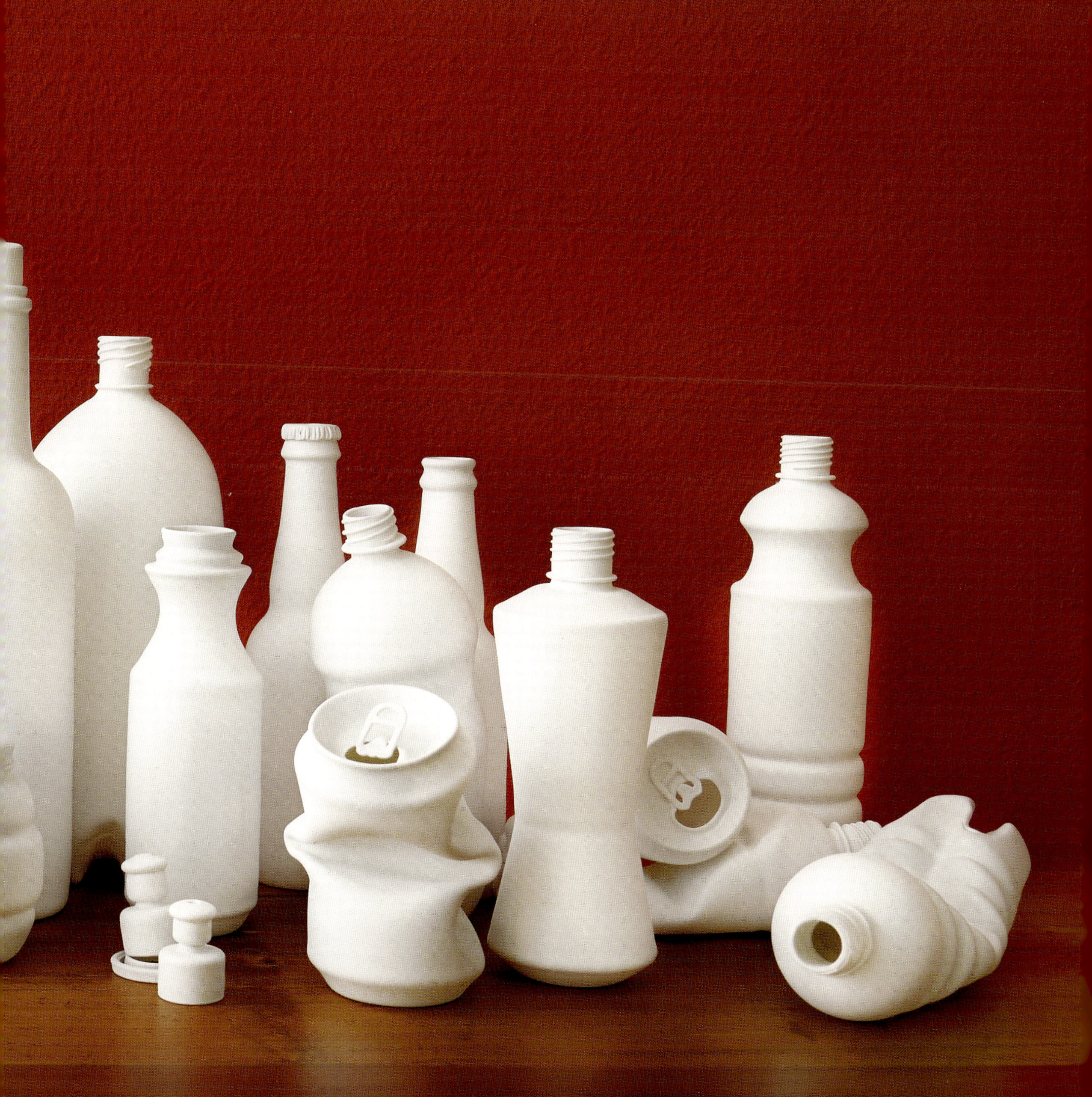

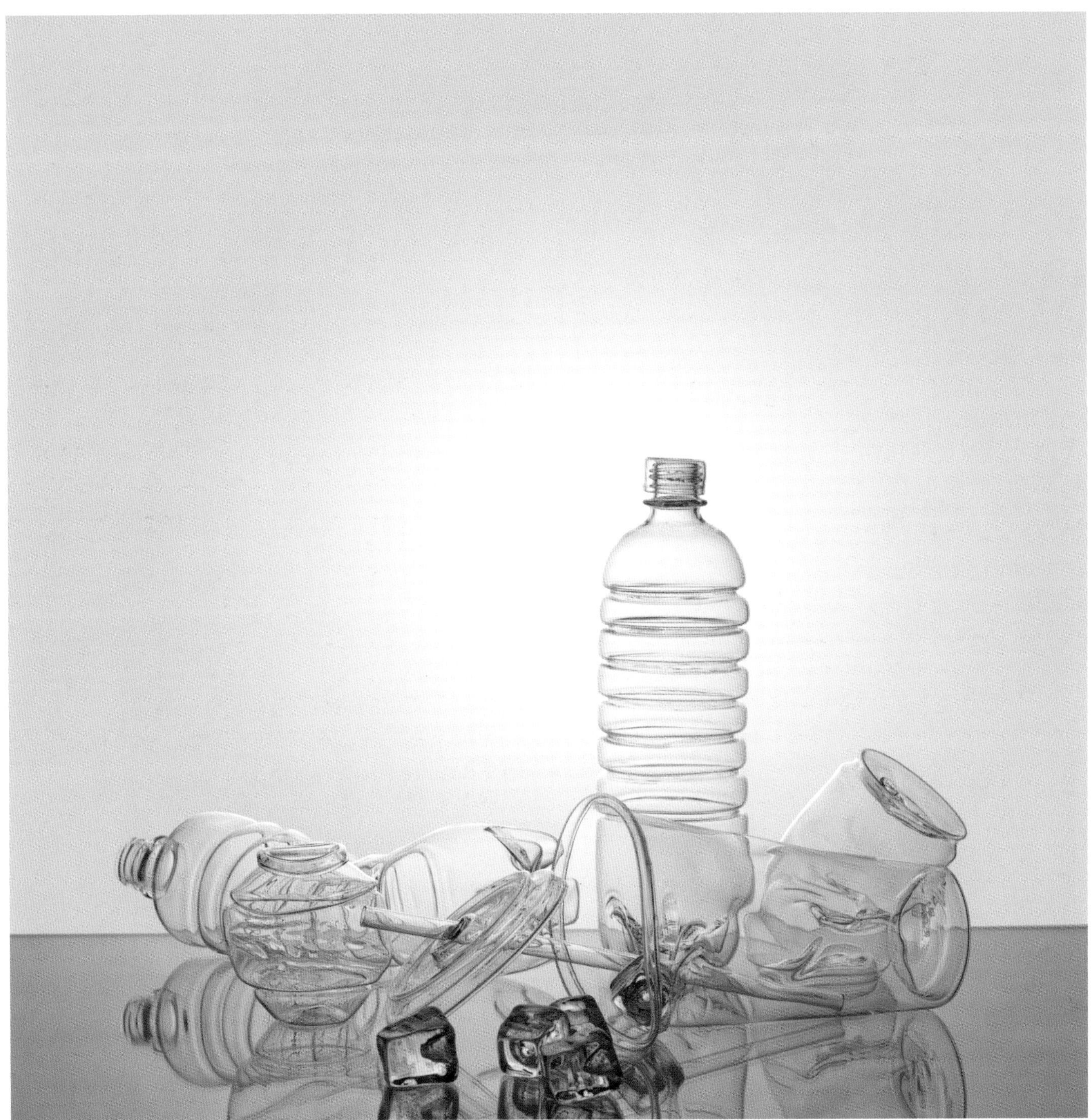

me hard. In the initial stages, I made a lot of objects that were individual, then I started to make larger groupings of objects. I was aware of Beth Lipman's work and so I started thinking about making the groupings on tables. It made sense to have the glass on a very nice antique table, but I was hesitant because of my awareness of Beth's work. But, in the end, I really felt the work was demanding it. That moved it forward sculpturally, and critics started to look at it differently. In general, though, it hasn't changed a lot, because the source material remains the same. The installation changes, really.

MM **Why is it important to mass the objects, to present multiple objects together?**

ME It's the impact. There are so many different forms. But you also see it a lot. Go to a festival, or in the airport, you see my sculpture over and over again in the trash-cans. Visually it has impact; it's more interesting with the lines and shadow, it's formal. And then, it gives the idea that there is so much of this in the world. It's overflowing. It reminds you there is too much waste. We're too lucky; we have access to too much.

MM **But, you're making waste into a precious object, especially when you are placing it on the tables. How are you thinking about that?**

ME Sure. If you've seen the series that is mirrorized, it's two birds with one stone. I love the finish and was looking for multiple ways to treat the glass. But then, the finish underlines the idea of it as a valuable item. I didn't think about it ahead of time—that they would be seen as having more value, but that happened.

MM **You experiment with the finishes throughout the various series, though.**

ME Yes, in the first pieces, the finish was really about being pragmatic. It was really easy to make things out of clear glass, and so I applied the color after. It's more difficult and expensive to use colored glass. Clear was the easiest way in the beginning so I painted them with oil paints. A lot of people use oil paint and then wipe it so that it's translucent and there is a consistent texture. I laid mine on with a brush, though, so that you see the brushstrokes. I liked that because I felt it tied it to the history of the painted still life. I've also painted with spray paint because I like it as a dirty, quick method of applying paint. More recently, I've powdercoated the work, because it is a thick, shiny layer that is more archival. The mirrorizing was really good for me because I had a finish that I really liked while it played with the notion of value. The realistic series is geared much more toward making the work "pass." I was exploring mimesis rather than representation. People get a thrill that they can be fooled by the work. I wanted to explore that. It's pretty nice if the viewer is excited in some way. This was also exciting for me because it was a challenge.

MM **So in your trashcan works, is everything glass?**

ME No, if you see beverage containers, bottles, cups, that's going to be glass.

MM **And everything else? The Skittles box?**

ME If you see paper, cardboard cartons, that's going to be paper and inks of some sort.

MM **So, you are still making everything in the trashcan.**

ME Yes. Everything. The only thing I won't have made are the caps and the labels on the beverage containers. But, if you see a cigarette pack, that took about six hours to make.

There Goes the Neighbourhood, 2012

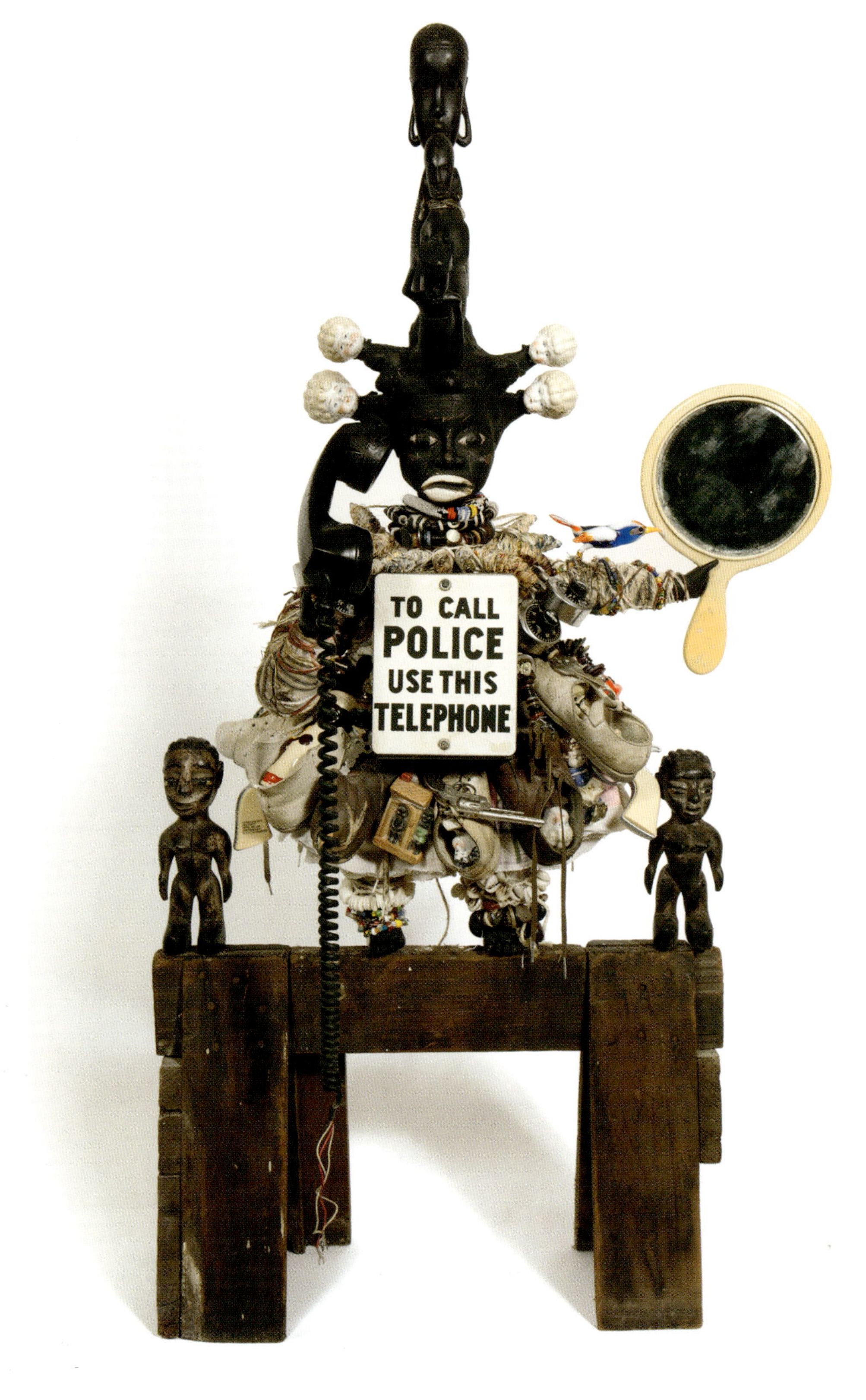
TO CALL
POLICE
USE THIS
TELEPHONE

Vanessa German (b. 1976) is a transdisciplinary artist, poet, performer, and activist. She is based in the Homewood neighborhood of Pittsburgh, Pennsylvania, where she collects the discarded remnants of the residents' lives and uses them to fashion potent "power figures." Her sculptures are composed of mass accumulations objects and doll parts that, for German, lift the detritus of forgotten lives to a higher plane and, in doing so, honor those lives. Borrowing from African and African American experiences and traditions, she invokes shared histories in an effort to build communities through transformation. German has performed and exhibited widely at institutions that include the Andy Warhol Museum, Pittsburgh; the American Visionary Art Museum, Baltimore; and the Carnegie Museum of Art, Pittsburgh. She is represented by the Pavel Zoubok Gallery, New York.

Vanessa German

MATTHEW McLENDON **You are largely a self-taught artist, but you come from an artistic family; your mother is a fiber artist. When did you start creating art?**

VANESSA GERMAN I started creating in the home with my mom and my family. My mother, growing up, we were familiar with her practice. She was collecting fabric, buttons, and notions and had a specific space in the house for transforming these raw materials into something else. Sometimes it was things people asked her to make—she made clothes and costumes for shows—and sometimes she would make what she wanted to make, she would design and create it. So, I grew up understanding that you could have an idea, almost the thirst for an idea, and surround yourself with the ingredients, feeling this internal vision, and you could make that come true. I grew up understanding that that wasn't novel, that it was something called "crafting," that it wasn't a hobby. It was just part of your life because I watched it be a part of my mother's life. In our house, we didn't have a lot of money. Anything that we had was second, third, fourth hand, or our mother made it. If we ever wanted something, our mother would tell us to make it. If you wanted a book, or a dress, or new shoes, my mother would be like, "Yeah, you're going to have to do that yourself." So, we would write books and plays and songs. We'd try to adapt our garage sale shoes into something that wouldn't be humiliating to wear to school. I found, for me, as a kid, there was this grace period while creating. My whole body and my mind felt like no other time, when I was involved in the process of making. I recognized it was happening, but didn't necessarily give it a language or even recognize it at that point.

MM **Spoken word is a large part of your practice. Did you start out writing and performing, or did you start out making objects? Or, were they always linked together for you?**

VG We never compartmentalized any part of our lives. I just knew life as life. I didn't ever know, this

Reality Check: To Call the Police Use this Phone, 2013

is time to write, or this is time to make art. We were home schooled. We didn't start school until a little later, and we started at higher grades because of it. In Los Angeles where we lived, we had a bench in this hallway that was very cool. There were no windows, and in the middle of the day when it was really hot and my mother probably wanted us to go to sleep, we would go to this bench called "the reading bench" and we would all have to choose something to read. I remember reading poems from a children's book of poetry and also Edgar Allan Poe poems. I had a very good memory, so I would memorize these poems and I found that when my mother would make us clean—there were five of us—and it would take an hour to wash the dishes, I could repeat the poems I had memorized and it would feel like I would start washing the dishes and then just be done. I would go into the world of the rhythm of words and let myself be alive inside of these poems I had memorized. So, as fundamental as my mother telling us to make what we wanted, and telling us to write songs and plays, whether it was words or objects, it was always my mother enabling our creative courage.

MM **Creativity in the broadest sense was simply your day-to-day.**

VG It really was, and it was a part of our mother's day-to-day, and we were a part of her creativity. My mother would drive into the alleyways behind fabric stores, and the kids would have to go into the dumpsters to get the cardboard and winding wheels for ribbon and fabric. We were totally the tools of her collecting, of her material process.

MM **Well, that leads to your process as a sculptor. When did you start creating these sculptures?**

VG It has been a process. It's difficult. I started to want to give shape and dimension to these sensations I was experiencing when I would touch certain objects or would see certain things. I could feel what I wanted to do, and to make, and to build the substance of these feelings, these collective feelings. I had an almost incessant desire to create these substantial, wavy, cumulative figures, but I hadn't seen what I wanted to create. I mean, I would see a certain kind of broom, or a certain lightbulb, or a box, or a radio, but I never realized that I wanted to make sculpture or assemblage. It was a process of coming to the understanding. I didn't know anything about making sculpture. Then there was a Christmas after we moved from Los Angeles to Pittsburgh, we were all together in my mother's studio and she wanted us to do a family project together. She wanted us to make Christmas tree angels with these half-bodies of a doll that we would put on a plastic cone and then embellish with ribbon, and fabric, and beads. So we're working on these angels, and I wanted to make what I felt, not the example we were given. So I took some self-hardening clay and formed it around my thumb and used a knife to carve the features of the face and then put it into a wine bottle. Then I went outside the studio, which was an old stable, and there were all of these rusty nails on the ground. So, I started picking up these nails, and trusting my instincts, and put the nails into the clay head, using them for hair. Then I strung beads from the eyes and made it this weeping angel. Then my sisters and my mom looked at it and they were like, "Vanessa, you did not make the angel! Why is it so scary and crying?" And I told them I wanted to make what I felt. I wanted the process to do something with me. That was really the first time I wanted the process to do something for me and the product to do something

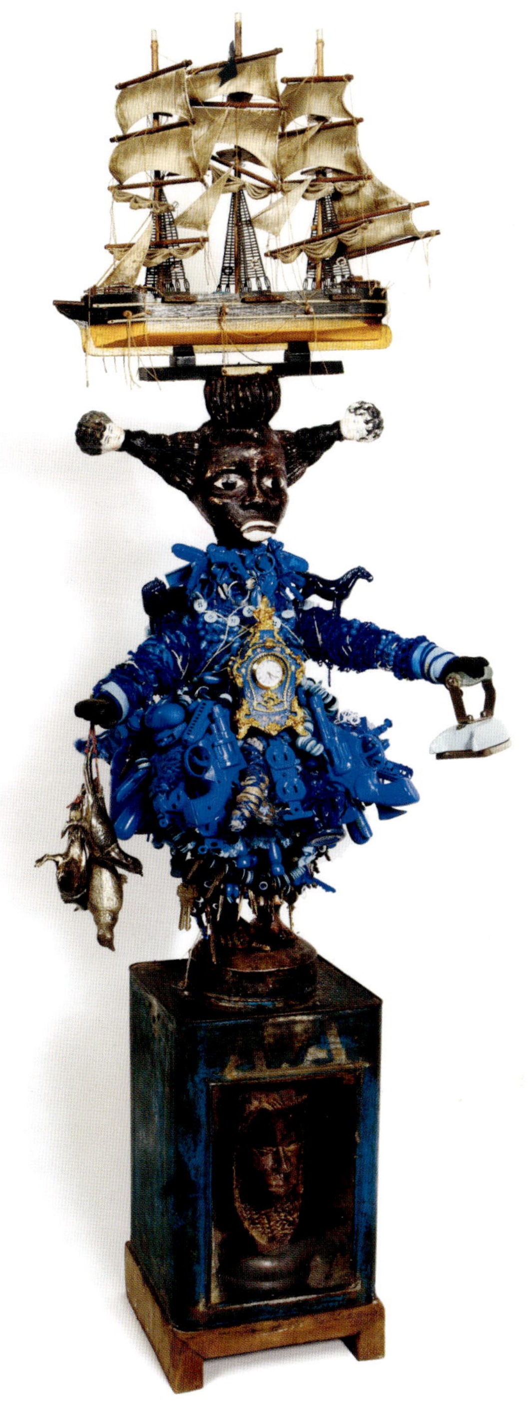

with me. Then, I took it to a Black history craft fair and someone saw it and told me I was using nails like they did in African power figures, and I didn't know what they were talking about. So I looked it up and it made sense to me. I knew why they were doing it and I felt connected to this tradition. That made me start to wonder what else is inside of me that is ancient but still present in the most original parts of myself. So I moved forward with that process, wondering what would be revealed if I refused to obstruct my instinct.

MM **Your process has certainly continued to evolve. You are continuing to collect from around neighborhoods like you were when you were collecting as a child for your mother.**

VG I live in a place where there are a lot of vacant lots. In another era, there were row houses off of alleyways, most of which are gone. So, there are these long alleys that people use as dumps. So, when I walk my dog, I take bags and see what's been left. When I collect things, I do not take them immediately into my house. I feel like that, you know, they could be dirty. I leave them on the porch in the sun and let them get air around them. I let them get rid of the spirit of their old place and become new and useful. I'll pick anything up, because I've had deep regret in the past for not picking things up because I was worried what people might think. Now, I really trust that even if I don't have a specific use for the object at that time, it will be put to use by the fact that I was drawn to it. Recently, I've brought home a lot of skateboards that are worn out and left in the streets. That's been a great find: skateboards that have been played with to the point that they are tattered and bedraggled; they might only have two wheels left. I love those. Then, because I'm not

Self Portrait of the Artist with Physicalized Soul, 2013

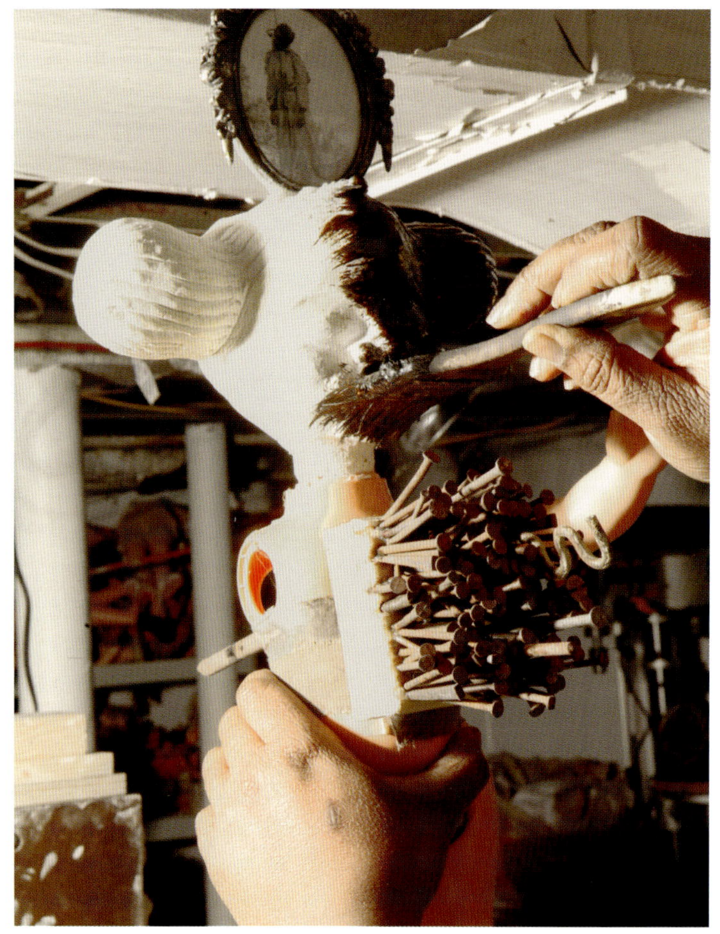

detail studio photographs

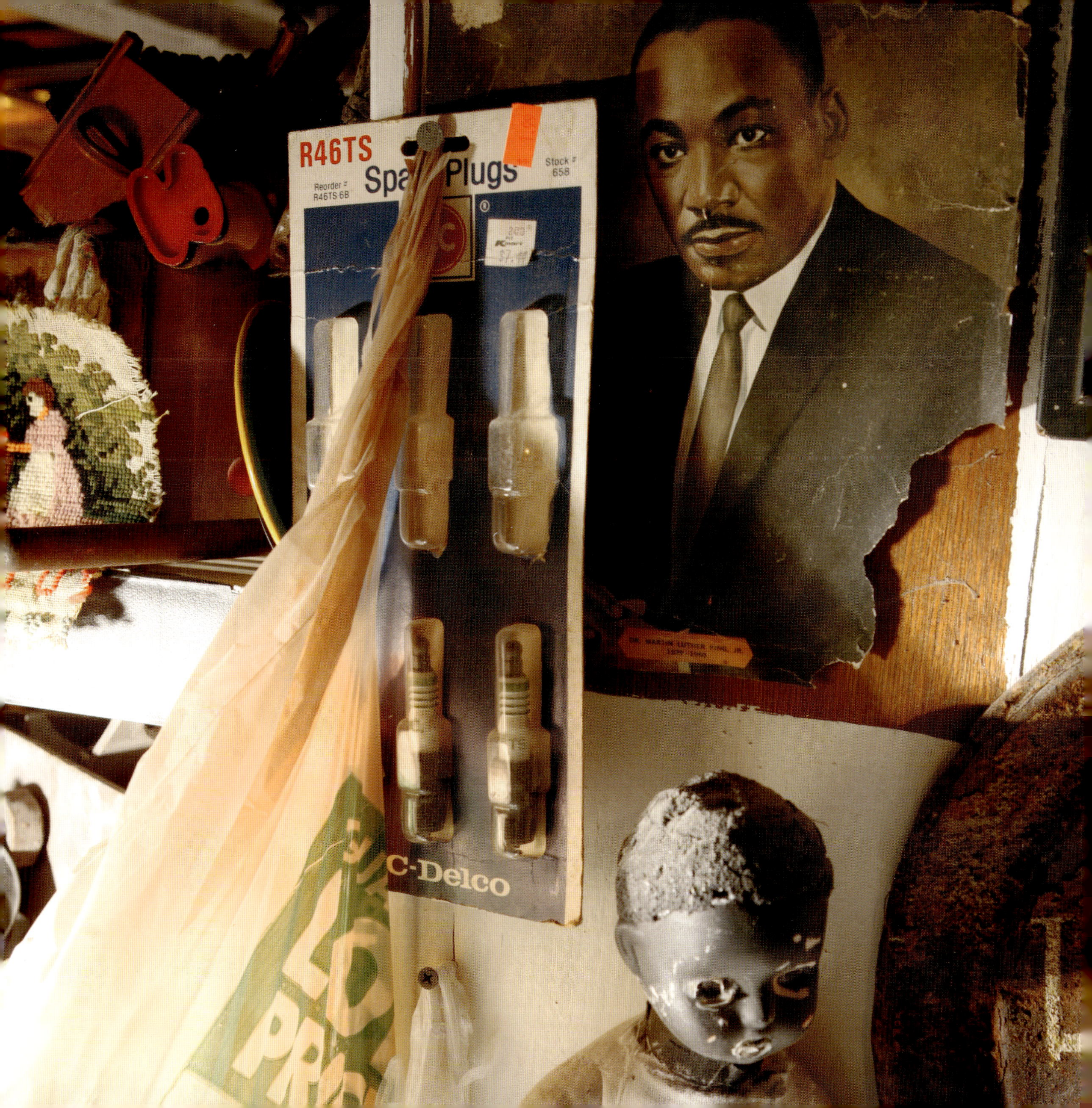

R46TS
Reorder #
R46TS 6B
Plugs
Stock #
658
C-Delco

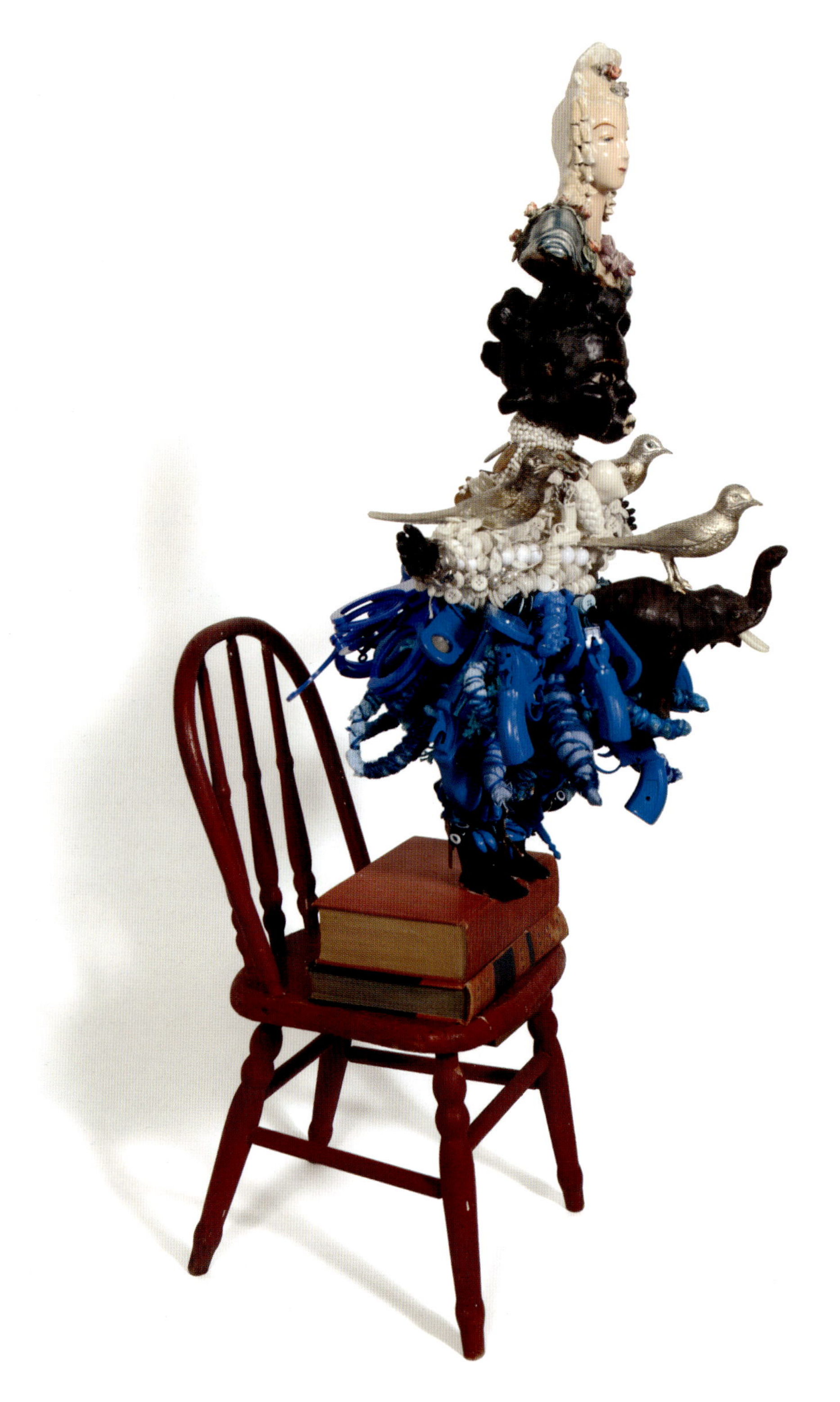

as poor as I was when I first started, I will shop for things at flea markets and flea-tiques, you know, flea market antique stores. I don't use anything that is too precious. Now, I'll look at a lot of things and I look to see what I am inclined to touch and pick up. I have a conversation about curiosity with myself—a conversation about what it is that I am specifically drawn to. I'll buy almost anything someone shoves in a Ziploc bag because there is a lot of it and I'm addicted to that. I just bought hundreds of very small fuel gauge levers from weed whackers or lawnmowers. I know what I'll do with them and I had to have them. Yesterday, I brought home this great old oak chair that the prostitutes have been using in one of the vacant lots, but they haven't been around and no one is using the chair anymore so now it's on my front porch. I feel like I won the chair lottery. I was walking three dogs and carrying this old chair—and a gardening hoe because we got attacked by another dog once—so that was the scene. And I look at this chair and I'm so excited because of what will come.

MM **Do you have more of a conversation with yourself when you're buying something as opposed to when you are picking up something someone has discarded?**

VG No, no not really.

MM **So it's still instinctual?**

VG It is instinctual, and the thing is, I feel like what's great about flea markets and flea-tiques, is that I get to see so many great things, and I get to let my soul select. I'd never be able to engineer that variety.

MM **But surely there is some difference between what you buy at a flea market and what you collect around your neighborhood. The bought items have a certain level of anonymity, don't they?**

VG There is a difference in the conversation when I pull things from my neighborhood [the Homewood neighborhood of Pittsburgh], because I see everything there. I see the effects of every kind of system on the neighborhood. The alleyways that I pull stuff from, one is called Formosa Way, but it's famous through the FBI crime stats as "the killing fields." For years, when there were still the abandoned row houses and there was so much drug and gang activity, the gangs would take sides of the alleyway and they would cut holes in the walls of these abandoned buildings and stash bodies in them. Then they could walk through the holes between the row houses and not be found by the police. Some of those places still feel creepy. These alleyways run the length of the neighborhood. When I'm getting things from there, or on the street where people have been evicted—rental properties, single mothers—when I take those objects it is with a sense of reverence and uplift, honoring these human lives that have been treated as though they are disposable. In my neighborhood there are these wanted posters for young men who have been murdered, and there is so little reward money offered. So, when I see that, I think about taking these objects and placing them in power figures and putting them on pedestals so that they are literally raised up. I got a lot of sheet music from an abandoned house and I gilded it as a way to literally give weight and honor to these lives. This is the material that made up the everyday living.

MM **You call your sculptures power figures. How did you come to call them that?**

VG People were looking at them and saying, "Oh, that's just like this." And I would have no idea what they were talking about and they'd say, "You need

The Story of America in Pictures, 2013

to look at this in Africa," or "You need to look at this tradition in North and South Carolina." Then I would research that and then feel connected to these places by dent of my instincts, like a hand rising through my instincts, and I'd honor that. Then I had conversations with a professor at Carnegie Mellon University, Dr. Edda Fields-Black, who works with pre-colonial African history and the Gullah Geechee, and she told me that the Africans who came to the United States as slaves primarily came from the Congo and Sierra Leone, and that was fascinating to me because I know my ancestors were slaves and that most of them came from these two places and, then, that one of the places [Congo] is where these power figures with the nails were made. I felt really connected to that. I felt, why wouldn't there be insistence and presence of my past linking me to my family who were sculptors and creators? I am still made of these strands of DNA. Why wouldn't this information still be there? And then, living in this fast and slick and colorful and violent world, that's distressing and depressing, so sometimes the only thing keeping me alive is working on minute detail in sculpture. The work that I was creating literally held this power—the power keeping me alive. So there is this whole spectrum of why I call them power figures. I have to use them to assert love into the world; they are beautiful.

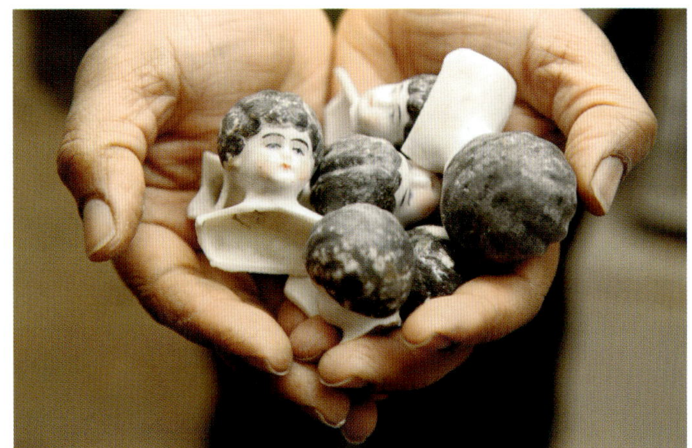

MM **There are aspects of the sculptures, however, that call to mind painful aspects of our history. There are parts of them that are not beautiful.**

VG What is not beautiful, Matthew?

MM **You refer to some of the sculptures as "tar babies" because they literally are. You paint the doll parts with tar. You are referencing some of the darkest, most violent moments of our past with that; that is not beautiful. What are you trying to transform through these power figures?**

VG Yes, they literally are tar babies. I think of them as reckonings. For me, transformation is a very complicated thing that is a complex series of events—intellectually, physically, politically, and spiritually—that has to take place for transformation. But, inside of transformation there must come a place of reckoning, so the juxtaposition of the language of "tar baby" and what that calls to mind, the disgusting, disgraceful, shameful, and haunting systems and actions are called into reckoning, into the dialogue with these other objects. Then, through the juxtaposition of all the objects in the sculpture, these ideas are elevated. None of my sculptures have their feet on the ground; they are raised up. With the tar babies, do you raise up something that is debased or do you try to hide it? Here, they are raised up. If we look at what is happening in the piece, there is a reckoning by sight that will ignite an internal

detail studio photographs

reckoning. Why is the tar baby adorned in gold prayer beads? What does this mean? What is the poetry of these objects? So, it's not just one level. It's not just a one-stop thing. If you're in therapy and you have a breakthrough, it can be painful. You have to cry, but when you get to the other side of that breakthrough, you get to have more of your whole self. That is the reckoning. And that, that is an exquisite beauty, to be able to be more of yourself. It is the journey; it is the reckoning. We get to be more exquisite in our wholeness.

MM **So this leads me to ask, and I don't mean this negatively in any way, but are you making these sculptures for yourself, or are you making them for others?**

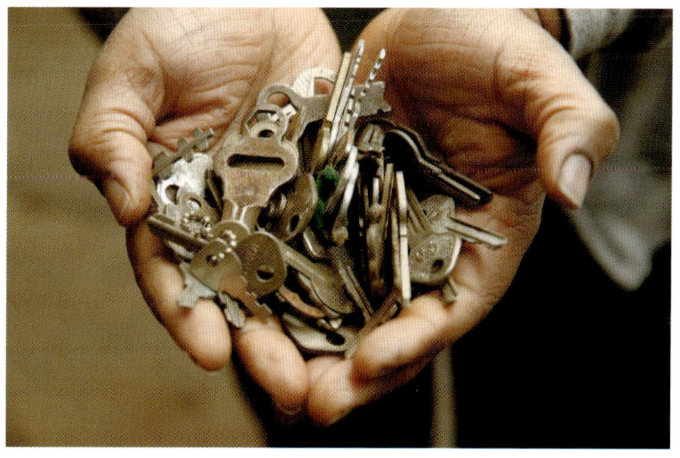

VG Oh, that is not a negative question. I don't do anything just for myself. I feel that we are all connected. We are tied in an inescapable garment of mutuality. More and more I am convinced we are all interconnected. I don't believe my life is just about me, ever. Matthew, it is the known unknown. So, I am completely and utterly selfish. I have shaped all the parts of my life that I could control so that I can have as much time as possible in my life to create. But also, I recognize within that, that I could not create unless I was inspired to create—that known unknown, that soul, that connects me with generative empathy with other people. So I'm completely selfish; I make the sculpture for myself, but we're all connected. All of this enables me to help the community.

MM **Do people send you things to make power figures for them?**

VG Yes, but they also send me things just so that they will go in the figures. Stuff shows up in the mail, at my front door, on the porch. People are honored to think something they gave could show up in a power figure.

MM **One of the recurring themes as I do the interviews for this book is that a number of artists talk about people giving them things. It seems like a very powerful act.**

VG Yes it is, and as I think about it I can't put my finger on who is the giver and who is the receiver. Where did the moment of inspiration start? I'm so glad to know the other artists are experiencing that.

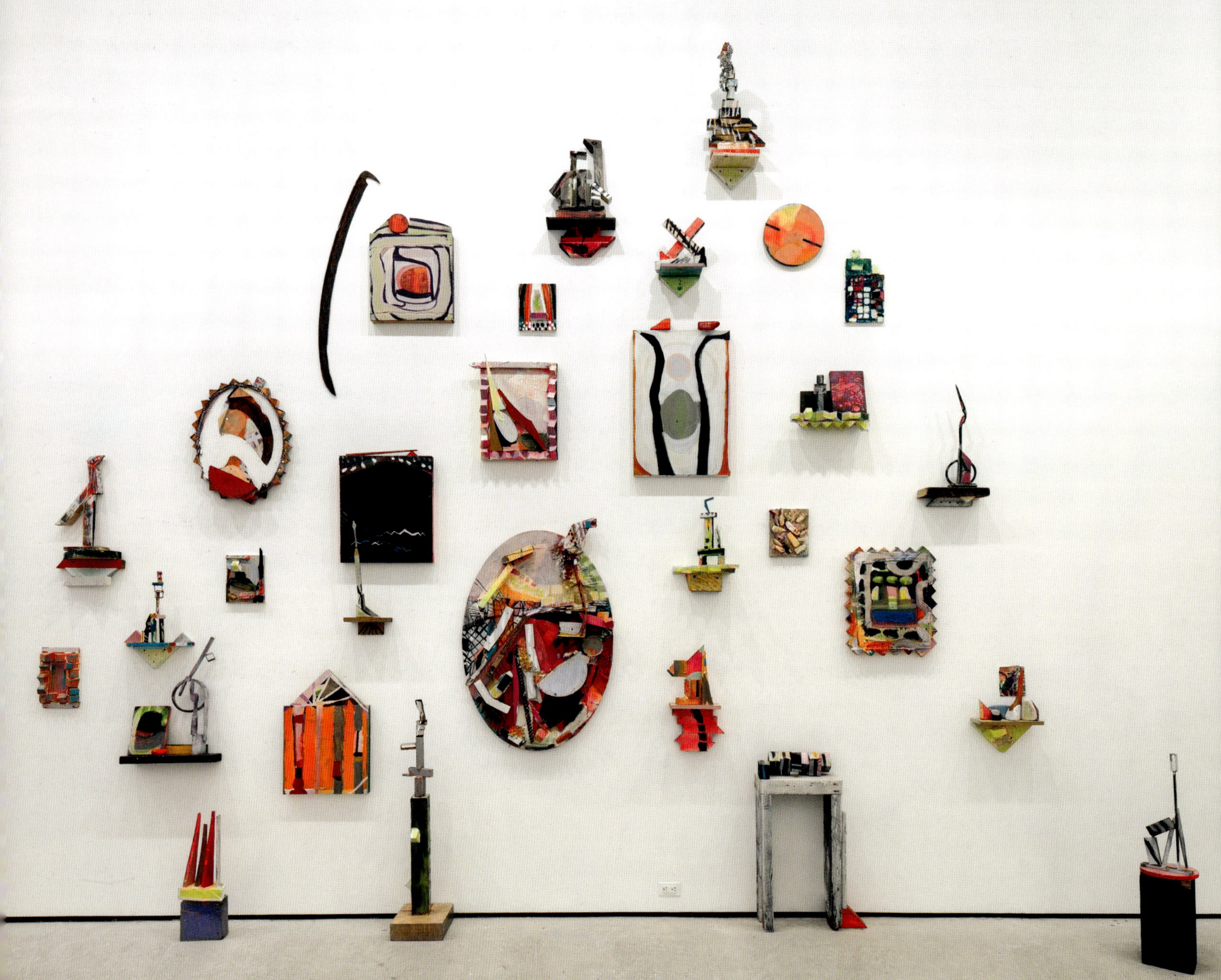

Emily Noelle Lambert (b. 1975) works in both 2D and 3D and has exhibited in numerous group and solo shows. Based in Greenpoint, Brooklyn, she is known for her use of exuberant color in complex combinations. Lambert explores movement and placement throughout her work, and her sculpture practice has focused on stacked, totemic constructions, largely composed of found objects that, for Lambert, retain strong narrative or biographical associations. She received her BA from Antioch College and her MFA from Hunter College. Lambert was a fellow at the MacDowell Colony, The Lower East Side Print Shop, Dieu Donné, and she has expanded her practice into the making of multiples. Lambert is represented by Lu Magnus Gallery, New York.

Emily Noelle Lambert

MATTHEW McLENDON **I want to start with your origins as an artist. You work in a variety of media, so did you start off sculpting, or painting, or printmaking?**

EMILY NOELLE LAMBERT Well I started painting, but actually even before I studied painting in school, I really did start as a maker. I think that's a big part of it. I grew up in a household in which my mom was an artist, painting textiles, sort of wild and wacky, out of the pattern and decoration movement. Fairies, and polka dots, and flowers, and creatures, painting on silk that she would then sew into dresses and kimonos. My Dad, as well, was building and making stuff all the time, furniture and functional things, not a fine craftsman, but it was out of his love of making the objects around us. So I grew up with that around me in Pittsburgh, and my mom was involved with the center for the arts there, and a lot of their friends were artists. It was the background.

MM **So you grew up around "making."**

ENL Yes, and my mom's studio was the attic of our house and it was connected to my room. When she wasn't up there, I could go in, and this was the space where you'd come to make and draw, whatever. I understand that as a very important part of my development as an artist.

MM **And, you were in Pittsburgh, so were you going to the Carnegie museums?**

ENL Yes, from the age of eight or nine on, for art classes every Saturday. So I had not only the craftsmanship but also walking through the halls there with Picasso and Matisse, and Arthur Dove, and Milton Avery, Giacometti—that was the other part of the education.

MM **What classes were you taking as a child at the Carnegie? Were they traditional?**

ENL Yes, it was your basic museum education program: you would meet as a group in the hall of architecture with all the plaster casts of the great monuments and then either go look at paintings and then up to

Curio Logic II, 2014

the classroom and work on colors, or you'd go to the natural history part and look at birds, observational drawing, and collage, and I remember doing these great cut-outs and printmaking. That must have been fourth grade until high school, then I went on to Carnegie-Mellon programs.

MM **When you got to college, what work were you making then?**

ENL I went to Antioch, and the art building was an old airplane hanger, a huge building with these glass ceilings, and I worked in printmaking, etching, ceramics, and then painting. As a liberal arts student, I studied it all, 16mm film, typography. My degree says "visual arts" and it really was this expanse, but painting was really where I settled. I worked with a great teacher, Daniel Hignite, who had just finished at Yale and this was his first teaching job. I fought against what he wanted us to do, but it was really great. He really taught me how to paint in a great way.

MM **We'll talk about the influence of painting on your sculpture in a bit, but before that I want to focus on your use of the found object. Have you always been collecting discarded things, for lack of a better word, to use in your art?**

ENL Yes, yes, always picking up things. I think that's all part of it—seeing. Seeing form and color in the world and then translating into painting. Or, seeing scraps of color, images, strange pieces of wood. I started looking at the world around me and taking those pieces back to the studio. Now it's literally taking the pieces, the found objects, found forms, really, and putting them into the work.

MM **So, you are really thinking about this not as found object but rather as found form. That is a crucial distinction in your practice, I would think.**

ENL I don't know if I've ever really said that before just now, but that really is so much a part of it. I love the thrift store and the flea market. I'll actually dream of those things and gravitating toward strange shapes and vessels, and forms, bright colors. Those are the things that I hold on to.

MM **For me, one of the fascinating things about your sculpture is that each piece has its own story. So, was the narrative aspect of the pieces always an aspect of the process, or did it evolve over time?**

ENL I think that the story part, the history of the forms, has evolved. But, I think that knowing that they are almost souvenirs of certain places I've been to or things I've seen, somehow, this combination of the sculpture and the story come together. It's about walking down the street and seeing a strange circular form, like an old cutting board with a hole in it. Then, I'm like, "Whoa! What made such an interesting shape? How can I work with this?" Then, it's about combining and recombining these forms. So, I think, the initial collection is about form and shape, where they come from, and their heft, too. The more I'm building, the more I think about what I need. I see these huge construction beams that the New York City Department of Transportation uses, these huge orange and white beams, and I think, "Where can I get those that aren't as heavy but are kiln dried?" That then becomes about calling out to my brother or my dad and saying, "Keep an eye out for huge beams I can use."

MM **So it becomes a family affair.**

ENL [*laughs*] Definitely! My cousin who lives out in Oakland is a huge collector as well, and he's always telling me to come out with a truck because he has all these painted pieces of wood for me that he's found on the beach. So, yes, I'm collecting from all these different places.

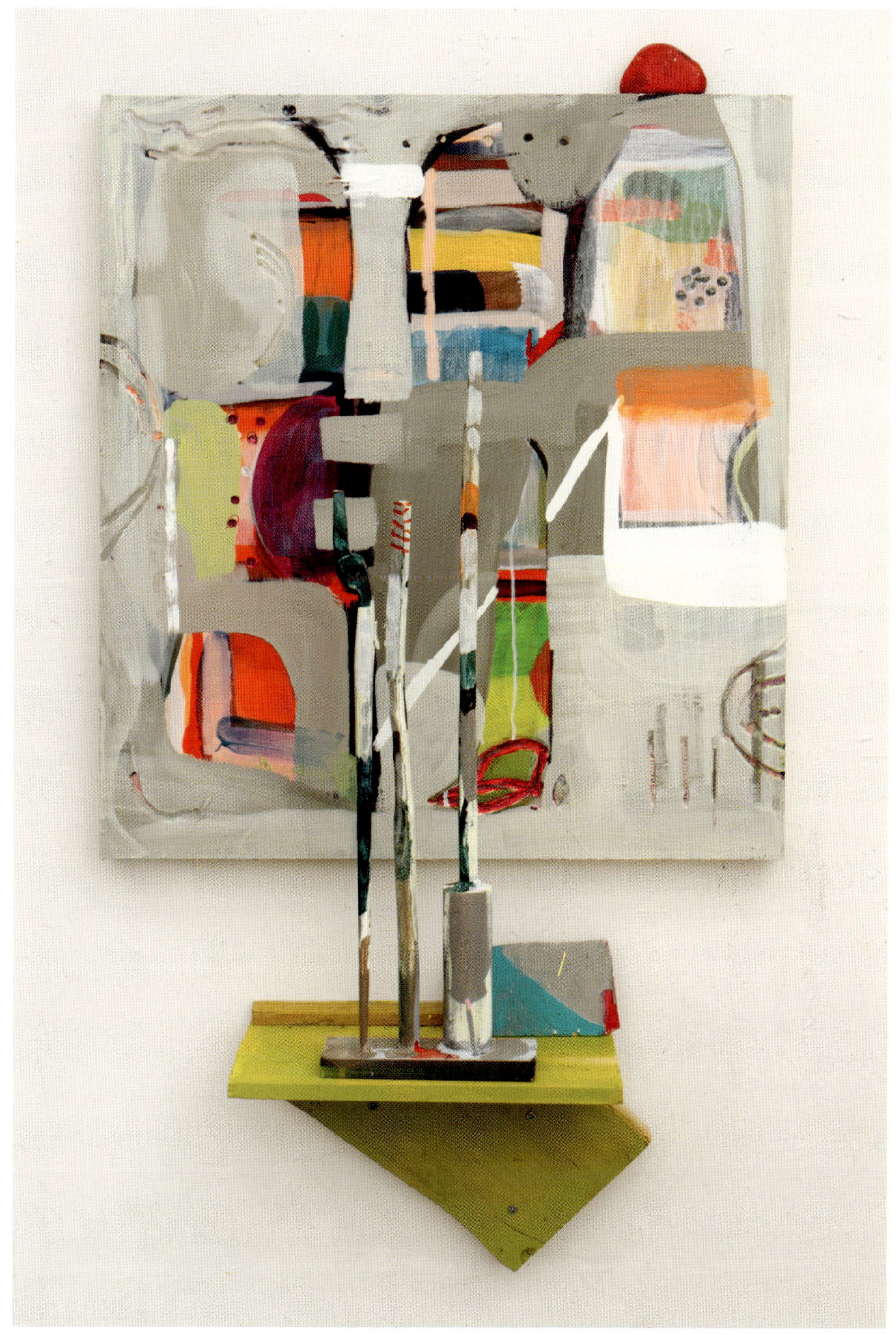

Road Path Way, 2014

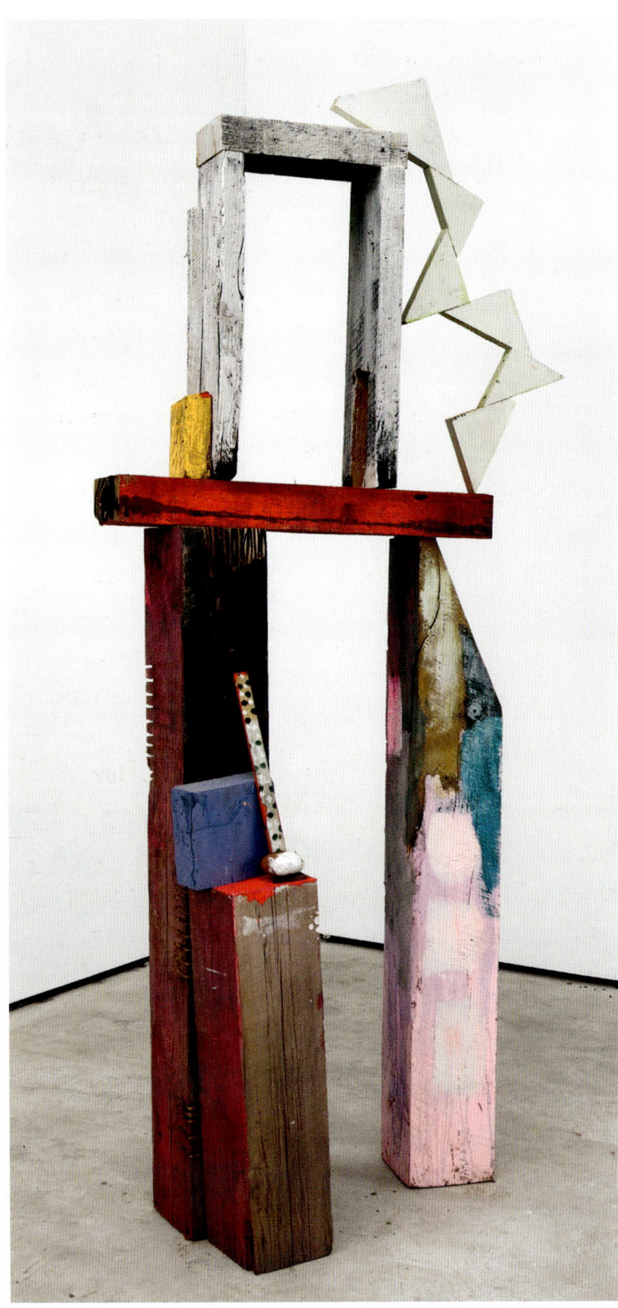

MM **If I'm following you, you see these huge beams that the city is using that are too heavy for you to carry back. So, are you carrying back the look of that beam in your mind and then searching for something that approximates it?**

ENL Yes, definitely.

MM **So it's a mental collecting as well.**

ENL Yes, and I'm thinking when I'm walking down the street and the sun is hitting a corner where there is a bit of graffiti and part has been pasted over and a yellow stick leaning against it, and an orange piece of paper floating—I see these moments of decay, and accident, and purposefulness. Something that had a use but no longer has a use, this is a composition. I think some of the pieces of wood retain some of this. At some points, the natural wood comes through, at some points paint comes through. It's in the same way that accidental arrangement, detritus, purposefulness, all these things are swirling around in the outside world, but that's also what I want. I want to find those moments within the sculpture and the painting.

MM **I've really loved two phrases you've used in our conversation: found form and accidental arrangement. How much chance do you leave in your process as you arrange the work?**

ENL Yes, and I think I have to say that's what sculpture gives me that I don't have in painting. I can try and surprise myself in painting, I can put the painting away, I can turn it upside down, but it's still always me creating the forms and building with those forms. But when I'm collaborating with the pieces of wood that I find, then I have an exterior collaborator.

MM **I love that you see the wood as a collaborator.**

ENL Yeah, because it's giving me something that I wouldn't have come up with on my own. It's giving me something that is not totally determined by me.

Triumph, 2012

MM **Do you view your work as indexical, or archival?**

ENL Yes, certainly indexical. Especially now since I started the sculptural work in 2009, there is definitely this history: these are the pieces that came from my residency on Long Island on the South Shore, this is from Montauk, this is from my friend's studio when he was getting rid of pieces of wood, this is from the shop down the street—so, they do tie to periods of time from 2008 through now. Whatever moment comes through that. And then, they change and link together. Is this the South Shore buoy or is this from Miami? So indexical is a good term, but I don't think archival, because they will continue to change.

MM **Yes, and that is an important aspect of your work. You frequently rearrange the constituent pieces from various sculptures to create new sculptures.**

ENL They are made to be modular, to come apart, and then come back together. When they leave the studio in one form—unless I'm very sure it has a trajectory beyond my studio—when they come back, they come into pieces again. I live in New York City, not a giant barn, so my studio is a place of experiment. They are not all open to reshuffling, though. Today I was photographing three pieces that came back from Kalamazoo, and there was this other piece that had been sitting in here not quite finished, and today I saw something that had not come together before, and then it's working really well with this painting I have going on. A painting is set until I change it, but the sculpture can fall apart and come back together. I can forget one piece and substitute another and it's even better, like building blocks in a way.

MM **Right, and each iteration is valid for you. How does the meaning then change for you when you are collaborating with the wood in this way?**

ENL Well, I think that's where the indexical quality falls away and it's about the form. It becomes less about what and where they are from and more about how they speak to one another, how the color and the texture work. But, where these pieces are from is so much about what they look like, so the indexical doesn't totally fall away. And, these voices mix when they come back together. I think that's the notion of time and the trajectory of the work. I may make a series of work for one show, but to re-envision it or reassemble, if it comes back into the soup of the studio it will become something else.

MM **Another great turn of phrase, "the soup of the studio."**

ENL I say that to my students: It's really how I think about it. I keep things stirring in the studio—big paintings, small paintings, big sculpture, small components of sculpture. I work between them all and it does feel like a soup.

MM **When I had my first studio visit with you, what I found most intriguing was the color of your work and how you spoke about it. In many ways, I think of you first as a colorist and then as a sculptor, a painter, a printmaker. You paint the wood first and then create the sculpture. It's the form of the wood, then you paint the form, and then you compose the sculpture, so you're really creating the sculpture like a painter thinks.**

ENL Right, but this isn't all down pat.

MM **No, I don't mean to reduce this to a formula: "This is how Emily makes art."**

ENL No, I'm enjoying the conversation, this helps. It also helps that I'm here in my freshly cleaned studio looking at things I just arranged this morning, and I'm thinking to myself that it did come about through these color choices that are happening in it. Going back to painting, so (A) there's the collaborator, but

(B) it's saying in a painting, "I want this large form to feel very light, and I want this form to be very sharp and bright, and I want this form to feel soft." Then again, the wood forms dictate that. The character of the wood gives me so much more, then it can become about arrangement, balance, texture. Yes, definitely, without a doubt the color.

MM **You have these great evocative titles as well. Where do those come from?**

ENL They come from all over. I think some of the titles are from poetry; I love Rilke. I think across the board I see such a parallel between making artwork and making a life. I'm always seeing how I approach my work and how I approach my life—they are very similar. I like seeing those metaphors. I like to think about words that can convey multiple meanings in the titles. That's one aspect. I also want the work to be multiple things at once. One of the other things is that the sculpture exist in my studio as these characters, they become like characters hanging out in the space with me. I refer to them as guideposts, or guardians, or watchers. Fortress, I love that word. It can either be keeping people from coming in or it could be keeping them from going out. There is also the play between Fortress and Forest. That play back and forth I find interesting. I had one piece in the studio for eight months, and no matter how I arranged it, it always had a figurative quality. So I gave it a name—Walker—because it had this presence in the studio of moving.

MM **Because you go back and forth among printmaking, and sculpting, and painting, do you think of them as separate practices, or is it all simply creating art?**

ENL No, it's all the soup. Really, they all inform one another, work together, speak to one another. I think that is really the place I am excited about being in. I will focus on one for a while, and then I'll move my focus, but they are all really happening simultaneously. I started the sculptures around 2008–2009; they gave me so much more freedom, and bravery, and exploration, and then I brought that back to my painting. So, then it was: "How do I build this painting and how does that inform how I make a sculpture?" Then in this last year, focusing on prints, the simplification of form then informs the sculpture and then comes back into the paintings. Maybe the sculpture really is the exciting force with all of this. I've never taken a sculpture class, and yet I'm using it with that kind of sense of "How do I do this? Let's try it out." That continues to reinvigorate all the aspects of my practice. And I should also say that now I'm experimenting with stacking my paintings in arrangements on the wall, and when I was at The Ringling, I was walking through the Gothic gallery and seeing how everything was stacked on the wall together there. That gallery, I was shocked by it, and then I read the description—that whole notion of the curio, the curiosity, the great combination of the relief sculpture with the painting. That was a great surprise and it is what I've been experimenting with.

MM **Well that leads me directly into what or who do you see as your influences?**

ENL That is, of course, such an important question. It is vast. To say one or two, you can't. It's a continual process. I said a little bit about growing up and the collection at the Carnegie—certainly Diebenkorn and color, and Matisse, and Picasso, Arthur Dove, Milton Avery, those were really important figures for me, and Giacometti. But then, I go to the Met in New York and I look at South East Asian art and then the rooms

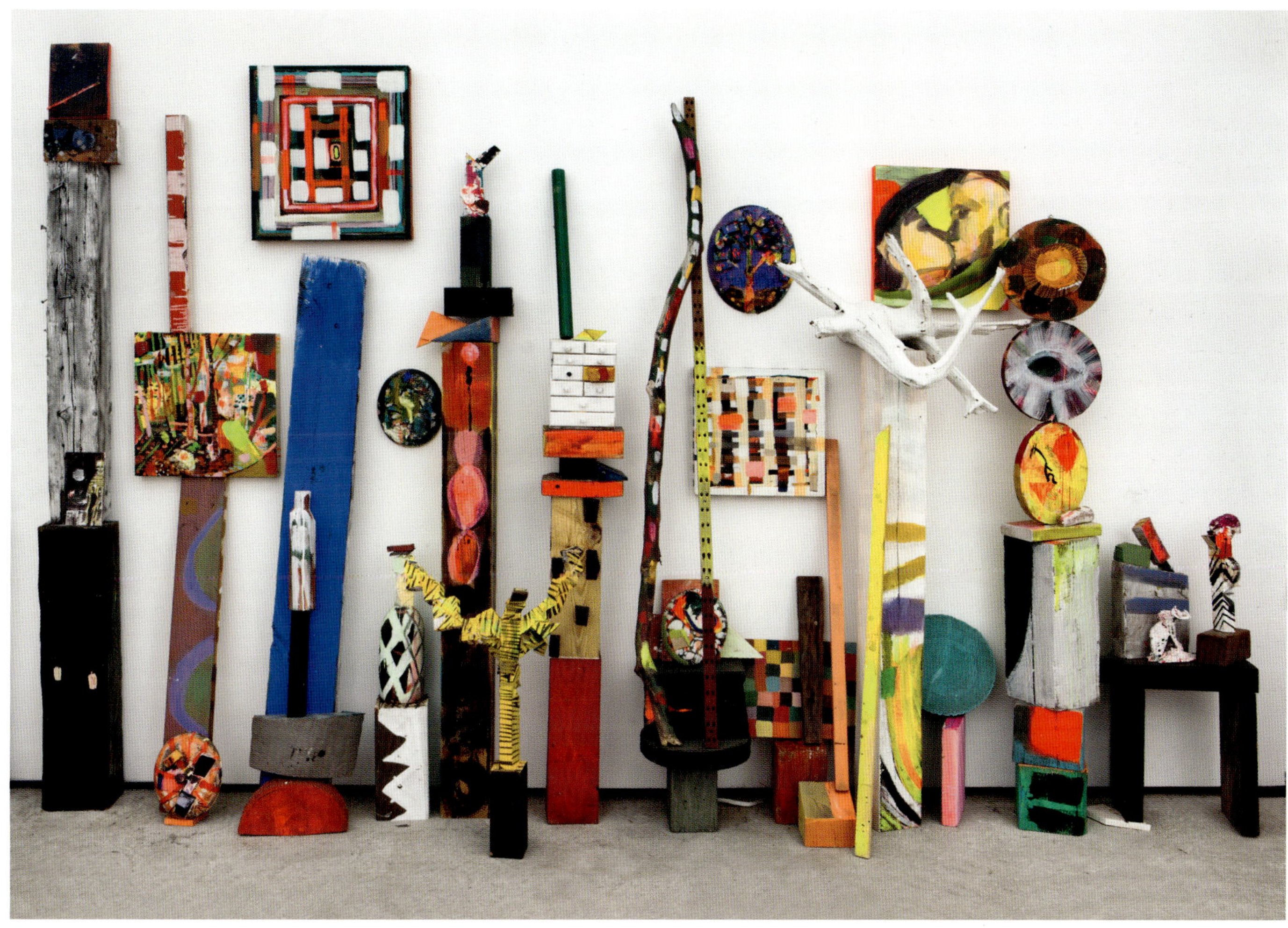

with the large totem figures. That work is really exciting to me. And I remember the African sculpture at the Carnegie with the nails, and whenever someone was sick they would hammer a nail into the sculpture, and I loved that participatory sense. That says art has a possibility to have some effect, at least that's how I viewed it growing up. Then I traveled around Mexico, and India, and all around Europe, but I had never been to Italy. So, when I finally made it to Italy in 2009, to Rome and Florence, and sat in the cathedrals, it was, "Oh my God, I'm sitting on art, I'm standing on art, I'm in it, I'm smelling it." It was an incredible, surrounding experience. It was installation art.

MM **Right, so it's when art pervades every aspect of your life. It's literally on every street corner in Florence.**

ENL Yeah! Yes! So I think that's a big part. I do continue to look back to the early Renaissance paintings

Fortress, 2012

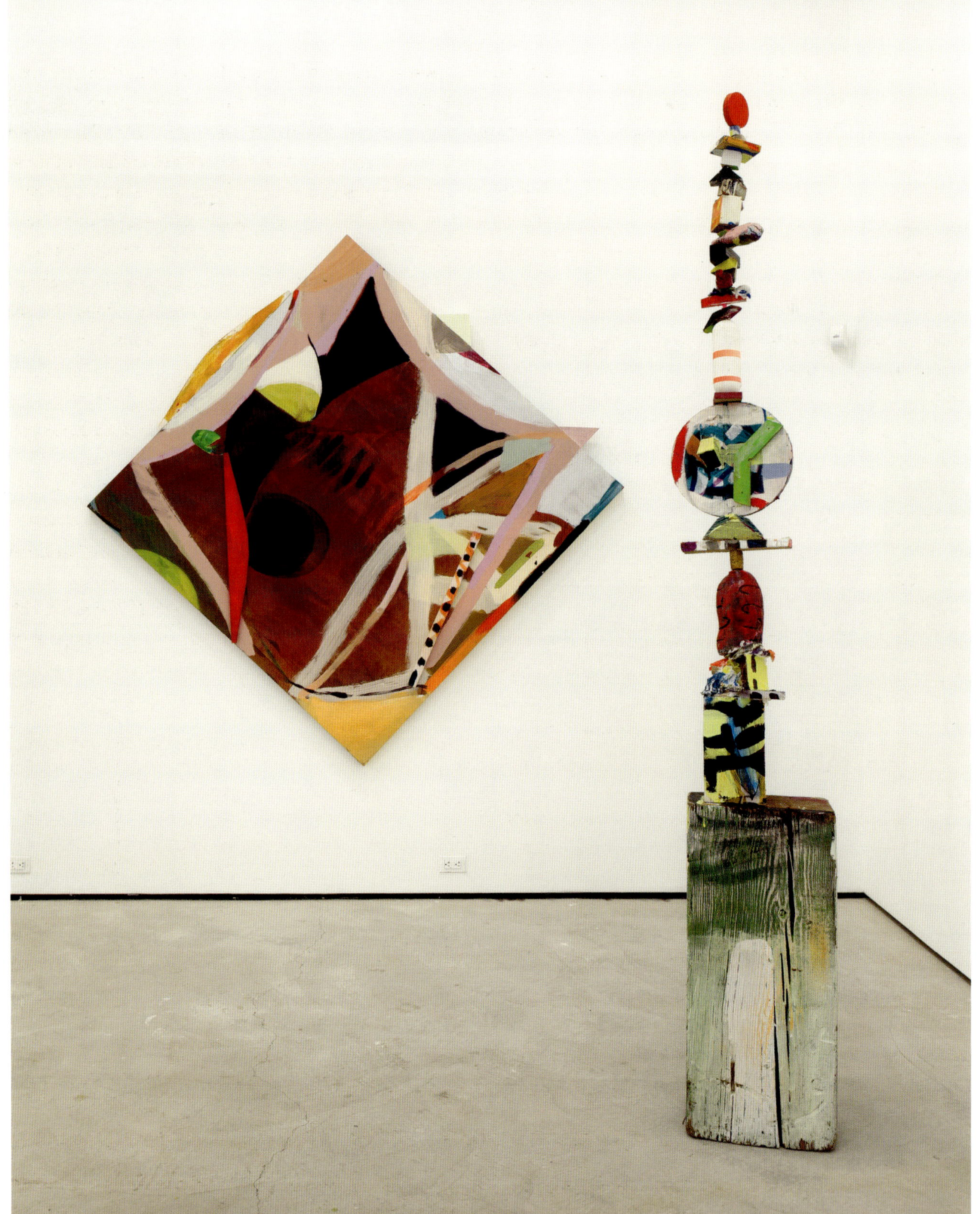

where they are figuring things out. So, there are no specifics, but it's all of this.

MM **Yes, these are all things that come into this soup that you talk about.**

ENL And then it's being in New York, and being with my friends and seeing what they are making. This incredible community of artists I have. It's a back-and-forth conversation.

MM **Right, and as we discussed in that first studio visit, I was so interested that you painted the wood before you made the sculpture because when I first looked at your sculpture I thought, "Ah, yes, a continuation of Nevelson." But, of course, Nevelson painted her found wood sculptures after she brought the forms together. She talked about the paint as a skin. You are doing something radically different.**

ENL Right, right. I was so glad you said that.

MM **And, then as we talked more, this recombining of the forms reminded me of Brancusi who created the bases for his sculptures and frequently reconfigured the bases, which, ultimately, were an important part of the sculptural whole.**

ENL Oh yes, I love Brancusi. I love that room at MoMA. That always stops me dead in my tracks. He has the marble, with the plated cast forms, [added] to the wood. That combination, I think about it all the time whether it's conscious or subconscious.

MM **So, for me, it's important to frame you in that art historical context. You are definitely a part of these conversations, but you are working so differently. That, for me, is the real interest.**

And so, finally, we should talk about your relationship to the "found form" that you use as discarded material, as trash. Do you think about that?

ENL Oh sure, I mean we generate a lot of trash and this is a way of finding these things and giving them a new life. I remember being a kid and a certain night of the week we'd drive around in our VW van and we'd find all this amazing furniture, and bits and pieces. We found this great Barcelona chair, you know, this incredible stuff. I've stopped doing it after the big bed bug scare, but this was a part of my life.

MM **Well, this brings up the fact that we'll need to have a future conversation with our conservator at the museum, because all of the work that is included in the exhibition comes from "trash," it's found, it's scavenged, and so, we have to be mindful of this. So those of you working with organic material, we have to gather as much information as possible to determine any risk. I think the saving grace with your found wood, though, is that you paint it. Keep painting and sealing everything in.**

ENL And a good portion of it has been inside for a long time. I do think about that. Believe me, the thought of bringing something questionable into my studio, I really think about it.

MM **Yes, it's one of the particular things we have to think about with contemporary art. Nontraditional materials create nontraditional challenges for the museum.**

Grand Whirl Stream, 2014 and *Desire*, 2014

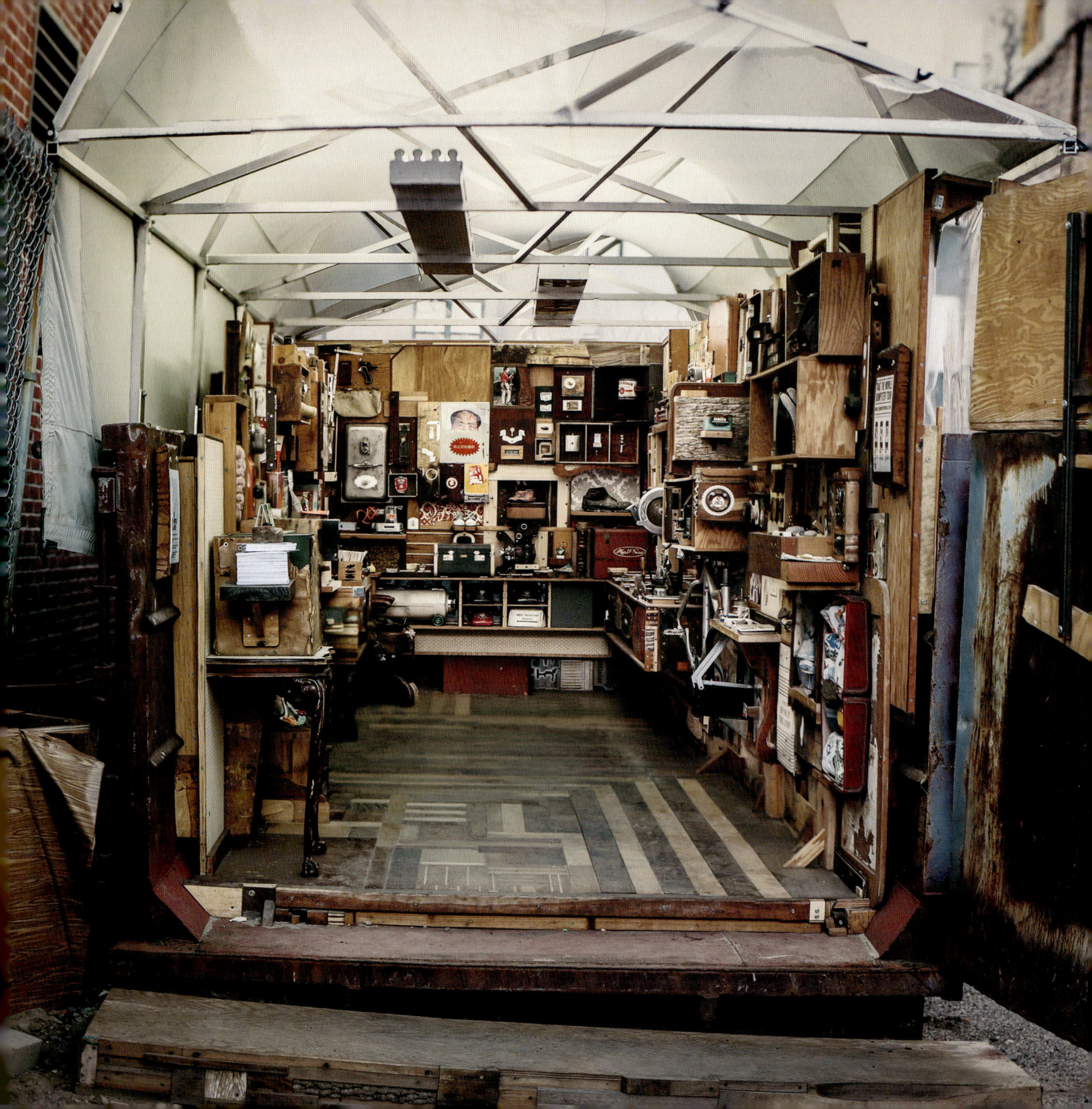

Mac Premo (b. 1973) is an American artist and "stuffmaker." Premo graduated from the Rhode Island School of Design in 1995. He has exhibited in New York City, Los Angeles, Miami, Washington, D.C., and Belfast, Northern Ireland. Premo has won seven New York Emmy® Awards, including those for best commercial, best photography, best set design, and best PSA. A 2008 NYFA fellow in video, he currently works across media. Premo lives in Brooklyn with his wife and daughters. He is represented by Pavel Zoubok Gallery.

Mac Premo

MATTHEW McLENDON **Let's start with the origins of *The Dumpster Project*. It begins in 2010–11?**

MAC PREMO Great question, "When did it start?" Well, actually, it started in 1973 when I was born [*laughs*], but the project came about in the spring of 2011. I had to move out of my studio. I was sharing a studio with Oliver Jeffers and Aaron Ruff. It was a great studio, a one-story garage space that had housed myriad things, but it had held hot dog carts just prior to us moving in. We busted down some walls and put in a wood-burning stove, and just really made it our own space. But then the roof started to cave in and the heat really sucked and then our landlord, who was super cool, decided to sell it. It was going to be turned into a doctor's office, and it was time. Oliver and Aaron found another space relatively quickly, and it made sense for us to find separate spaces. I make a lot of dust, and dust doesn't really go well with paint. So at the time it was like, "Crap, I've got to find a new studio and I have all of this stuff." So I found another temporary space, but it was about 30 percent as big as the former space. So I had to figure out what to do with all of the stuff, and thus began a process of deaccession.

MM **I love that you refer to it as a process of "deaccession," as that's the term we use in museums when we remove things from our collections. Already the link between your work and the museum as a repository of collections is becoming clear, but we'll explore that more later.**

MP Yeah, I could have stored it, but that would have been anathema to the whole idea. Essentially, I had been keeping all this stuff to make art out of. So the question presented itself: do I collect and keep stuff to make collage art or do I make collage art in order to facilitate my desire to collect and keep stuff? But when my feet were put to the fire it was the former, because I didn't want to keep all of this stuff. It was things like my daughter's first shoes, I didn't want to just keep them, I wanted to use them.

The Dumpster Project, 2011

MM **Did you start to throw anything out? Did you throw anything out?**

MP No, no I didn't because I came up with the idea first. If I'm going to put them in a dumpster, I'm going to do it my way. And the joke was always, if it starts to go pear shaped, I can just call the carting company to come take it away. So, that's how the whole thing started.

MM **So, you had been collecting all of this material starting in your childhood.**

MP Yeah, I had a lot of stuff from childhood. My mom moved out of the house I grew up in around 1997 and I took a lot of stuff from there. And I watched her put a lot of stuff in storage; in fact, I think it's still in storage. And, I remember thinking, "Well, you might as well just throw it away." To a degree, I mean that's how I was thinking. A lot of people put stuff in storage, but that feels like purgatory to me, and once you get to purgatory, you don't generally come back to life.

MM **Right, so what do you feel drives you in collecting? When you were a kid and you were collecting things, was it already with a mind to create art out of it?**

MP I always made art, but growing up I was doing a lot of tight pen-and-ink stuff. But I look back at my room and when I was in sixth grade, I was really into cars, so I'd buy *Car and Driver* magazine and my walls were covered with cars. Then very shortly thereafter that transferred into skateboarding and for the next four years my walls were covered with skateboarding images. So, I always, sort of, built a collage in which I lived. I didn't even apply the collage that I surrounded myself with into the art-making I was doing from ages thirteen to seventeen, but as soon as I got to college (RISD) and really engaged with collage, suddenly the way that I organized the world around me visually, and the art that I made, started to meet and it really hasn't turned around since. Subsequently, all of my environments have been not only places I live but also potential sources of material.

MM **Were either of your parents artists?**

MP No, neither of my parents are artists, but my grandfather on my mother's side was an engineer and there are some artistic leanings in my family. My mother has the most beautiful handwriting in the world. I grew up around a tremendous amount of encouragement. My mom raised me that it was mandated that you follow your dreams, if you're lucky enough to have one, and she encouraged and supported my art-making in terms of, you know, she would drive me to classes at the Corcoran and my father was incredibly supportive, too. He's one of my closest friends. But I remember we were talking a few years ago, at a bar, and I leaned back and said, "You know, Pop, I don't really know what it is you do, and you don't really know what I do either." And he looked over, and laughed, and said "Nope." And it was one of those great moments, because, I mean, I know what he does and he knows what I do, but we don't know what the other does in terms of process. But even with that, both of them have been absolute champions of me. They've always treated it as though it could become a reality.

MM **That's great. So it starts out with you creating these collage environments you were making as a kid, then you go to RISD to study illustration? What were you making during college?**

MP When I first got there I was still married to the tight pen and ink that I knew I could do, but that crashed quickly. So I didn't technically graduate with enough credits in illustration to call it an illustration degree. I found a loophole, and I took a lot of animation classes, so in a sense, the degree was a type of collage. But what happened is, in my sophomore year I went to study in Mexico, and at that point, I don't know if I became

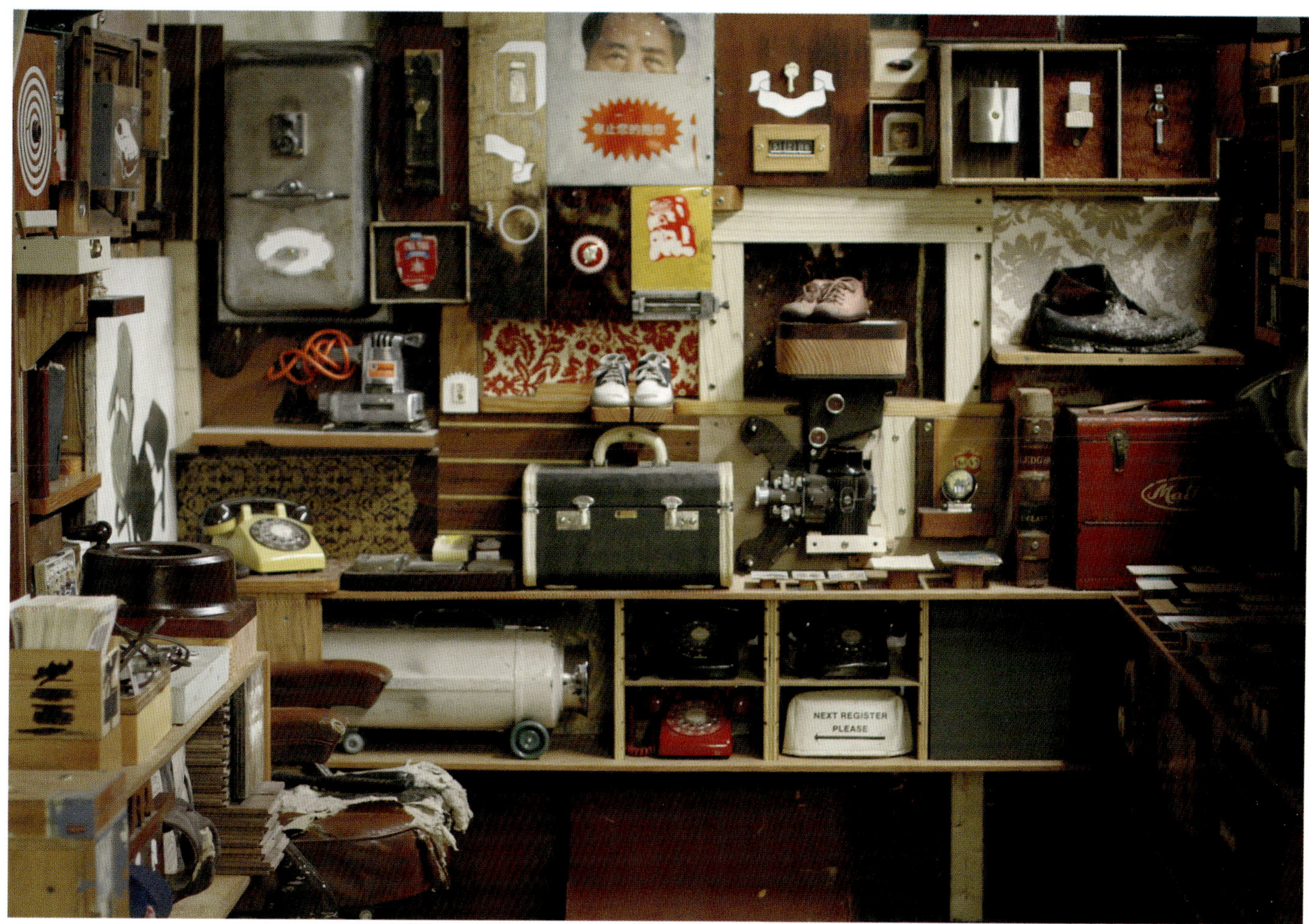

inseparable from that method, or if I just realized that was my calling.

MM **Was there anything particular in Mexico that brought that out?**

MP The textures and the colors and the fact that there's an aesthetic in Mexico that is collage, and by aesthetic I don't just mean the way it looks, I mean it in the true sense of aesthetic, across the board. Everything, the reasoning, all the way to the final output, the whole empirical sense. I remember being in Mexico City and feeling I was in a collage, from the lack of building code and the ad hoc creation of a building system around me, to the colors and the patterns that were put together seemingly without any regard to each other, but then the more you get to know Mexican culture you realize the deep regard to each other. And it just sort of felt like my understanding of collage shifted from the way something looks to the whole reason something is created,

The Dumpster Project (detail)

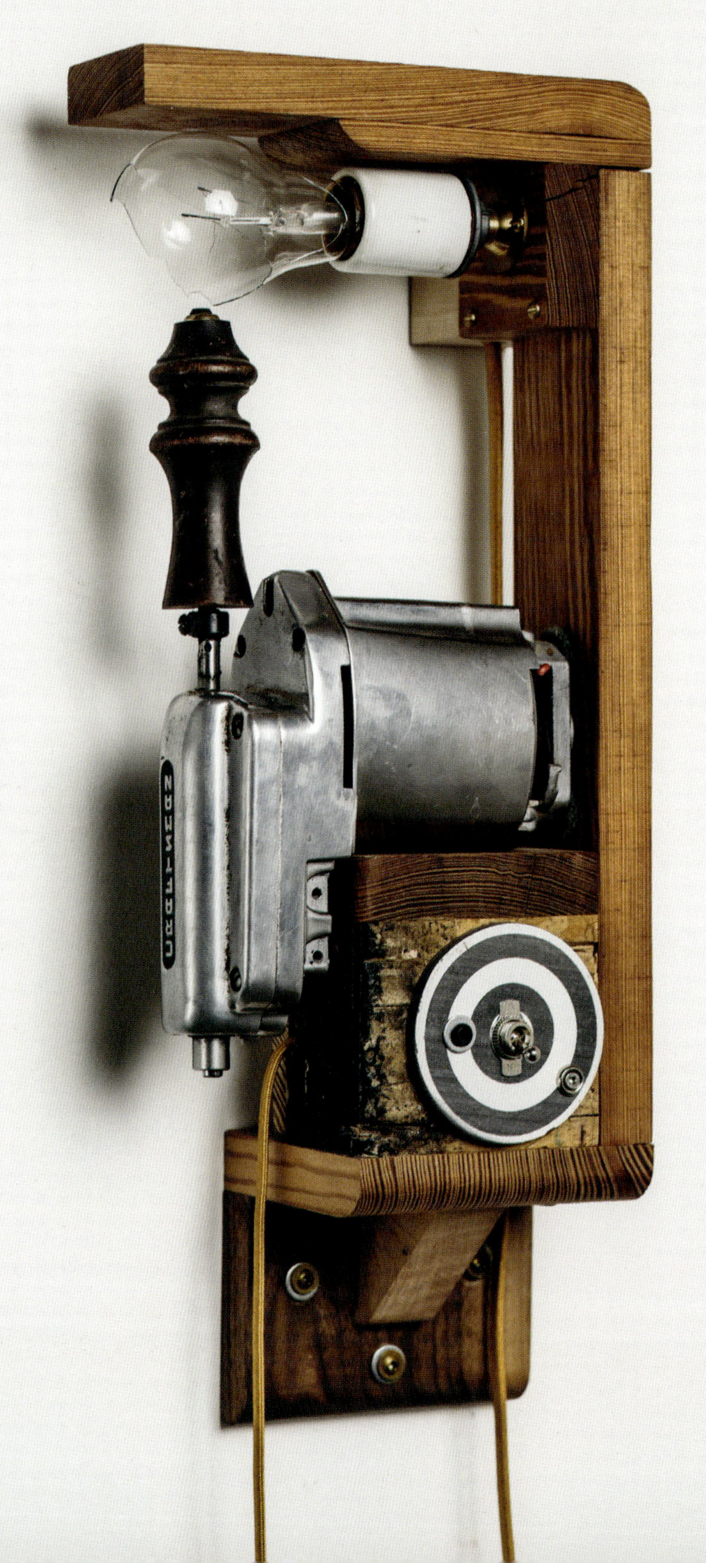

the whole process, the way of looking. Disparate does not mean that things do not get along; disparate means that there are two ways to measure those things and they might be tremendous next to each other. That was a revolution in my brain I still haven't gotten over.

MM **That is so important, because I wanted to discuss that you have a very open use of the word collage. The Oxford English Dictionary still defines collage simply as pasting of papers or things onto a surface, but you refer to your whole body of work as collage, your sculpture, the dumpster. So what does collage mean to you?**

MP That's such a great question. I went down to Mexico City about three or four years ago with my friend, Oliver, with the intent of recreating the Popol Vuh. The idea was to do a group project, so we did this workshop with a publishing company and Mexican illustrators down there and talked about basically doing a global (meaning participants) version of the Popol Vuh. We met with some resistance from the old-school dudes; some of the younger funky dudes were into it, but nothing ever happened with the workshop. It was a fascinating project to be a part of. And there was this one guy who kept referring to everything as a concept, and it became a kind of joke—everything was a concept—so to me collage is a concept. I look at the stuff that I do—I just wrote and performed a one-man play, I do animation, I do film stuff, I do carpentry and two dimensional collage in its traditional form and three-dimensional sculptural woodworking—and I think collage means it's less about the materials and more about the method.

MM **Alright, then, describe your method.**

MP Well, it leads with concept. What's the idea that I want to investigate, the question I want to answer, or the question I want to pose? What do I want to say? Then in a weird way it becomes the path of least personal resistance. That certainly doesn't mean the easiest way, but I start using the methods and forms around me that make the most sense and, in a very personal way, lock into addressing the problem I posed. And so, sometimes when I have an idea I'll start by making a little wooden sculpture and it will end up becoming, for instance, a play. That's what happened with this last play: it came out of this series I made called *Smashbulb*. What I posed with making these pieces was a question that the process wasn't answering in a satisfactory manner for me, so I looked for different forms to present the problem in. The process means being open to whatever form best suits the concept I'm trying to tackle. Obviously, the form isn't all over the place; I have a form and visual vocabulary that I've been building, but within that it varies among drawing, filmmaking, woodworking, etc. So collage to me is being open to the materials being dictated by the message.

MM **That last bit is very interesting. I like that you're saying whatever it is you do—the initial impulse is a question. So, with *The Dumpster Project*, what was that initial question?**

MP Why do we keep the things we keep? Why do we collect the things we collect? What is the value of an object?

MM **And what did you ultimately determine for yourself?**

MP The things that we keep and the things we collect are more than just mnemonic devices, but they are that, too—what they allude to, if that's what a mnemonic device is. What it alludes to, what it reminds us of, are the narratives of our life. The objects we keep, the things we choose to collect, ultimately become a taxonomy of our existence. They become a map of who we are, and they point to the web of narratives that make up our identity.

MM **So, do you see *The Dumpster Project* as a personal archive or index?**

Smashbulb (Portrait), 2013

MP It's a taxonomy; it's a taxonomy of my existence.

MM **One of the themes explored in this exhibition is an idea that comes out of archaeology. Archaeologists talk about "object biography," which, loosely, is the accumulated narratives arrived at through the shifting contexts of the object; the object takes on its own "biography." What is really interesting to me is where the object biography comes up against the artist's biography and the biography of the viewer.**

MP That's the one thing I never expected—the biography of the viewer. That's what, for me, was so humbling about this whole project.

MM **How do you mean?**

MP When I finished this thing, first of all, I looked back and saw all the support I had in making this. My family; my wife; Oisin Dineen, my assistant from Cork, Ireland, who helped me build the whole thing; the Frank Collective, a production company I work with who gave me seed money to buy the dumpster. It really was herculean on so many people's parts. So, what happened is I finished this thing and was showing it at the DUMBO Arts Festival and I kind of had this idea that I would stand in the back and hold court and people would come in, ask me questions about all these things. But, as people walked in, I realized two things: one, there's not a lot of room in the dumpster so I eventually got squeezed out, and two, eventually I realized that I was totally unimportant. It was important that someone made it; it seemed very important to the project that a person made it, not a collection of people, because it was an examination of a life through objects. But, it didn't really matter who made it, and it certainly didn't matter that the dude was standing around waiting to talk because what people brought to it was their own experience, their own sense of narrative, their own sense of curiosity. Well, what does that mean? I can't tell you how many times

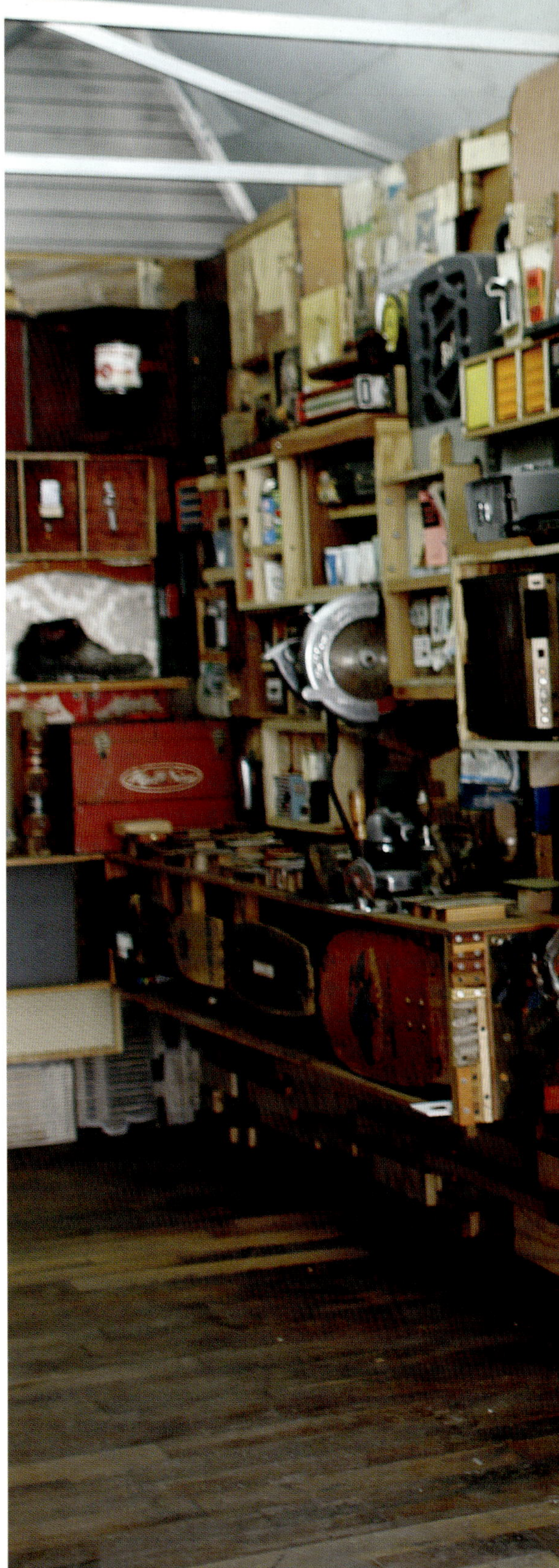

The Dumpster Project (detail)

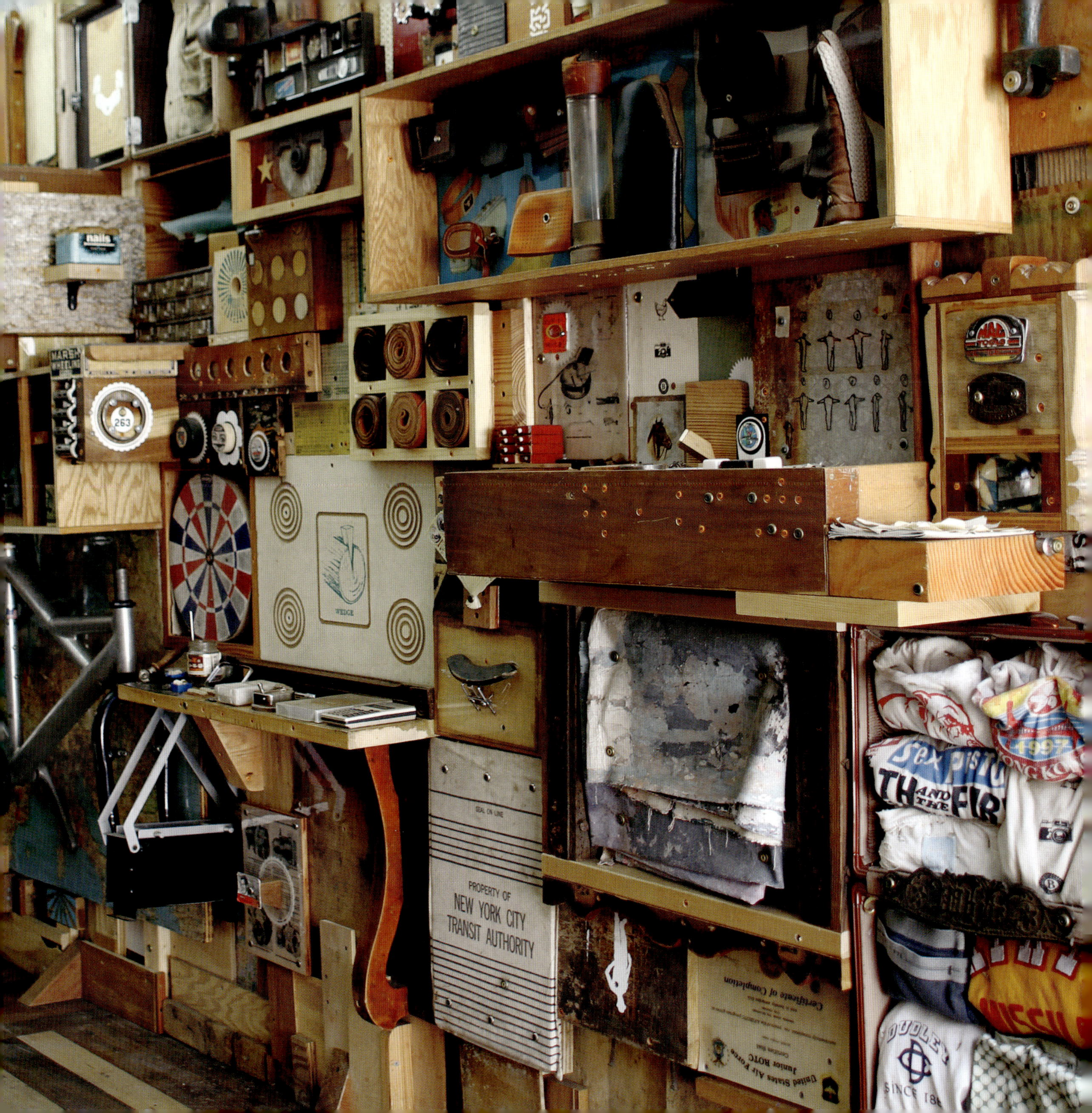

nails
263
WEDGE
PROPERTY OF
NEW YORK CITY
TRANSIT AUTHORITY
Certificate of Completion
United States Air Force
Junior ROTC
1997
SEX PISTOLS
THE FIR
DUDLEY
SINCE 18

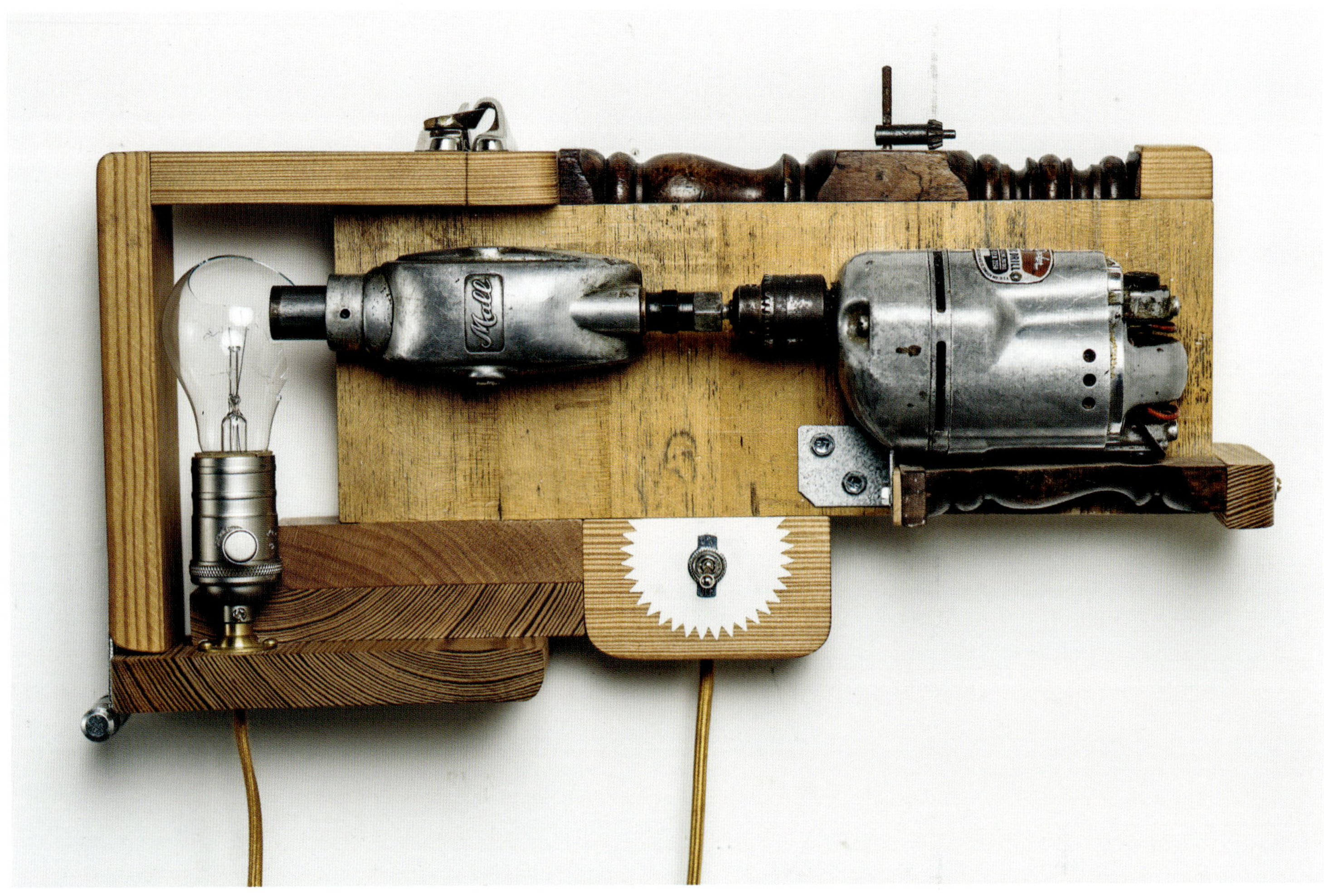

I heard, "I had one of those!" Then suddenly, my whole object biography, while relevant and maybe fascinating to some people, is just in itself a mnemonic device to someone else's narrative. But, the whole thing ended up being about stories, either mine, or what mine reminded other people of—their stories.

MM **Again, it's important I think that you talk about the individual objects as "mnemonic devices" because of course that is a linguistic tool. Language plays a large role in your art; there's quite a bit of text that makes its way into the work. Where is that coming from?**

MP I'm a big fan of philosophy, and semiotics, and linguistics. I have a fun time poking holes in it, to a degree. I mean, I don't have a PhD in it, I probably couldn't hold my own in a conversation with Bertrand Russell, but I enjoy it. I made a piece a few years ago where I spelled "failure" wrong, and I thought that was kind of funny. Moving back to the whole point of my

Smashbulb (Landscape), 2013

relationship with objects: it is about what they mean, and the most effective way we have to describe what something means is through language. But that's two things, it's fallible and it's not terribly poetic.

MM **Language plays a big part in *The Dumpster Project* because you have meticulously catalogued every object and written the equivalent of a museum chat label (didactic label) for the objects that is available for the viewer. So you are making the museum of your life.**

MP I'm close to being done with that. It's so interesting: I took maybe a year and a half off. I wrote maybe three hundred labels, maybe three hundred fifty of the roughly five hundred things. At some point, I'm just going to power through. For a while I was doing one a day pretty regularly. Writing doesn't feel all that different to me from collaging—same language, just a different method. So I have a pretty particular writing voice, same as I have a pretty particular craft voice. All started out as imitation. When I was fourteen I tried to write like Kurt Vonnegut, my early collages were like Robert Rauschenberg. Then you find your own voice eventually, so the writing aspect didn't feel so much like a separate thing, or addendum; it always felt integral.

MM **Were you thinking of precedents for this project? Were you thinking of how this fits into a particular history? Or were you doing this intuitively?**

MP I really did at the time have my back against the wall, I had been part of a startup, the whole thing folded, and startups don't tend to end cleanly, and so I realized through *The Dumpster Project* that in all ways I was an artist. Because, when you come up with a solution that's a bigger pain in the ass than the problem, you get to call yourself an artist. The big question was, if I had a big enough space to fit a dumpster in, would I really have to get rid of all my stuff. And the thing is, I found that space: someone donated that space based on this idea. I think I had this idea for a while: what if I put it all in a dumpster and got rid of it? Then when I had to move out of my space, I realized how much I didn't want to get rid of the stuff. Now, frankly, I would like to get rid of the dumpster—not throwing it away, I would like it to go somewhere and be a part of a program or collection. I don't need to spend time in it any more. I've made my peace with all the objects, but I had to go through that process of it becoming art. I had to photograph every object, move them around, get the right light on them, glue it or screw it onto its own little stage, and write its story. So, I wasn't thinking about any precedent; it was pretty much tunnel vision.

MM **It's always so humbling for me working with artists, because as an art historian and a curator, *The Dumpster Project* speaks to the whole history of the museum, collecting, the cabinet of curiosities, et cetera. And when it is at The Ringling, a monument to a collector, it is placed even more in this context. But, of course, as the artist, at least in this case, it didn't really even enter your conscious mind, this history. You were creating a impractical solution for a very practical problem.**

MP It felt weirdly very, very practical.

MM **Sure, but as object biography, if we come back to that, we can see the history of the museum within *The Dumpster Project*.**

MP Yeah, it's funny, I don't think I had ever heard of the cabinet of curiosities or Wunderkammern prior to making the dumpster. Then a lot of people were saying it's like a cabinet of curiosity.

MM **Well, it is and it isn't. It might be a bit of a superficial assessment. The cabinet of curiosities was about amassing the knowledge of the world, embodied in objects, in one place. It was biographical, perhaps, through the selection of things collected, or if those objects had been collected by the owner of the cabinet. So while *The Dumpster Project*, with its mass,**

its bricolage of "stuff," may visually recall the notion of the cabinet of curiosities, it's actually, I would argue, far more autobiographic. It's the archive of your life.

So, one of the last things I want to discuss, is your relationship to the material we discard. You stopped short of discarding all these objects, but many had been discarded by others and then collected by you, correct? Or, perhaps the question is, are you collecting or scavenging? Is there a difference for you?

MP Perhaps a semantic difference. I think scavenging serves a more functional purpose. If you're scavenging for stuff you are looking for stuff to use, whereas if you are collecting you are looking for stuff that holds meaning. I think I definitely do a bit of both. A lot of the wood I use is found on the street—there's a house being renovated. What kind of beams are they using? That's nice stuff to use. That's definitely scavenging. But, it's weird, there is a crossover. Collecting implies, I think, that you have a notion, or a base object criteria. You're collecting baseball cards. Most of the stuff I find on the street, 98 percent of the time I'll walk by something, I will have seen it, and two steps later I'll turn around and pick it up. So, I don't know if that's collecting or scavenging; I think it's less scavenging because I'm not looking for it. I just sort of walk with my head down all the time, and that may come from skateboarding; you always have to be aware of what's in front of you. That's the stuff I've found on the street. The stuff I've decided to keep; for instance, there's a Mr. Tayto bag in there, from the night I first told my wife I loved her. We were in an Irish pub, in the Lower East Side, and I kept that because it was immediately emblematic and I knew one way or another it was going to be a momentous event in my life. It turned out momentous in a good way. I saved that on purpose, I noticed it in the moment. It felt like a character in the narrative.

And then there's the stuff that people give me. I've become this repository of crap, and it's great, I never say no because once you do that, you shut all the doors.

MM **How do you describe your aesthetic?**

MP I like stuff that has the ability to show its history in its material. I like wood stuff because it takes on character, it scratches, it wears, it weathers, it takes on form that shows its context. So I think my aesthetic is using stuff that sort of hints at its narrative.

MM **You use the word "stuff" a lot.**

MP Yeah, I do. I call myself a "stuff maker."

MM **Is that conscious? Why "stuff?"**

MP Yeah it is. Stuff is everything. As opposed to, how do I put this?

MM **Is it because it's so generic, it's inclusive?**

MP Yes, it doesn't discriminate. "Objects" sounds a little fancy. It already implies that there should be a meaning. Whereas, "stuff" is powerfully ubiquitous.

MM **I love that, "powerfully ubiquitous." I think the final question for you is, what is the difference between collecting and hoarding?**

MP Hoarding is when you project yourself onto the object, and I think collecting is when you appreciate the context. A hoarder sees the stack of envelopes and says, "I should hold those, I can use those later." For what context? It's voided away in a desperation. Or I took a sip of this coke can and part of my life force is in it so I can't throw it out. Where with collecting, I throw out a lot more than I keep. It might not look like I do, but I do. Subsequently, there's already a curatorial process, before it even makes it to my studio. So, that, albeit not terribly apparent, process of discernment is what separates the two.

MM **So, it's a level of investment.**

MP Exactly.

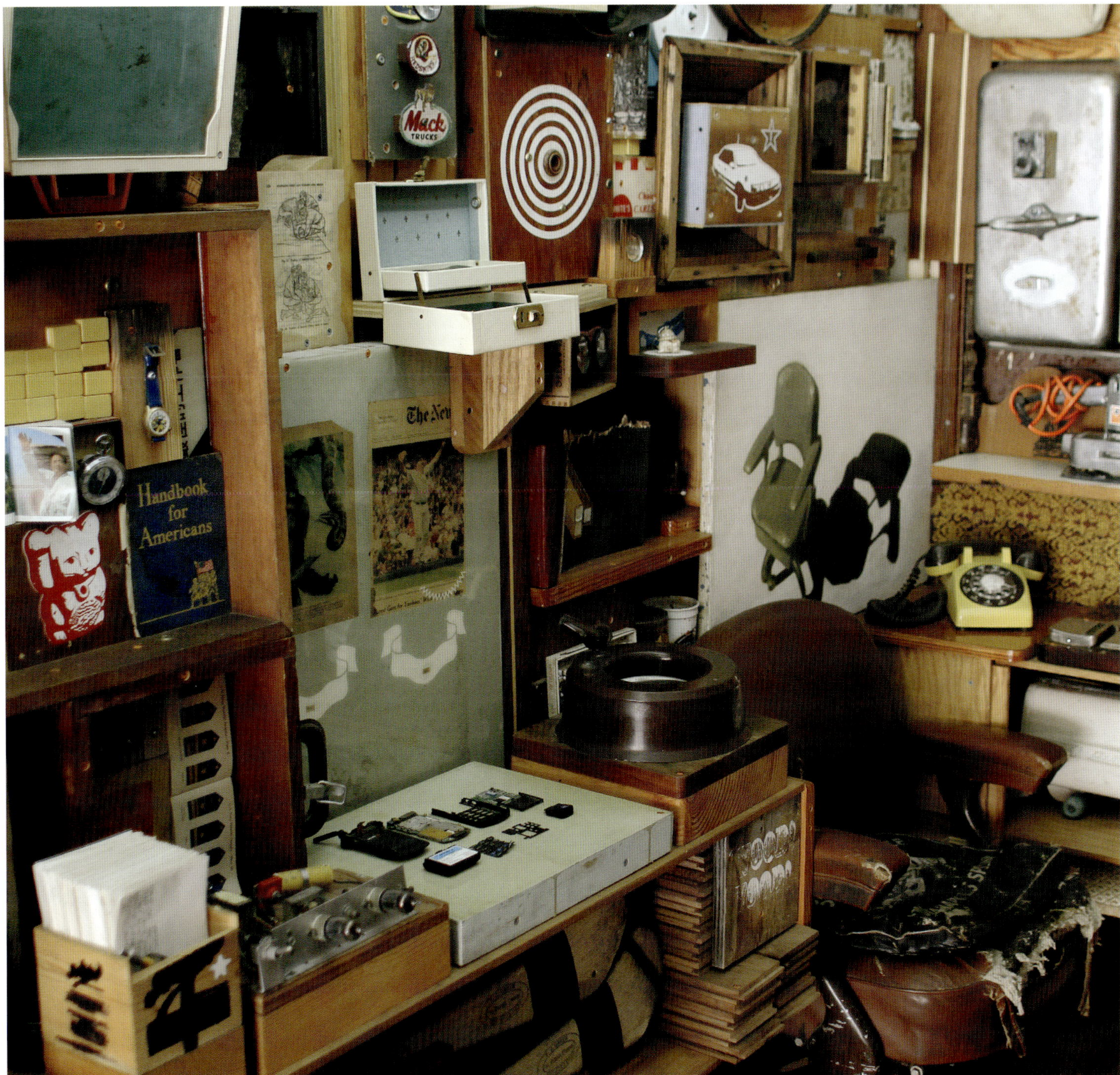

The Dumpster Project (detail)

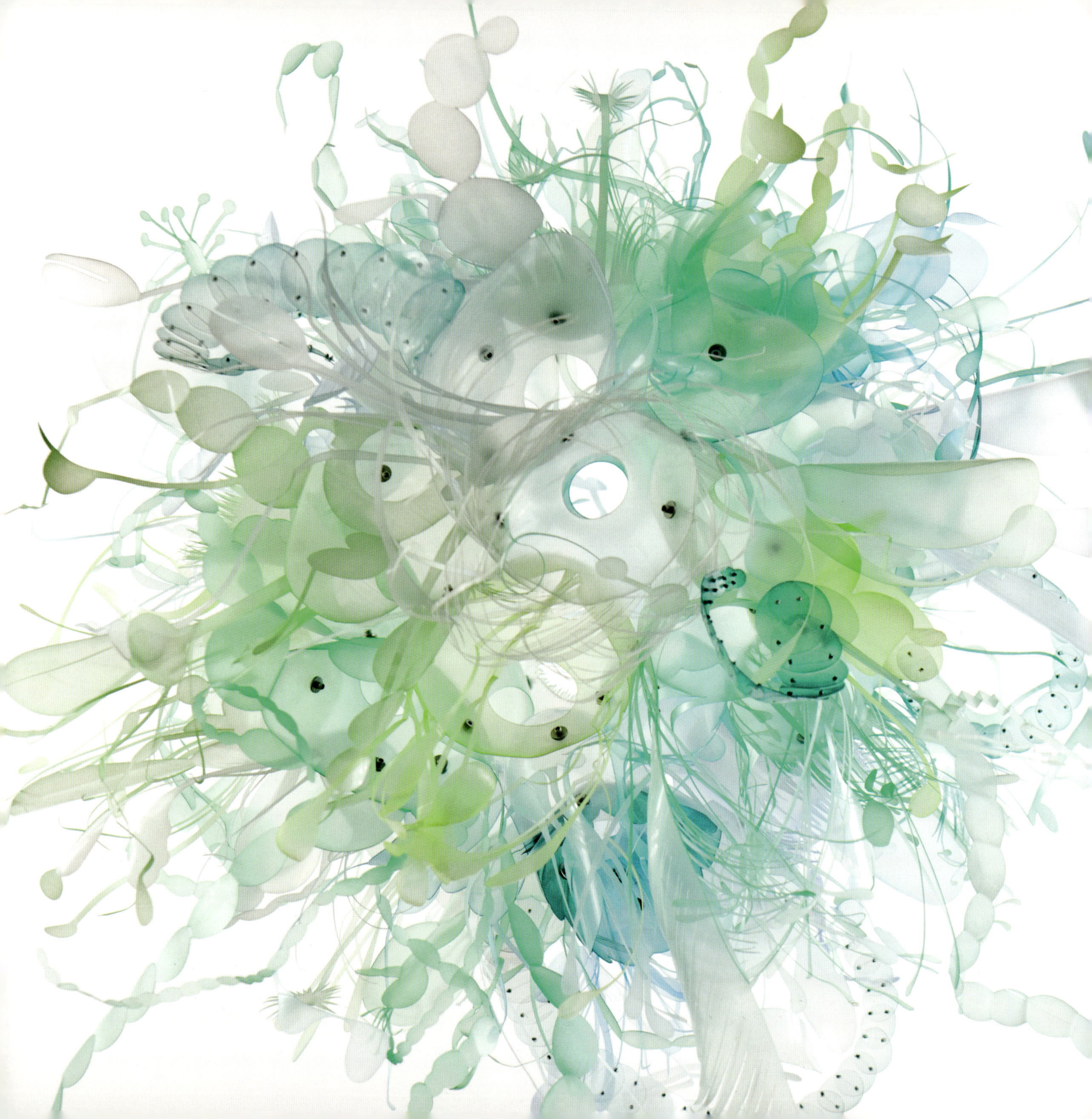

Aurora Robson (b. 1972) is a multimedia artist known predominantly for her transformative work that intercepts the waste stream. A Canadian, Robson was born in Toronto and grew up in Maui, Hawaii. She has lived and worked in New York for the past two decades. She earned a BA in visual arts and art history at Columbia University, and was named the Elizabeth Kirkpatrick Doenges Scholar/Artist for 2012. In addition to her artwork, Robson lectures at institutions around the country, and she has also taught photography, welding, and sculpture in New York City.

Aurora Robson

MATTHEW McLENDON **How did you come to work with PET bottles? You have to accumulate a lot of them for your sculptures and installations. Have you always been a collector? Have you always been accumulating?**

AURORA ROBSON No, not so much. I'm not a natural-born hoarder. The way it happened was almost cosmic in a way. I don't know what other word I could use. It was like when someone is trying to get your attention with a mirror and a light, that kind of distracting light. I was working on paintings in my studio and finally I stopped to see what was causing this sparkling outside my window. I was marveling at how grotesque and how careless people can behave by throwing trash everywhere; there was literally this giant pile of trash outside my window. I was on the ground floor in Brooklyn.

MM **This was litter? This wasn't garbage waiting to be picked up?**

AR No, just litter. And, it's not like that everywhere, but at the time I was living and working in Williamsburg and it was really industrial and there was a lot of crime. It was where the Brooklyn Strangler's victims were found. I was across the street from a cement factory. Now, of course, it's a very upscale part of Brooklyn, but then not so much. So I was noticing the light shining off of the PET bottles, and they are very reflective. It suddenly dawned on me that these objects have complex curves, are diaphanous, and had similar qualities to what I had been trying to render in these two-dimensional works that were basically a mapping out of the nightmares I had when I was a kid. It was a formal response.

MM **You were painting before that, but you had studied sculpture, right?**

AR Yes, I had done a lot of sculpture in college. Before I went to Columbia and studied sculpture with John Kessler, I was a New York State–certified welder and had been doing a lot of work with motors and sculpture, kinetic sculpture. Welding was my livelihood for a while. I had a welding shop in the Meat Packing District when you could still actually slip on a piece of meat walking down

Thundering Typhoons, 2013

the sidewalk, and I did it because I had dropped out of high school, was doing all of these random jobs, from waitressing to bartending to antique restoration, dog walking, and I had a complex about my lack of education. I'm lucky to have an older brother who gives really good advice and he suggested I learn a trade and take up welding. So I went to a vocational school; at the time, there were all of these ads on the subway for Apex Technical School for HVAC [heating, ventilating, and air conditioning] and welding and all these technical trades. So, it was me and a bunch of guys learning to weld; there were maybe three women total. It turned out I had really good hand-eye coordination and a natural aptitude for welding. Actually, most women are better welders because they have historically had more experience with detail work like crocheting. I was doing window gates and balconies, staircases, for money, and then was doing my art for fun. This was before college.

MM **So, then you transferred those skills readily into studying sculpture. You've talked often about your imagery coming from your childhood nightmares. It seems this creates an immediate juxtaposition, or perhaps discordance, with the viewer because, to the outside observer, your sculptures are quite beautiful and delicate, almost ethereal.**

AR Sure, it's interesting because I have felt alienated my whole life. I had this very unorthodox childhood. I grew up as an "illegal alien" and now live in the United States as a "resident alien." Even among artists, I feel a weirdo. These nightmares I had, I always thought they were this weird thing, until a couple of years ago. I was invited to do a series of lectures for K–6 students who were the ages I was when I had the nightmares. Before that, I had only talked to college students and adults. I would ask had anyone ever had dreams like this and maybe three out of every hundred might have some recognition. But, when I did it with kids, at least one third of each class was saying, "I had that dream last night!" One little girl, she must have been eight, came up to me after a slide lecture, gave me an unsolicited hug, and said to me, "Thank you for making me not afraid to dream anymore."

MM **Wow, you can basically just stop there. That's as good as it's going to get, right!**

AR Yeah! I think it's some kind of childhood response to stress. It has all of the formal qualities intact. The only thing I really change is the palette. There were no vibrant, pretty colors in the nightmares. The nightmares were dark, very little color.

MM **And were these forms entangling you and consuming you?**

AR Yes, and everything was suggestive—suggestive of form. It was this constant state of being in this semi-familiar, yet foreign, entangled morphing atmosphere. It felt very suffocating and I'd wake up afraid of the blobs. I guess most adults forget about it. It's not like I'm haunted about this anymore. I feel that my practice is taking something with negative energetic qualities and shifting that to the positive. It started as a meditative process. How can I take these nightmares I had as a kid and transform them into an inviting space? And, is that worthy of deliberate practice in and of itself? It turned out to be something I really enjoyed and other people responded to it. This perpetuated the activity for me. Then, I ran into John Kessler at a thrift store in Brooklyn. I was excited to tell him I had quit my day job and I was going to do art full time, and I had a body of work and a website. I was so excited to report back to him, and he said, "What are you making? Paintings? Works on paper? But you're a sculptor." I was so upset. Come on, I felt, I'm not connected to anyone in the art world. I don't have the finances. How am I going to be a sculptor in Brooklyn? It's just impractical. And then it was within a week that I found the bottles. I think that was in 2002.

Be Like Water, 2010

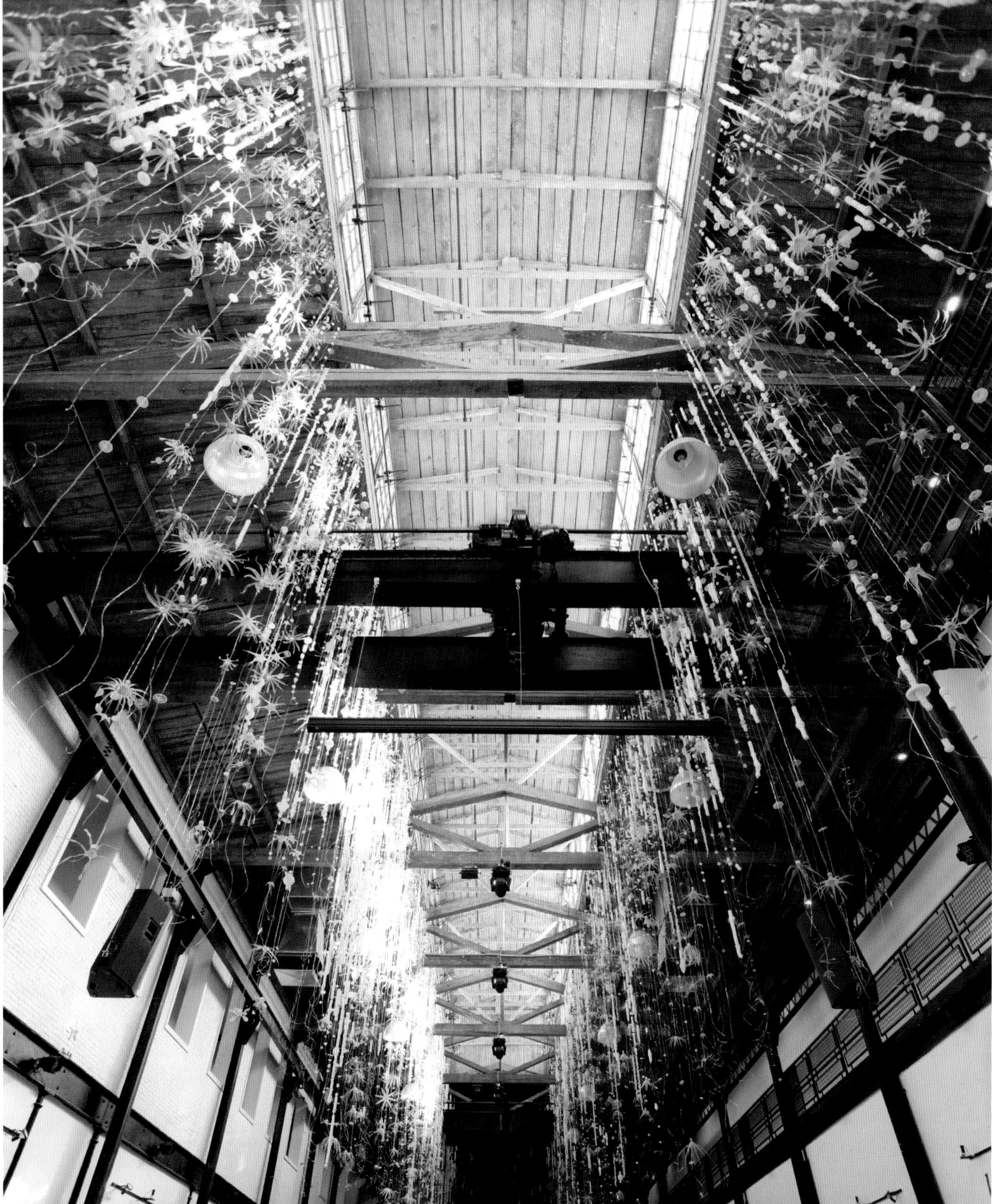

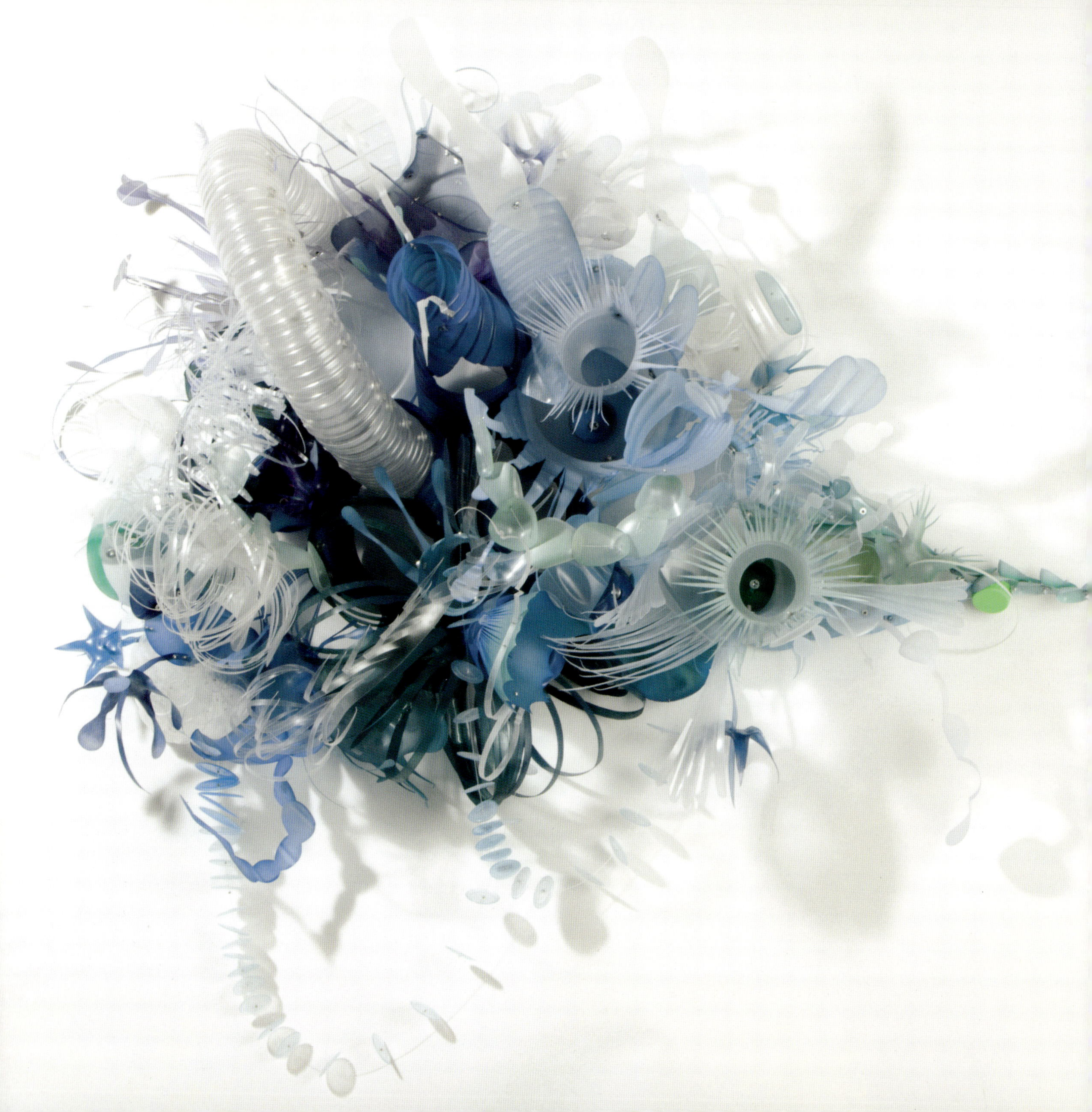

MM **So, your practice is transforming a negative energy into something that is positive, first with your childhood nightmares, and now with garbage, and a particular type of garbage, one that is destructive. How do you approach that?**

AR It has been a really interesting transformative experience with me. I didn't know anything about the environmental problems with plastic when I started working with it. Then, as I started working with the material, it was like, oh, these bottles have archival integrity, but, wow, this is really bad for the environment. We're throwing out millions of them every hour in the United States that aren't getting recycled. [*Estimates are that 2.5 million plastic bottles are thrown out each hour in the United States.*] The statistics are horrifying. The moment I started working with the bottles, I could tell something was going to happen in terms of the work opening up while maintaining its personal meditative qualities. It involves communities and is grounded in society; it goes beyond those fortunate enough to study art and makes it relevant to a lot more people, which I like.

MM **So, your practice continues to be community based.**

AR It has become more community based. It started as personal. Part of it, of course, is the sheer volume of material. Initially, I started working with homeless people in Brooklyn. I would hire them and they would bring me the bottles they would clean out from the streets, instead of having to walk twice as far to the recycling center, and I would pay them more, so it was a win/win/win. I got an endless stream of supplies, it cleaned up the streets, and it benefited the homeless. I could impact a few other people. Then it was addictive and I thought, "What if I can impact a lot of people in my lifetime?"

MM **What do you feel is the impact? Is it the message that comes from the material?**

AR Well, yes, but a lot of people won't read about the work. A lot of people just can't be bothered to read and discover. So, it's a visual experience, and it usually elicits some sort of "ah-ha" moment because I try to transform the material. I take something people think is useless, or waste, without potential, and then I change that completely so that they have an experience of desire, or coveting. It's taking capitalism and consumerism and twisting it around for a much better purpose.

MM **Yes, but if they're not reading about the work, how do you arrive at that experience?**

AR Initially, I was thinking through the art alone. Like reading a book. Each time you read it you have a different experience. So, some people might look at a piece and think it looks like sea urchins, and then later when they look at it again they might think it looks like an asteroid. It gives them a sense of where they are at that moment and helps them to shift their perception of value and matter, and their relationship to matter. But the way I think I have more hope at this point—and more excitement building for me—is a course that I've designed and am trying to integrate into the education system.

MM **Talk to me about that course.**

AR It's called Sculpture and Intercepting the Waste Stream. It's trying to tap into our preexisting education structures. Basically, there are colleges everywhere, there are bodies of water everywhere. All rivers lead to the ocean. There is a real disconnect in terms of material and value, I think. What I'm trying to do is take the typical model of a student in high school or college. You go out and get resources, then you transform those resources into what may or may not be art, and at the end of it, it might go on your mother's wall. If you're lucky, it will stay there for a while, and then eventually it migrates into trash. This is terrible. I don't think any student is happy with this model, from what I experience. There is this real lack of vital relevance in our education experience.

Fermi, 2012

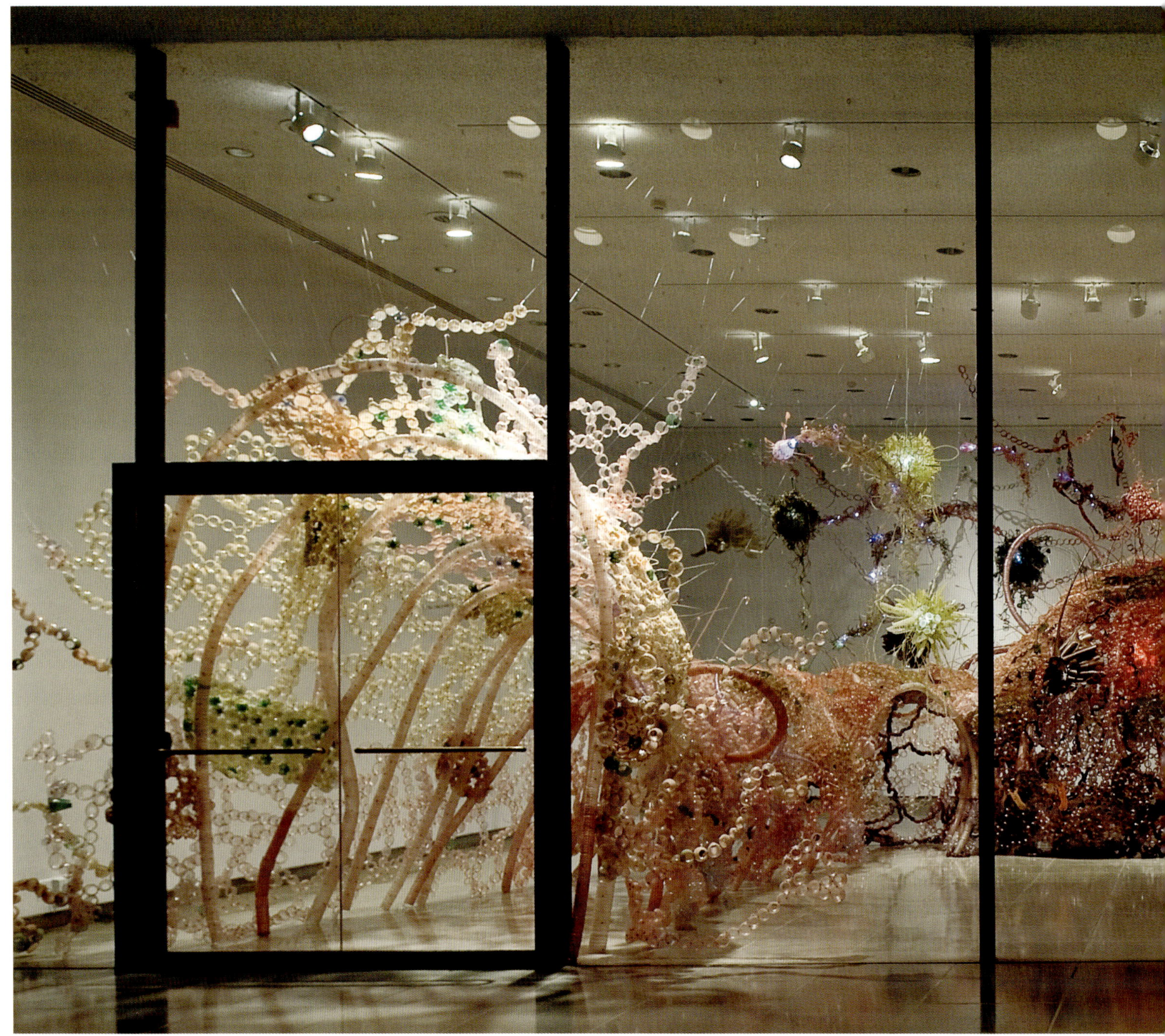

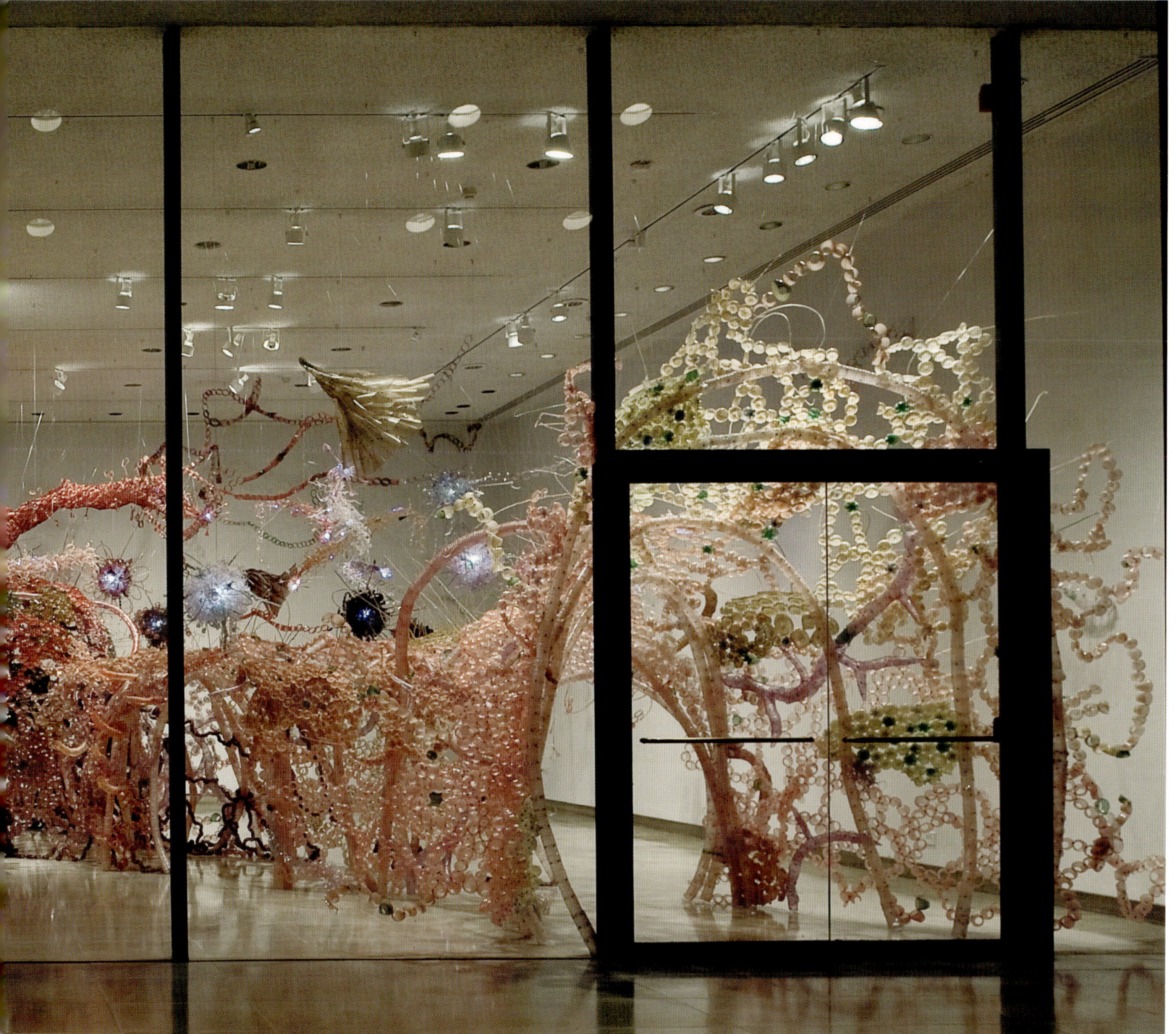

The Great Indoors, 2008

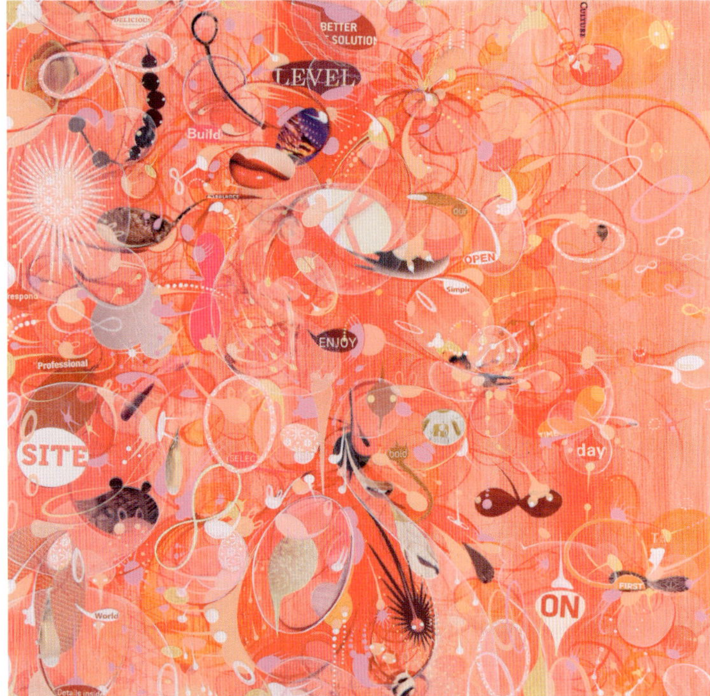

Thundering Typhoons, 2009

I remember feeling this myself in college, the feeling that this is not applicable right now in the world. In college, they are in a place that they have resources they are paying for, they have a community, and work like this is depressing unless you do it with a community. So, the model is they do a shoreline or roadway clean up. Then, they take the materials from the clean up during the semester and transform it into one object that cannot be confused with garbage. The process includes cleaning, and that is important. The process of cleaning slows them down, and they establish an intimate relationship with the material. What kind of properties does it have that can be used in sculpture? This is a very challenging exercise in creativity, and creativity is certainly the leading characteristic in our age. At the end of the course they have an exhibit with a silent auction. All of the proceeds then go to charities to keep cleaning roadways and shores, gradually expanding that creative stewardship among academia, environmental organizations, and the students. It's a different way of working.

MM **And community is again involved.**

AR Yes, that's very exciting. It expands the community that wants to support this type of activity, it broadens the art market. The entry-level collector is formed here. The first time we did it, every piece sold. People who had never bought art before were in bidding wars over student art. So, that makes me feel that there is potential. Otherwise, this is very David and Goliath.

MM **One of the things that sets your work apart from other artists who use refuse to create art is that you radically transform your source material. Without looking at a label, I don't think anyone would guess these are PET bottles. Why is that transformation important for you?**

AR I'm asking a lot of people. I've been able to support myself with my artwork for the last twelve years. I have incredible kids. Considering the cards I was dealt, this makes no sense. I should be in a gutter. So, the fact that people are willing to support this work and basically buy back their garbage, I put a lot of love in it. I also want to impart that there is value through effort.

MM **Sure, would you also say value through beauty?**

AR Yeah, I love beautiful things. I want to live with them. I don't want to live with a bunch of stuff I don't want to look at. There's enough depressing stuff in the world. It's so easy to be ironic, and sardonic, and nihilistic. It's so easy to indulge in dark thoughts. I'm trying to inspire myself and other people to stay focused on the light and remember how fortunate we are. I am dedicated to beauty, absolutely.

MM **Are you far enough removed from the nightmares now that you see them as beautiful?**

AR Well, I've done a lot of portraits of them in a really flattering light [*laughs*]. They really haven't disturbed me in a long time, and now I really am grateful because I wouldn't have the work without having that experience.

MM **Intercepting the waste stream is also a major part of your practice. But I've wondered what happens to a sculpture or installation if it doesn't sell or become permanent in a museum or collection. Does the material get reworked? Do you repurpose the already repurposed?**

AR I store things. I take care of them. I try to honor and value effort. A lot of time and human effort goes into making these experiences and installations, and it's not just my effort. For instance, *Being Water*: there were seven schools in Philadelphia collecting bottle caps for that. So I take care of it, I move it around. If I feel something has been out in the world enough, and it still hasn't found a home, then I'll transform it into something else.

MM **Through this process, how has your relationship with the wider ideas of garbage/trash/cast-offs, whatever word you want to use, changed?**

AR Well, I think I'm at a place where I'm not going to be working with PET plastic anymore. It has educated me as to how big a problem waste is, in some parts of the world more than others. For instance, Sweden has to import garbage for its waste energy program, which is amazing to me. Here, we're pretty far behind. So it has come to my attention that PET plastic is a big problem, but industrial plastic waste is a much bigger problem. I'm starting to work on my first outdoor commission using HDPE [high-density polyethylene] plastic, which are these giant barrels they use for shipping things like oil, honey, and beverage syrups, and they use them once. I mean we sterilize and reuse our surgical equipment that goes inside our bodies, but we only use these plastic barrels once. They're fifty-five-gallon drums and larger that are used for agricultural materials. I feel like I'll forever love the PET plastic, but it's almost like I've been practicing a decade for scaling up.

MM **But, still art with a social purpose.**

AR Yes, art with a social purpose, but it's art first.

MM **That's important.**

AR Yes, it's art first. The social message people can take or leave. The course I've developed is more about social message, giving people the tools. The beauty of it is that it exercises your creative muscles. If you go to the art supply store, it's all laid out for you. But here, you have to figure it out. You have to find it and be smart about it; it's all there. Then to bring it to a level where it is not garbage anymore is an important lesson for young artists.

MM **I think that would be important for artists at any point in their practice. It seems like those are the basic building blocks.**

AR Yes, and I should also say, I know everyone always discusses my work as environmental, but to me it's just mental. How do we fine-tune our relationships to ourselves, to each other, and to our environment so we are not such destructive creatures? It's about consciousness. Why have we become so perverted that we think bronze is more valued than plastic? It's our value system that is at question for me.

Hefty
050972
051982
the map
zipcard

New York–based artist Daniel Rozin (b. 1961) is known for his interactive installations and sculptures that change and respond to the presence of a viewer. Individuals become active participants in the creation of image, as his installations respond in real time to the viewer's presence. Using his version of the mirror, the body and gesture are explored through interactive technology as a changing surface becomes the platform for a meditation on identity. Rozin has been the recipient of many awards, including the Prix Ars Electronica, I.D. Design Review, Chrysler Design Award, and the Rothschild Prize. He is an associate arts professor at ITP in the Tisch School Of The Arts at New York University (NYU). He earned a BD at the Jerusalem Bezalel Academy of Art and Design and an MPS from NYU. He is represented by bitforms gallery, New York.

Daniel Rozin

MATTHEW McLENDON **Your practice has been based in making interactive works of art. Why did you decide to pursue this avenue?**

DANIEL ROZIN I began my career as an industrial product designer. I did that for more than ten years and then I went back to school to study what was then considered "multimedia" or "interactive new media." That's when I acquired the skill to alter things on computers. Before that, I was using computers to design, but it had never occurred to me that a computer could be a platform for expression. That ability to add a layer of computation, or "smarts," to a static object was one that I found really exciting. When that happened, my work became this idea of participation or interaction. There are a few things that are important to me in my work, and one of the central ones is participation. The idea that the work changes for a viewer or, sometimes, doesn't even exist without the presence of a viewer, or depends on the point of view of the viewer or viewers. I think that is in all of my works, regardless of the platform.

MM **And does that interest come directly from your background as an industrial designer because, as an industrial designer, you are taking the human factor into account?**

DR I think that the background as an industrial product designer definitely brings with it a sensitivity to communicate and interact with an audience. Some art forms, more so in the twentieth and twenty-first centuries, don't feel the need to be very accessible to the audience. Sometimes, they have layers of symbolism or of communication that are almost private for an artist or a very limited audience in the know. Maybe coming from a design background you are always trying to maximize the audience or the accessibility and the communication of the piece. So, I guess when I stopped working for clients and started employing the same disciplines for my own self-expression I brought with me that idea that I do want

Trash Mirror No. 3, 2001–11

to communicate, that I do want to include as many people in the viewing and the meaning of my pieces. And, interactivity is a very potent tool for engaging people, for explaining a piece to people, for allowing them to gain a feeling of ownership over a piece. It is a shared experience between the artist who creates the premise of the piece and the audience who completes the piece at the time of viewing.

MM **So, you said interactivity is one of your central concerns. What are some of the others that work their way through your body of work?**

DR I guess another one that exists in all of my pieces is that all of them are visual—the main sense I am engaged with is sight. Something that is of great importance to me is the creation of the image, the creation and the perception of the image. How can you create an image physically with different materials, different techniques—digitally with vectors and rasters, or using sculpture or mirrors. I try to see if it is an act of subtraction; how much can I take away from an image and it still be recognizable. A lot of my mechanical pieces, if you look at them as digital images, they are very low-resolution. They have hundreds of pixels where a typical image you get from a camera has millions of them. I'm constantly trying to see what's the least amount of information that makes an image. It's almost a matter of economy. Where is the line between "yes image" and "not image?"

MM **Well, that certainly relates to your *Trash Mirror* series, doesn't it?**

DR Yes, if you want to talk about *Trash Mirror*, that one definitely has these two layers, or two levels of image. When you place the piece in the museum, you first see it at a distance and you don't really know it's there to be a "pile of trash." What you see is a ghostly reflection of yourself; you might be far away enough not to know what's going on. You may just come to the realization that it's you, that the piece is moving with you. Then, when you get closer a second layer is revealed, and that's the layer of the detail. If you're very close to the piece, you've lost the ability to see that meta-reflection—you're too close now. But, suddenly you see the second layer of lots of wrappers, and boxes, and notes, and you can read what's written on them and you realize it's trash. You're getting a lot of detail, but you've lost the "big picture."
So, many of my pieces, either explicitly or implicitly, have that duality. I enjoy trying to pack more than one layer of information or image into one surface.

MM **As you are talking about optics and creating images, you are talking about it in a very participatory way, this relationship between the artist and the viewer. You are trying to see just how little you can give and still create an image. So, the image making is still based in participation.**

DR Right, and it's an act of choreography. I'm choreographing the act of viewing the piece. I try to make most, maybe all, of my pieces pretty. That's a superficial word, but it is important to me that my objects be "pretty." Again, if we look at art as a whole, art of the twentieth and twenty-first centuries, a lot of conceptual art is not concerned with making things "pretty." For me, as a tool of engaging an audience, I think the first thing you see at a distance is that, oh, it's a pretty object and maybe you gain a few seconds of interest in your piece. Then through interactivity, or kineticism—once again, you draw an audience to your piece. So, my core interest is the image creation, but then these other things that I've talked about may come up in the back of the mind of the viewer.

MM **Returning to *Trash Mirror*, I read that it was your first idea but not the first mirror you created. Why was that?**

DR That's true. My wife is a composer and she takes me to these contemporary concerts, and sometimes, I have to admit, I zone out, and I remember being at a concert and I started thinking that any object, given the right lighting, can become a physical pixel. When I thought about this, I wasn't thinking about a grid; I was thinking, let's make it as messy as possible and maximize this friction between the digital order and the messiness of the substance. The word that came to my mind was "crap." Then, as I was thinking about it a few weeks later, it seemed risky. At the time I had not built anything of that nature. So, I tried to simplify it. Maybe my background as a designer led me to think: let's simplify, we'll put it on a grid, let's use wood instead of trash. All the pieces will be uniform in color and shape and this will be more manageable. So, I designed the wooden mirror in 1999. After that piece was completed and shown, and I saw that the effect was possible and interesting for me, then I thought I would try and make the original idea. Then, I collected about five hundred pieces of trash, different colors and shapes.

MM **How did you collect these five hundred pieces of trash? Was there a great deal of thought behind the collecting, or was it more random?**

DR It was as random as any found object collage project you would find. You are, of course, restricted by what you find, that's the nature. But, you are selective as you collect. You know, there are all sorts of found objects that you start to think you can push toward your direction. Functionally, the pieces of trash needed to be not too big or too small, and they needed to be mostly flat. I have made several versions of *Trash Mirror*. The original is now retired and in my apartment. When I look at it, I think I was fairly conservative in selecting the pieces; it is more of a grayish blonde piece. I wasn't, at the time, sure if it would work if the pieces were too colorful or shiny. Every time I go out and search for trash for the later *Trash Mirror*s I get more and more adventurous. I like that the later pieces are happy and full of colors. Also, in the selection of the trash, I'm looking to give a mixture of items. There are very obvious brand items that are very recognizable. Other items are very personal. I do not find them on the streets. I find them in my pockets, so: receipts, notes, old ID cards, nametags from conferences. Some hold meaning only for me, some can have meaning projected onto them by any viewer.

MM **Were you thinking about the fact that these narrative possibilities—your narrative, the viewers' narratives—would all come together like this as you were creating the piece, or did that realization come later?**

DR I was definitely thinking that as you are creating this mosaic, it's a bit time consuming, and you're thinking about things that are very visual—the composition, the colors—but also in your mind, you're thinking, too many wrappers, I want to be more personal, I need a receipt here. So, as you are thinking about these visual components you are definitely thinking about a narrative of the piece and—like any piece that is time-based or interactive and not linear like a movie—how the gaze of the viewer will pass over the piece will be unknown to you. I don't think in a piece like this you can really determine the path of the gaze. There are these moments, though, when you see juxtapositions and you say to yourself: how nice to have this piece next to that piece.

MM **So, when you're creating the work, you are really thinking more on the micro- rather than macro- level?**

DR Well, yes. I have not made other work, but I think when you are working in "new media" or technology, it splits the mind, perhaps, more than in other media. There is a huge removal between what you want to get and what you need to do. So, if what you want to get is one of my mirrors and you stand in front of it and this sketchy image of you comes up, then what you have to do is learn programming, and sometimes you're searching the internet for a new library that came out from Microsoft. You're not thinking artistically, you're thinking technically. But then, the other side of the mind has to think like an artist. It's thinking about composition. And sometimes, you have to think sequentially. You start by saying, "I want to create a trash mirror with five hundred pieces of trash and mirrors," and then you have to spend months figuring out how to make that happen, and you depart from the "art" of it. But, like I said, this is the only type of art I've made. Some people find that very frustrating, but for me it is what I love about creating art with technology.

MM **So, on a practical level, how long did it take to collect the garbage for *Trash Mirror* #3?**

DR Well, actually, my daughter helped me to collect items for it. There is a note from her in the piece, and every time she sees it leaving she always asks, "Have you sold it?" She's very concerned about that one note that she made for me for my birthday. But, for a while you're a bit like a homeless person that you see on the streets, poking through the trash. It can be very unpleasant, but I always have a plastic bag with me so I'm always picking up stuff. So, there are a couple of months where I am building up a reservoir of material. And then I'm ordering the motors and building the frame, so it's several months and I have a few cardboard boxes filled with things I've

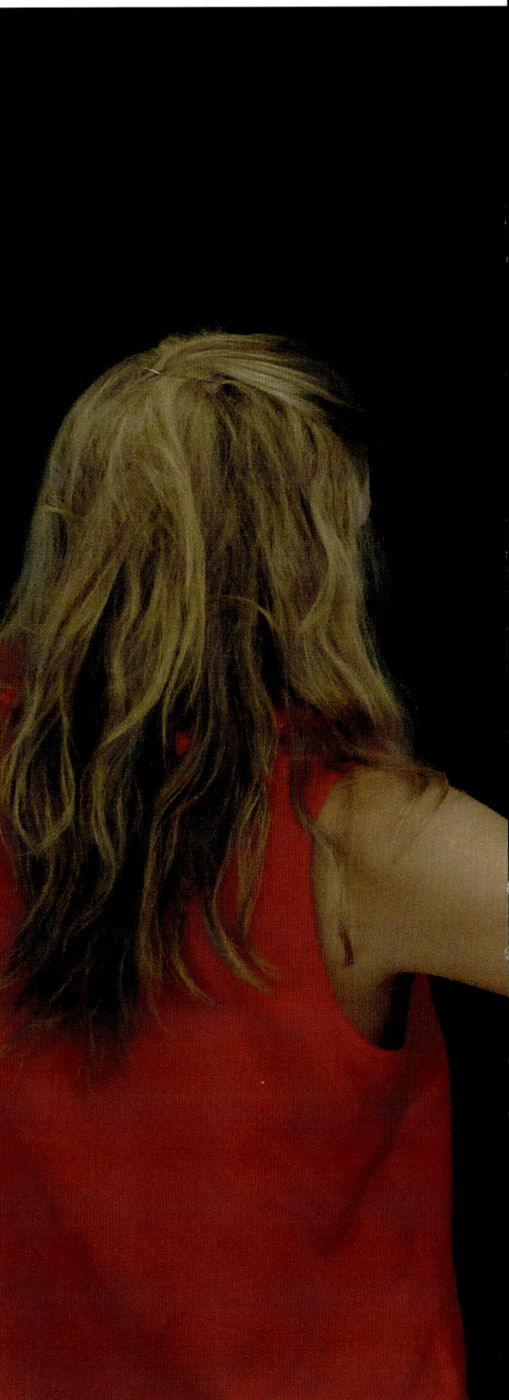

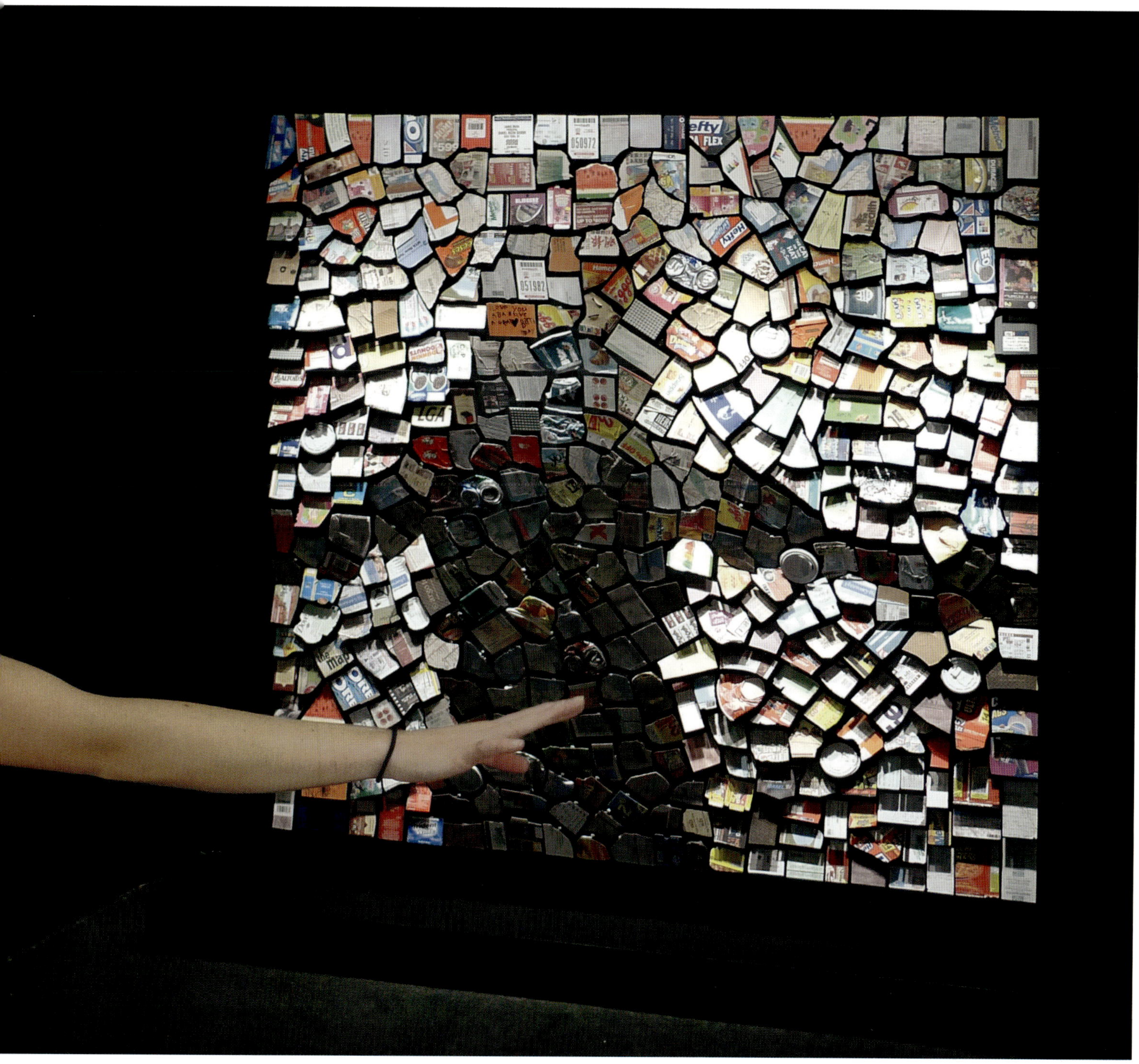

Trash Mirror No. 3, 2001–11

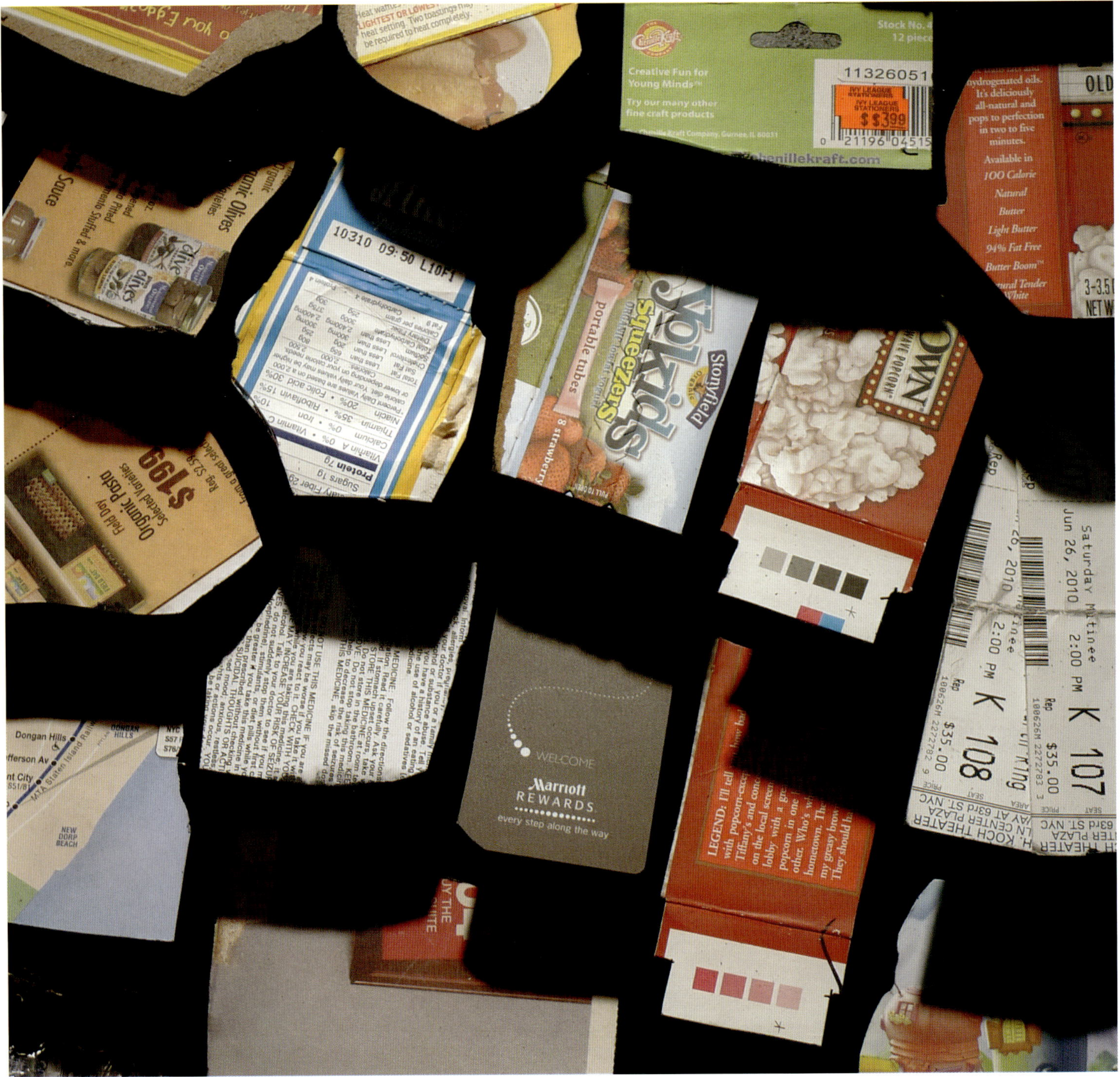

Trash Mirror No. 3 (detail), 2001–11

gathered. Then, usually, I don't have enough and at the last minute I'm going out to collect more. For #1, I had things contributed from colleagues, so people give me things, too.

MM **What is your relationship to things that have been discarded, that have been thrown away? Why did you want to make a mirror in which we see ourselves in "trash"?**

DR When you deal with "reflection" there is always this question of what do you want to reflect? It's simple to put a perfect mirror and place it in a setting, allowing people to see themselves 100 percent. I'm not sure if by seeing everything, though, you gain an understanding. My work is based on cameras, and the camera provides a very objective view of the viewer. Then I start subtracting from that and deciding what I won't show. So, I decide for each piece what I am going to reflect back to the viewer. You look at society and you might think the things we keep and put on a pedestal are good indications of what we are. But, on the other side of the spectrum, you gain a lot of understanding by looking at what they discard. We are as much about what we discard as what we keep, even, perhaps, more so, and it becomes very clear when you see more personal items, notes, movie stubs, and on the greater level, as a community, more what you see in the wrappers and boxes we discard.

MM **So, where does the reduction occur? Are you abstracting the image in the software you created, or is the image reduced and abstracted simply through the choice of material?**

DR The camera sees the world as a multitude of pixels and can be evaluated from black to white, as a grayscale. In digital technology we look at scales from 0–255. So we have lots of these points isolated from the space. And then you can minimize them. They come in the millions and we need hundreds for trash mirror, so you sub-sample them. Then in the end you assign corresponding pixels from the camera to every piece of trash. You say, this pixel, for example, it refreshes thirty times per second, so you think of it as frames in animation. Or, this pixel is 70 percent grey so I need to move the piece of trash 70 percent up with the electronics.

MM **Who or what are your primary influences today?**

DR I think most of my influences come from, for instance, visual artists like Picasso, and Van Gogh, and Chuck Close. When you look at my work you might see that I am interested in the things that they have explored. But, really my main inspirations come from science. I have series of software pieces that are about Darwinism and selection and evolution. I'm inspired by people like Newton and Einstein, and Darwin, and their ability to change the way we perceive the world through the power of their minds. Newton took the very messy world around us and used very simple ways to explain it to us, then Einstein came and questioned much of it. That kind of investigation into the way the world works—to build up or tear down our intuition about how the world works—that is what I find interesting, and that is what I'm thinking about when I'm creating.

MM **Sure, but in your work we certainly see taking the chaotic, garbage, and then using technology to create something very elegant and choreographed.**

DR Right, when I was doing it, the phrase I kept thinking about was "inflicting order" on something that was chaotic. Really taking digital, unrelenting order and "inflicting" it to trash, which is chaotic, which is not on a grid, which is not a system, and then create order with it.

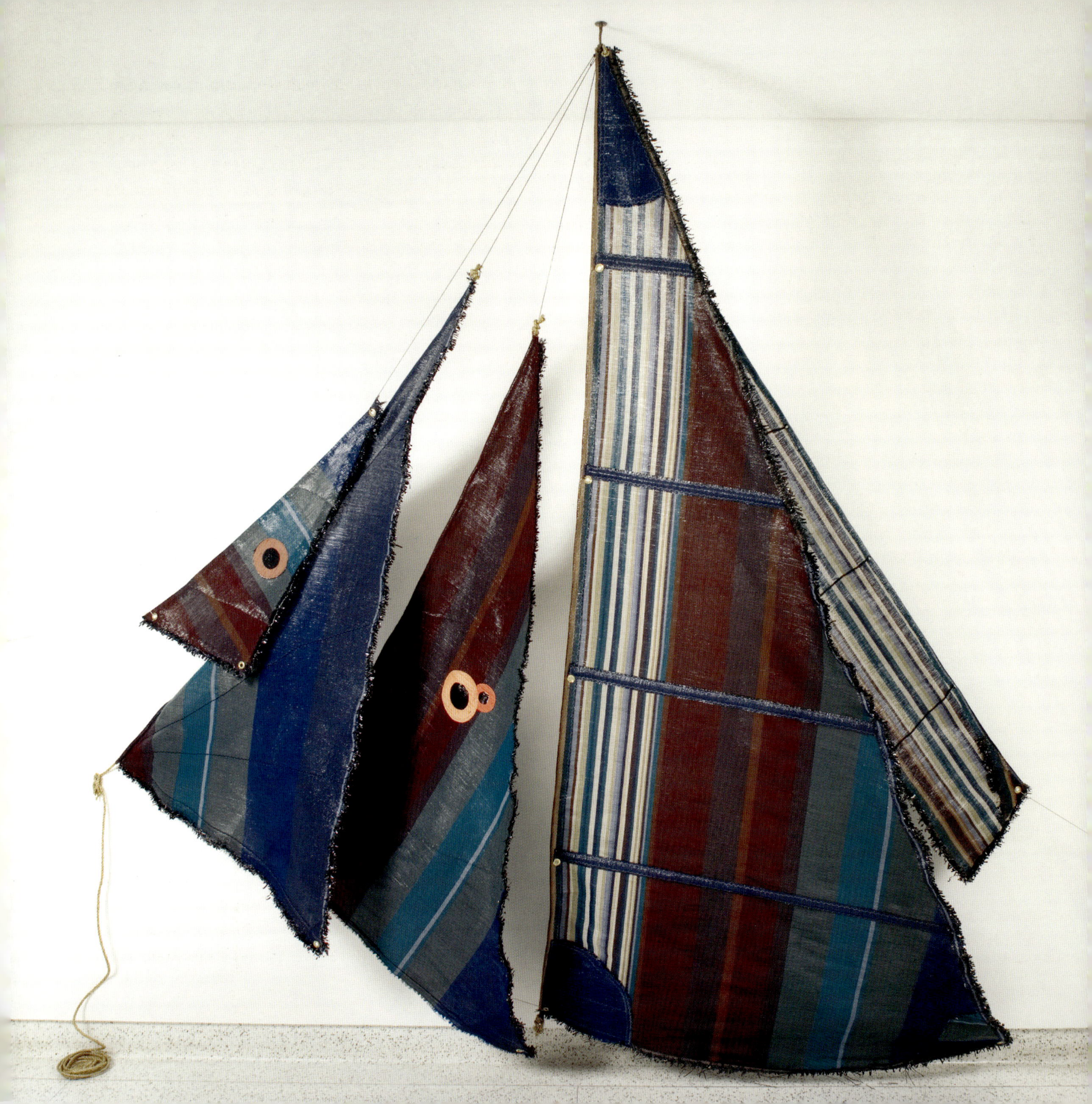

Alyce Santoro (b. 1968) is a conceptual and social/environmental practice artist, activist, and writer with a foundation in marine biology and scientific illustration. Santoro refers to her multimedia works as "philosoprops"—devices used to demonstrate a concept or spark a dialogue. Alarmed by what she sees as the direct relationship between the detached mindset cultivated in scientific research (and widely adopted by Western culture) and the destructive propensity of the technology that results from it, her works often offer subtle and deceivingly playful critiques of the foibles of dualistic thinking. Santoro's visual and sound pieces have appeared in more than fifty exhibitions around the world. Alyce Santoro is represented in New York City by Klemens Gasser and Tanja Grunert Gallery.

Alyce Santoro

MATTHEW McLENDON **Let's start with your background. You trained in scientific illustration at Rhode Island School of Design (RISD). So, how did you transition from that to working with discarded materials and found sound?**

ALYCE SANTORO Well, from an early age I knew I wanted to try and combine art and science. I was a musician; I started playing the flute at age ten. I loved art, and science, and music, and I just didn't know how in college I would make the decision to study just one thing. So, I decided what I would do is get a degree in science first. So, my degree is in marine biology, and then I decided that I would study scientific illustration later, and in the meantime I was still playing in bands and doing a lot of music. Then I moved to Providence in 1990 to go to RISD. Providence at that time was an incredible environment for artists. Real estate was very cheap; I was living in this incredible loft space. There were lots of people around making music, doing silkscreen. I was working as a marine biologist during the day at the University of Rhode Island (URI) and then going to RISD at night, and then completely immersing myself in the local scene. There were neighbors I played music with and silkscreened with. I think it was an organic process. I realized while I was doing scientific illustration, I needed more media than just pen and ink to be able to describe the wonder part of the things that I was illustrating. Science is all about the scientific method and detaching yourself from your subject. With scientific illustration, my illustrations were taking on the personality of the subject, and that wasn't very scientific. I wasn't a very good scientific illustrator. I was imbuing my illustrations with the personality of the squid or the flounder.
At the same time I was trying to take every course I could at RISD. I took sculpture and stone carving, letterpress printmaking. It seemed like every medium I tried, I was still making art about the same subject—the wonder of reality. With found objects, I'm really attracted to things that already have a history. I just love objects that are

Tell-Tail Thangkas (Sonic Sails, Musical Score Edition), 2007 used, an old wooden spoon with divots where the hands go, or a hand mixer that belonged to my grandmother that I can imagine her making eight thousand batches of pancakes with. I feel like I've always had an affinity to gravitate to objects that are well crafted and have a story. I love incorporating that story in my work.

MM **It's so interesting that you say that. Archaeologists talk about "object biography" and that is exactly how you are thinking about found objects. So, what is interesting to me in this exhibition is that you have the object biography that then has the biography of the artist layered on it, and these biographies in turn encounter the biography of the viewer.**

AS Yes, that's exactly it.

MM **Also, because of your background, I wonder, when you are creating, are you thinking in terms of "genre:" this is science, this is illustration, this is sculpture, this is music, or is it all simply the act of creating for you?**

AS I don't think in terms of genre at all. In fact, it's really funny to me because I belong to this eco art listserv where everyone is constantly talking about collaborating with a scientist, and there's like an obsession with medium and defining things. And to me, we just have to do what we know needs to be done. How it works out, is how it works out. I feel that part of my process is to live as simply as I can so that I have the time to dedicate to doing things in a way that it not necessarily marketable. I think a lot of artists—and this isn't a flaw—really have to do things that are going to sell. But, I don't think in that way at all, and I think the reason for putting yourself into a category is to market what you do. I had this giant solo show in New York in January 2013 and my work was an installation, but it was to tell a story, and really the story was the work. It wasn't really able to be commodified; you had to be present to hear the story. It's like you're saying: the person comes with their own story and that becomes part of the work.

MM **So, the process informs everything for you.**

AS Yes, absolutely!

MM **Do you find challenges beyond marketability when you are working across, or really outside of, recognizable genre?**

AS It's so interesting that you ask that. My partner Julian Mock, who's a guitarist, and I are both finding that over the course of the past two years what we're doing, as far as our relationship with the audience, is extremely challenging because the audience really doesn't know what to make of it. Even the shows that I had in New York, that's when the epiphany happened. When I was in the galleries telling the stories, that's when the work really came alive; that's when people responded and I had this relationship with the audience. That's when everything burst open. And, the same thing is happening with Julian. His music isn't classifiable. It's solo music for the nylon string guitar but what he's doing is so strange, that when people hear it, sometimes, when it's a like-minded

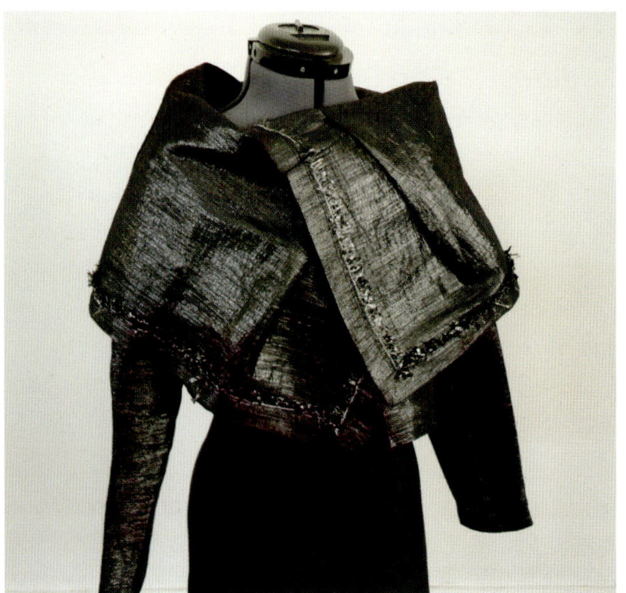

Cowl-Necked Jacket, designed by Koos Van Den Akker, 2003

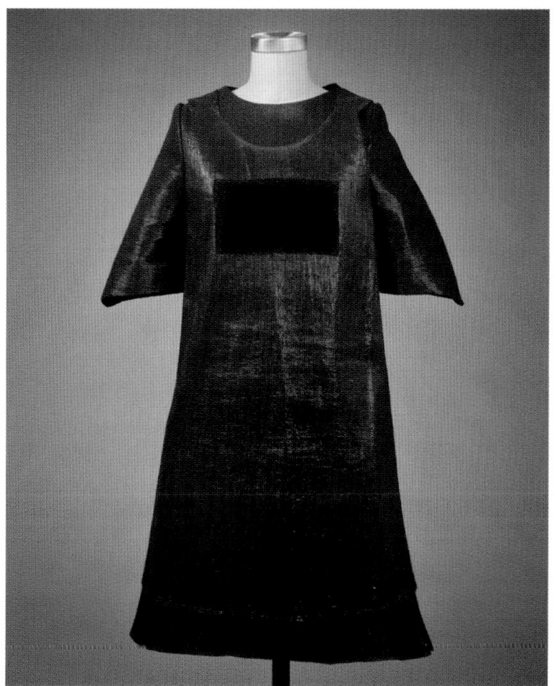

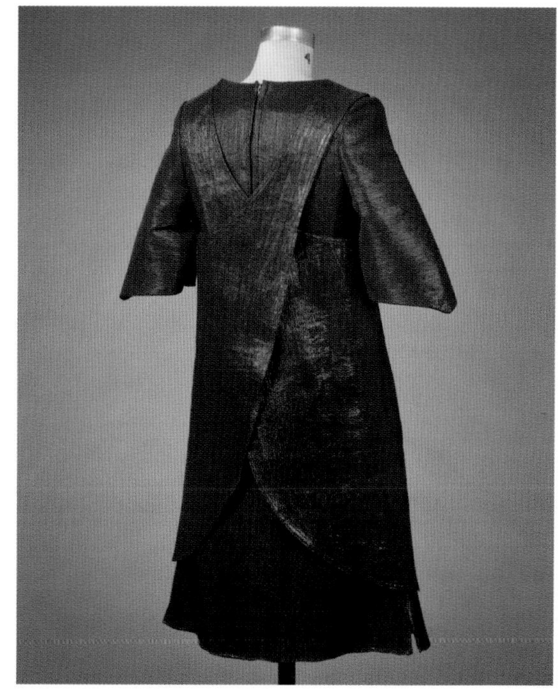

person, they are like "Oh my god, it's blowing my mind." But there are people who just don't hear it. A twenty-year-old guy gave him some feedback that there's no "hook" line—people are looking to be entertained. They assume that artwork or music should be there to amuse, and really that's not what Julian and I are doing at all. Really, we're just living in a new way. I think in our first email exchange you mentioned Joseph Beuys and I think that's what both of us are doing. We're responding to the way the world is right now, and we're creating a way to live within this context of all the strangeness—there's such a culture of fear, and a culture of struggle. There are so many negatives, and we're just trying to create a new path. I think it's hard for a lot of audiences to relate because what we are doing is not something that is familiar. Everyone is always trying to be marketed to. A lot of art that is out there is about emotional manipulation, and that's exactly the opposite of what we're trying to do. It's very challenging; it's a very strange time.

MM **That's exactly what I, as a curator, am always grappling with. This is something that we both really have to think about as we move forward with the exhibition and displaying your work. How do we display the work so that your message comes across; what are the tools we use? Because, of course, you won't be sitting next to the work telling your stories. What do you feel your obligation as the artist is in providing accessibility to your work in the broadest sense?**

AS After the show in New York, I realized I needed a catalogue that could travel with the work so that the stories could go along with it. So, I spent all of last year writing this book. I feel like this book, in a sense, is more the work than the actual work itself. I go through

Voidness Dress, 2007

every piece that I consider a "philosoprop" and tell the story of how it was inspired and why I decided to do it. I feel a great responsibility to make the work as accessible as possible. This book goes into the concepts of why I do not think art and science are separate, why separating them is causing rifts in the world and environmental destruction. This idea of objectivity, that we are separate from the world, is the crux of the matter. It is why we are able to exploit other people and resources. So now, the book is a part of the experience.

MM **Let's talk specifically about the Sonic Fabric. Where did the idea come from?**

AS As a kid, I used to race small sailboats and we used audiocassette tapes as a "tell-tale" tied to the mast. Then in 1989, when I was at University of California Santa Cruz, I learned about Tibetan Buddhist prayer flags. I was studying marine mammal bio-acoustics and I met my first Tibetan Buddhist who explained how Tibetan prayer flags work. They have a sacred sound or mantra silkscreened onto them that is activated by the wind. So, that's when I first got the idea to weave with tape. But it wasn't an urgent thing. I didn't consider myself an artist at the time, but I did start collecting tapes that I knew I would want to weave into a fabric. It wasn't until 2000 that I even began knitting with cassette tape; it took me that long to collect one hundred tapes I wanted to work with. The whole idea was about quantum physics—at the most basic level we are vibration, and we are all made up of the same stuff. I was imagining that I would have the Muslim call to prayer, Gregorian chant, Tibetan monks, Asian music, and African music, all of those cultures woven together. My vision was to travel the world collecting all of these sounds, but that never really happened. I was able to collect sounds everywhere I went for many years. Then in 2001, I was sitting in a café in Providence knitting with the tape and a friend, Philip May, came in, and he said we should try weaving that with a cotton warp at RISD. So, he made the first two samples of Sonic Fabric in 2001. Then I moved to New York with those, and it wasn't for another couple of years that I was able to make more. I imagined that the project was finished at that point. I had my hundred tapes and I had woven them into two yards of fabric and that was the piece. Then in 2003 I was accepted into a show of work made from repurposed materials at Felissimo Design House, and they asked me to make something out of the fabric, so that is when I made my first sonic shaman-superhero dress. Then designers started seeing it there, and they started asking for yardage and I was offended—you want yardage of my art? It took me a while before I was willing to say, well, maybe this can be a thing used in everyday life, and that's really important to me, too. I don't just want art to be something that is inaccessible. I would love for people to have and use it in their everyday lives. Then I found the mom-and-pop textile mill in Rhode Island, and they were willing to work with me, so it was in 2003/2004 that I was able to make more yardage.

MM **And is that when you switched from cotton to polyester thread to weave with the tape?**

AS Yes, and the reason we switched was that the polyester thread was much more durable.

MM **So, the first textile was made out of the one hundred tapes you collected, but now you're working with these large reels of tape. They come from a company that produces audio books?**

AS Yes, they produce audio books, and I think they had the contract with the Library of Congress, and they've slowly been switching to digital. And, they're one of the few companies left in the United States that has the technology to record onto these large spools of tape. Most

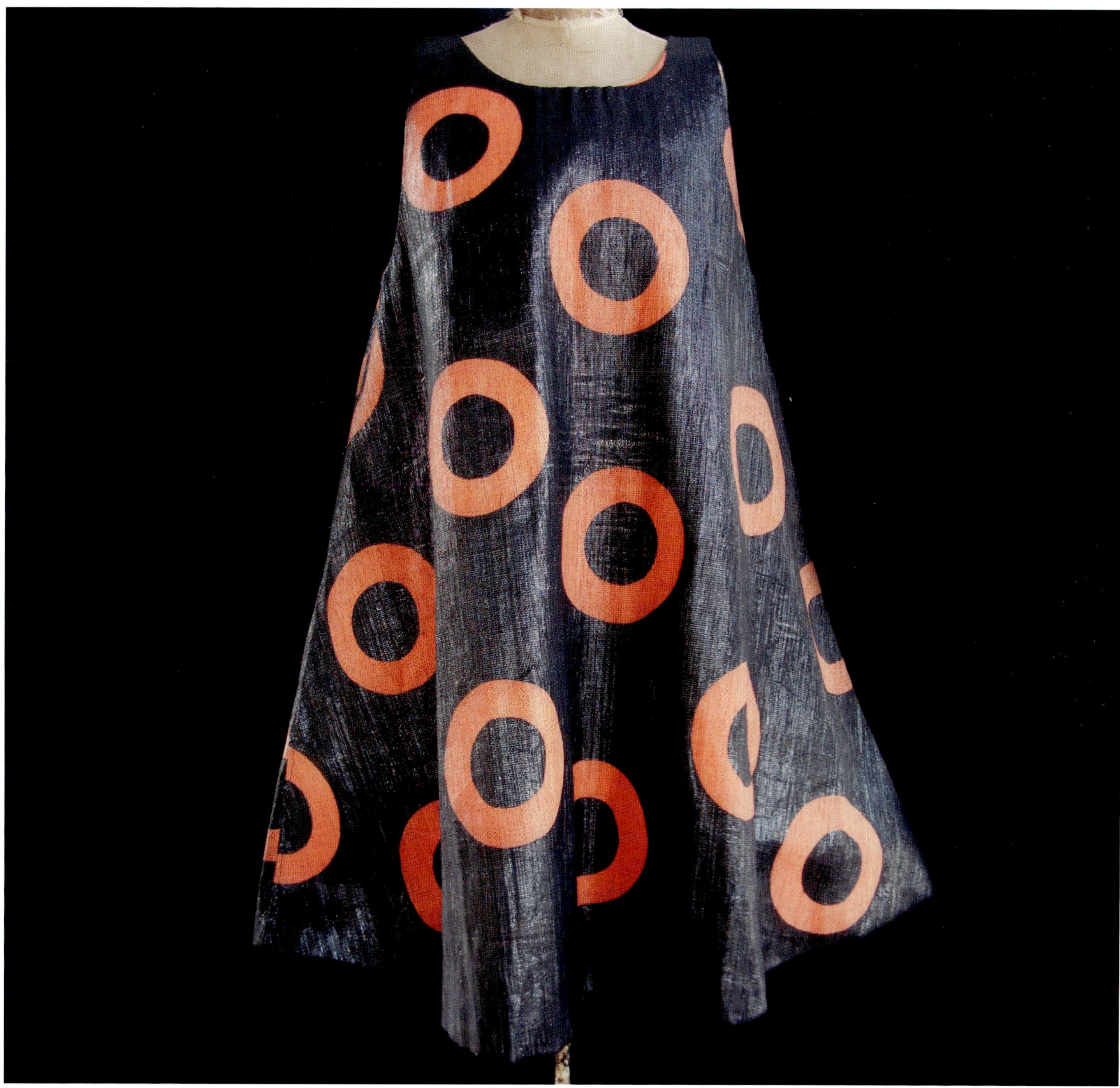

Jon Fishman's Sonic Fabric Rhythm Dress, 2003

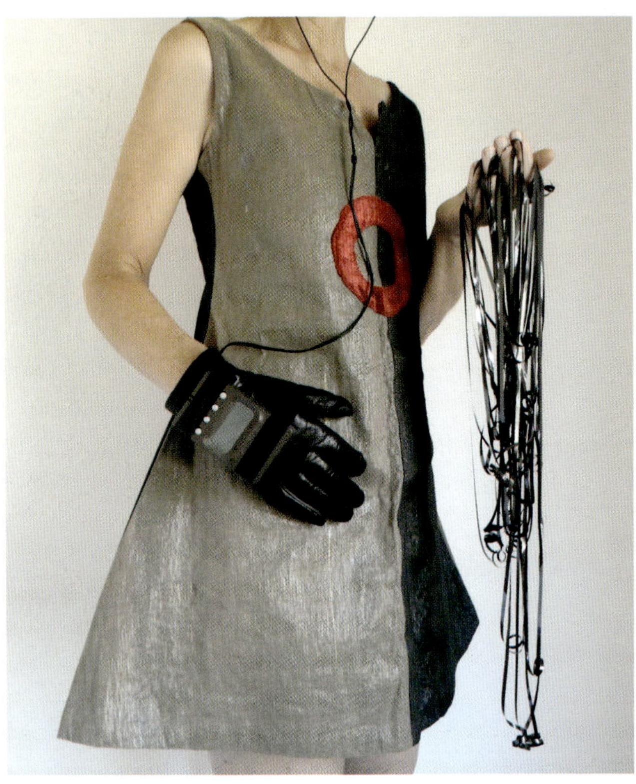

Sonic Superhero Dress #1, 2003

companies today, because they do such small volume, just get tape that has already been made into cassettes and copy directly onto the cassette. So, this company makes the giant spools of tape that are called "pancakes."

MM **Now, you're employing found sound to make the Sonic Fabric. Do you have the pancakes and record directly onto the tape yourself?**

AS I make sound collages digitally. When I first started, I carried a Sony Walkman recorder around with me and recorded the sounds that way. Then I would use an analog four track I've had since high school to make the layered collages. Now, I record digitally and then I create the sound collages digitally. I have this huge collection of samples that I use to make the collages. I just made one, "the calls to prayer." It's crickets and frogs, and the Muslim call to prayer, and Tibetan monks, all of these kinds of things, and I sit down and I make music out of the samples, carefully weaving them together so that it takes you from one sound to another. Then, all I do is email that track to the company and they are extremely meticulous in the details. Do I want the collage on both sides of the tape going in one direction? Do I want it on both sides of the tape going in opposite directions? They will record a forty-five-minute collage over, and over, and over again, and then those spools get shipped to the factory in Rhode Island where they are woven.

MM **Okay, you are partnering with the company. So, their interest in this is that this is becoming a redundant technology; they would be throwing these pancakes out because no one is using them anymore.**

AS Right.

MM **So, at the factory, on the loom, are you a part of that process, or how do you instruct them?**

AS Well, Millcraft Rhode Island, they are a specialty mill that weaves with odd materials: monofilament, rattan, et cetera. When I went to them, it was just amazing that they were just north of Providence and I could go to them with the tapes and they didn't think I was nuts for trying to weave with tape. It took them a couple of years to perfect it, and they ended up salvaging a loom from another mill that was going out of business, especially for Sonic Fabric. It's a 1940s Dobby loom with a special shuttle that picks up the tape with this little forked piece and presses it into the shuttle just right, gently pulling the tape across the warp. It's an incredible process. I've seen it, but I don't work directly anymore. Now I call up and they ask me what I want, what color I want. It then takes them about a week to thread the loom; it's a very complicated process. I have to do about 250 yards at a time, so usually it's when I have a commission.

MM **And the color comes from the polyester thread.**

AS Yes, well, I can choose from black tape or brown tape and then I usually use a black warp, but we can use a blue warp. I've only ever used a black warp with the brown tape, but with the black tape I've used blue, gray, plum—I've used a whole array of different colors. In fact the one set of sailboat sails that has the stripes, that's actually cotton thread, and each color is based on a sound wavelength to light wavelength conversion. Each color stripe represents a musical note. So, in a sense, that's a musical score. The musical score isn't woven into the fabric, it's on the surface.

MM **Is Buddhism something that influences a lot of your work? Do you have other philosophical influences that impact the Sonic Fabric? You've talked about Buddhism, you've talked about quantum physics, are there others?**

AS There is a lot of crossover, I think, between Buddhism and physics, but I think those are the main two for Sonic Fabric. Buddhism definitely influences my work. I don't consider myself a Buddhist per se, but I've done a lot of studying with Tibetan Buddhism, especially, and to me it just fits in with what I'm thinking about a lot of things.

MM **Are there artists who are influencing your work?**

AS Well, definitely Beuys.

MM **And with Beuys you said earlier, it was about forging a completely new way when perhaps people are not yet ready for it.**

AS Yes, well, I think Beuys recognized that there were parts of society that were not constructive or healthy, so a lot of his work was about trying to ritually create new ways of being. I feel like once we recognize that there are problems with society, we can begin to solve them by taking a step. That step could be a ritual, like planting trees or sitting in a gallery and trying to commune with a coyote. He's doing these things that are not necessarily directly solving the problem, but they are sinking into our subconscious. I think a lot of time the subconscious is where the work gets done.

MM **So how does Sonic Fabric fit in with that?**

AS Well, I feel that it's one of these things I make called "philosoprops." I make these philosoprops as a way of demonstrating that we are all connected at the most basic level. When we run the tape head over it, we get what I call an "exquisite cacophony." That's what I feel we all are as a culture, a society, a global community. That's what you get when you run the tape head over it—it's garbled. Everyone always asks me, "Oh, can I hear a word?" To me, that's not important. To me, what's important is the mixture of all the sounds. That's what we're all emitting as we go through life; it's a very subtle thing. If you tune in to the subtleties of the world around us, that's where the real beauty is.

MM **So each time you weave new Sonic Fabric, do you think of that as an edition?**

AS Yes. For instance, that first edition of Sonic Fabric was made up of my favorite influences from Laurie Anderson, to Bjork, to John Coltrane, to Allen Ginsberg. Then I did an edition for the Cidade da Cultura de Galicia that was all the sounds of northwestern Spain, and an edition for the drummer of the band Phish. So, each edition of the fabric is like an album.

MM **Is that a collaboration with each of those entities? Do they have influence on the sounds collected?**

AS Yes, yes definitely, and that has been such an amazing part that I could never have expected. Working with John Fishman, he just gave me his three hundred favorite tapes with people like Jimi Hendrix, and Phish, and Sun Ra. It was such an honor and privilege to go through someone's personal collection of tapes. This happens all the time. People just give me tapes all the time.

I used to work with individual tapes more often because I had a connection with these Tibetan refugee women in Nepal who would hand weave editions of fabric. It's such an amazing thing to look through someone's sonic history; that they would trust me with what influenced them. When we worked in Galicia, sixty tracks of sound were donated from all different entities, from traditional music, folk music that is very Celtic there, bagpipes, and a hurdy-gurdy, to Galician rock bands and classical music. These were all woven together. In fact, I didn't collect any of those sounds. They were all sounds that were donated. Then I got to go there, meet some of these people; we jammed with them. Then, that edition of fabric was made into garments inspired by the traditional dress of the region by the students at the University of Vigo. It was a wonderful cultural exchange.

MM **So, how involved are you in the construction of Sonic Fabric garments? Are you doing the tailoring yourself?**

AS Some of the early ones I did sew. Some of them my mom sewed. I have a dear friend in New York, Julio Cesar, who does a lot of it. I basically call him up with a vision, draw it out, and he makes it for me. He's much better at sewing than I am. When I was doing it, it was all A-line dresses; that was my skill level.

MM **So the fabric works as an index, or archive. What we discard is perhaps the greatest index of our lives and civilization. Do you see the fabric as a type of archive.**

AS Absolutely. When I first made it, I had no idea it would be playable. To me, then, it was this idea that you were capturing a moment in human history. It's literally like a silent, captured moment. Really the important part to me was imagining what was on the tape. The fact that you can have playback is interesting, but not as interesting to me as the fact that you are literally holding captured sound.

MM **So how did you discover it was playable? Was it by accident?**

AS Yes, it was sort of by accident. Louise Bourgeois used to have these salons on Sundays, and you could go if another artist invited you. When I first moved to New York a friend gave me the number for Louise and I called her up and she answered the phone, and it was amazing. I got to go to one of her salons. I get there, I have my two pieces of fabric and she calls me up to talk to her, and she said, "Well, what does it do?" And off the top of my head I said, "Well, it's for rituals." And then she said, "Do a ritual." So there was cognac—everyone was drinking—so I splashed some cognac on the floor, and I put the two pieces of fabric down, and I asked everyone in the room to pick an object and to think of a wish and then put the object down on the Sonic Fabric. I chanted "Om" over it, and then handed back the objects to each person. The objects were now empowered. So, another person at the salon said to me, "I bet that's playable." And I said, "What?!" And he said, "Yeah, we'll just go get a Walkman and unscrew the heads." So he told me exactly what to do, and I went home and, sure enough, the fabric made sounds.

MM **Wow, that is not at all what I expected when I asked that question. That's fantastic. It all came out of one of Louise Bourgeois's salons.**

AS It totally did.

MM **That's great. I'm a little discombobulated now. I think maybe we should end with Louise, there's really no way to top that.**

AS [*laughs*] Exactly!

Sonic Fedoras, 2007

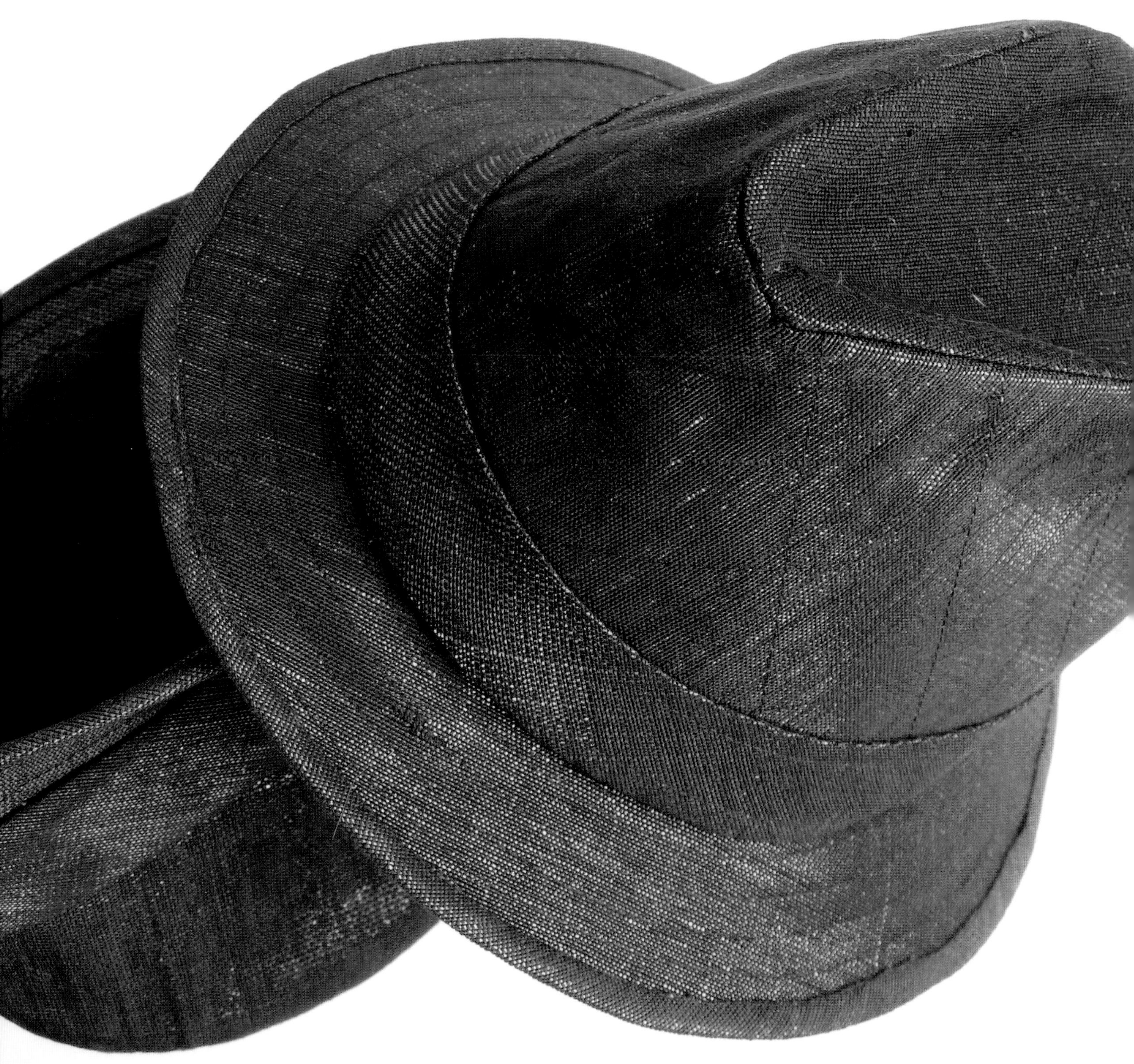

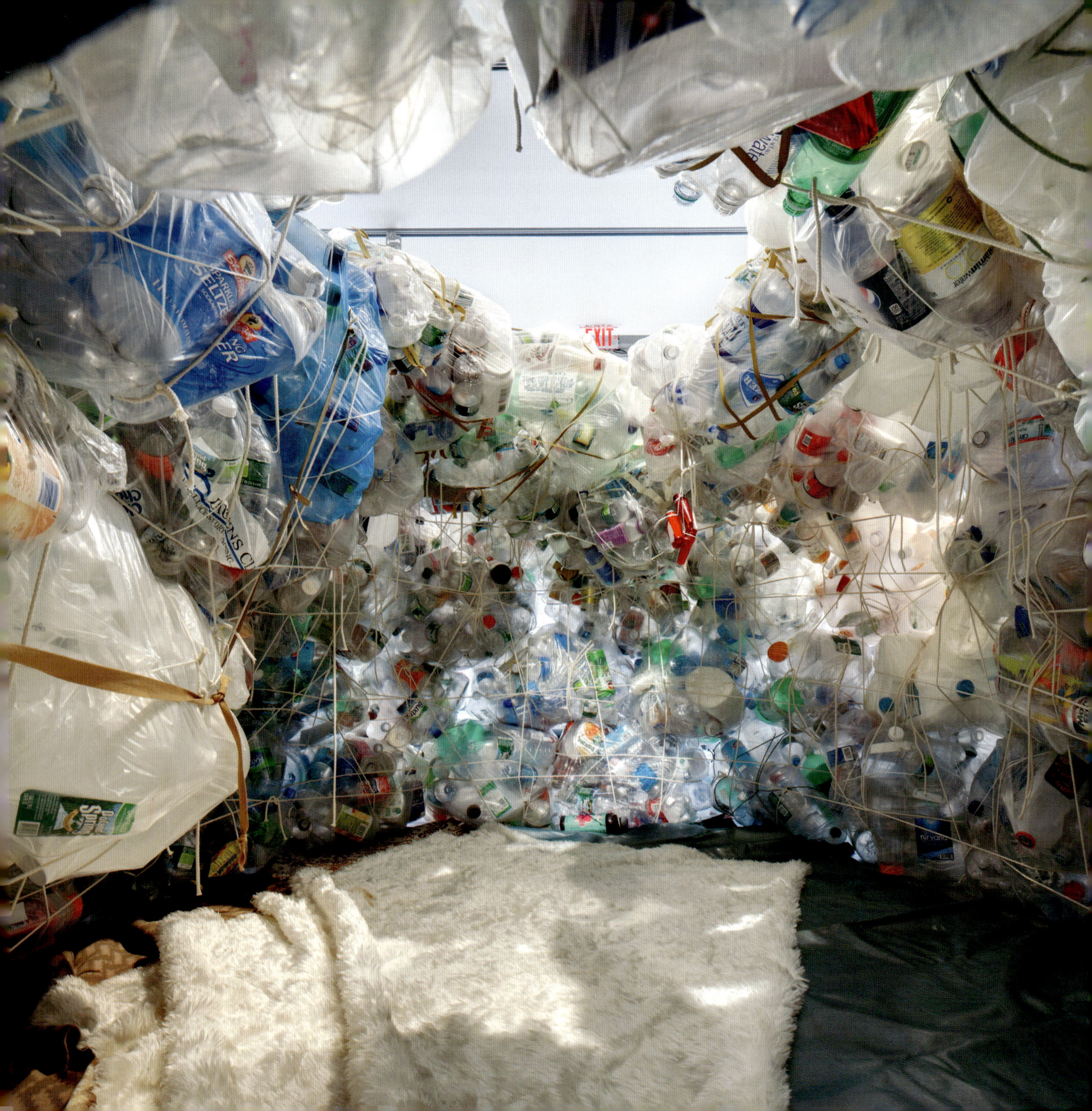
SELTZER
EXIT

Jill Sigman (b. 1967) asks questions through the medium of the body. Trained in classical ballet, modern dance, art history, and analytic philosophy, Sigman has been making dances and performance installations since the early 1990s. She is artistic director of jill sigman/thinkdance, which she founded in 1998, the same year in which she received her PhD in philosophy from Princeton University. Sigman is based in New York City and has been a fellow at the Center for Creative Research at New York University, a creative campus fellow at Wesleyan University, a choreographic fellow at the Maggie Allesee National Choreographic Center (MANCC), and a movement research artist in residence. She has made work for stages, galleries, abandoned buildings, armories, fences, drained swimming pools, bus stations, remote roads, and public parks. Sigman's work often involves audience interaction.

Jill Sigman

MATTHEW McLENDON **You began life as a dancer. How did you start dancing?**

JILL SIGMAN I wanted to dance starting way back. I was always very physical, and when I was a kid I read a biography of the ballerina Maria Tallchief (a Native American ballerina who rose to stardom working with George Balanchine) and I was hooked. I started taking ballet at age seven and studied intensively at the Ballet Center of Brooklyn and the Joffrey Ballet for the next eleven years. I began to study modern dance and eventually choreography in college, at Princeton with Ze'eva Cohen. And at first that was a difficult road—to shed the aesthetics of swans and princesses and all that I had been taught as a dancer, in search of new ways of being real and physical in the body. I was horrified by the ugliness of the movement and I would cry when I got home from class. But a dancer always wants to dance, so mystifyingly, I kept going. Something happened when I started reading Nietzsche. I was studying Humphrey technique (a modern dance technique created by one of the mothers of American modern dance, Doris Humphrey) and reading Nietzsche's *Birth of Tragedy*, which talks about the opposite impulses of Dionysian loss of self and Apollinian self-individuation. Humphrey's use of fall and recovery is based on her interpretation of these two poles. And suddenly it all made sense to me—how ideas could be physicalized and we could think through movement . . . how it wasn't just all swans any more.

MM **Is this history still there in your work in some way?**

JS Well, my work has migrated quite far from that beginning, but I guess I still always consider myself a dancer/choreographer first. Whatever I do, I see it that way, as an exploration of ideas through movement in space. Sometimes it's my own movement; sometimes it's the movement of materials; sometimes it's the movement of the public. But I am working with movement and helping us relate to the spaces we are in. Helping to create charged spaces so that we can be present in them.

And I guess my history has influenced me in that I know magic from way back. I love magic. The tree growing at the

Hut #8, interior, 2012

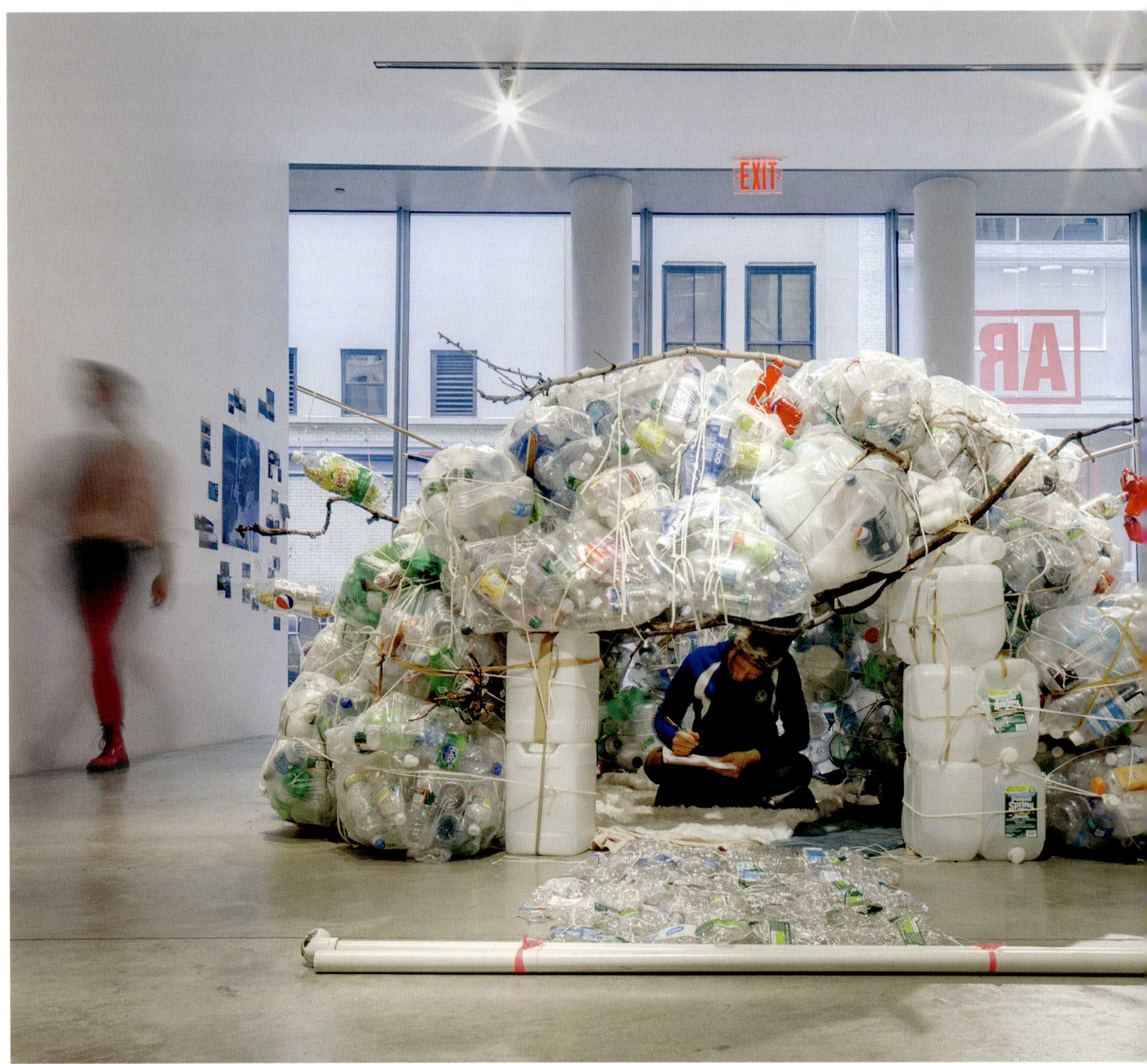
EXIT

end of Act 1 of New York City Ballet's *Nutcracker.* I love that tree. And my huts are my DIY version of that tree—a little sinister, a little magical, devoid of the consumerist trappings of the earlier version.

Because we don't have a category for that—art that is like the tree growing—my work ends up being considered "multi-disciplinary," an amalgam of dance, installation, and social practice. But for me these categories don't really make sense. It all seems like one thing.

MM **Before beginning *The Hut Project*, you were making small bundles, assemblages of wax and twigs, and old costumes, et cetera. Why did you make these? Where did these come from?**

JS Yes. I had made a dance piece called *ZsaZsaLand* in 2009. And for that show I also made an environment embodying the cultural contrasts I was exploring—technicolor fake consumer paradise and abject, physical objects that seemed like parts of bodies or bodily processes. There were knots of cast-off, dirty fabric dipped in reddish wax that looked like some sort of weird growths.

Anyway, after *ZsaZsaLand*, I was interested in how the artistic process could swallow its own detritus. I had all this crap. And what do we do with post-performance materials? We store them or we throw them away. But how could I feed them to my own process? So I started wrapping them—making these bundles of my own stuff that were wrapped in bandages and stray plastic and wax and otherwise sealed up in a sort of alchemical way. I was more interested in the wrapping and sealing, the containment, than in the form or revealing the contents. I began thinking about Vodou *paquet congo* and how these empowered objects derive their power from what they contain, the parts we don't see. I was interested in the histories of the objects I wrapped.

MM **What brought about the first hut?**

JS Well, then I started wrapping myself, too—becoming part of the assemblages and creating a moving component to the

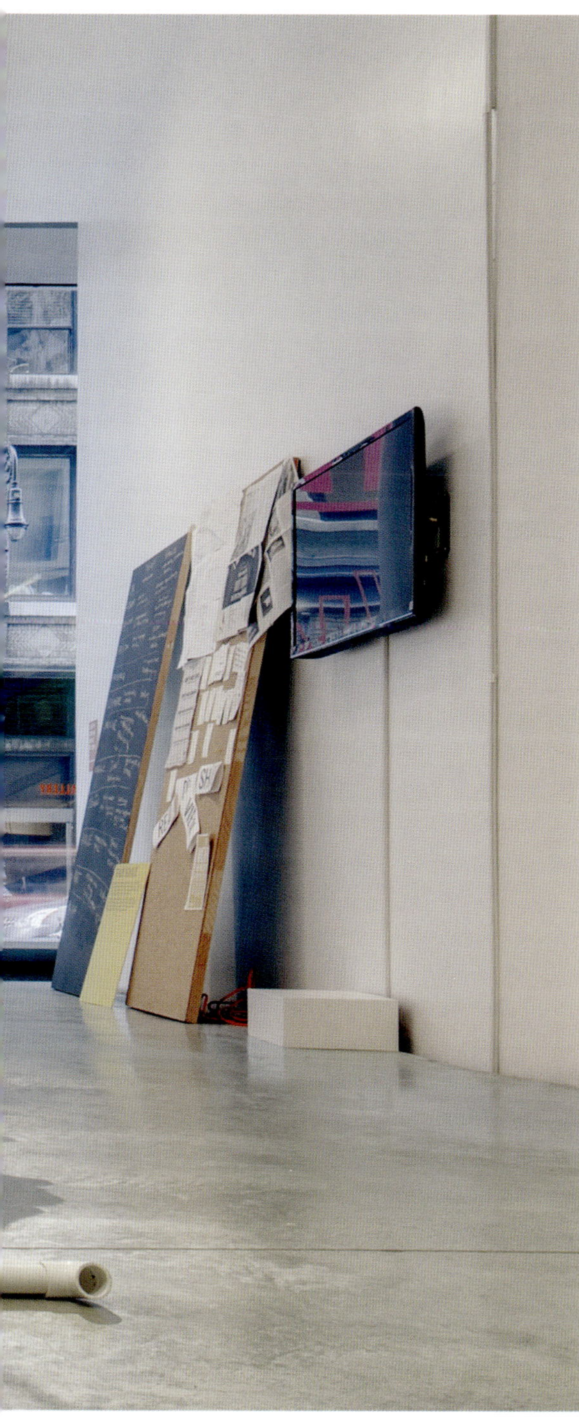

Hut #8, 2012

system. Like being part of a weird post-apocalyptic sundial. I made a piece called *Nu-Gro* for Movement Research. But then I began to want to wrap the audience, too, to wrap the container we were in, to hold the whole performance process in this bandaging that is both creepy and loving.

I also had this experience in which I made a portable performance installation about trash with composer Kristin Norderval (*Our Lady of Detritus*) and we toured around four NYC boroughs for six weeks to public sites like Van Cortlandt Park in the Bronx and Port Authority Bus Terminal. And that performance did something I wanted to do; it took the walls of the theater away and made the art open to everyone. And I was happy with the politics of that, the way it democratized who could see the work. But in another way I missed the walls. As a performance, it was so diffuse, and I realized one of the reasons why we have a theater—because we need a container for the magic. So how can we have a container that is still open and egalitarian in spirit?

MM **So where was the first hut located?**

JS First I built a structure out of found materials in my studio and just sat in it for a long time. It was a refuge. The first two huts weren't public. They were just about understanding what a container is, how these objects can hold the space. In movement we have this expression "holding the space" and I was wondering how I can get these objects to hold the space the way I do. But then I started to figure that out and they became public spaces and I was interested in the idea that once there is a place, people gather. They want to do things there—like have rehearsals for their rock band or hold staff meetings.

So I began to think of the huts as containers—for performance, and community discussions, and tea, and cooking with reclaimed food, and growing things, and workshops. I don't think there has to be one purpose; I think the beauty of it is in the holism and the fact that when people do things in a hut they have a different relation to the space and their own bodies and each other and their ideas about what is possible. And when I serve them tea, they are guests and not "audience" and that empowers them in a different way.

MM **Why are the huts a site of performance for you? How does the hut inform the performance?**

JS I think the huts are physically charged—through the physical processes of collecting the objects and building with them. I touch everything that I pull out of the trash to build with. Often I know the story behind it, or at least where I found it. So performance begins with the creation of the hut; that is a performative act. And then it follows naturally to do more—to activate the space, to let movement make the space around the hut the way a planet has a gravitational field. Sometimes I do that through my own movement, which is more purposeful in its choice-making. Other times I do that through the mass movement of the public. Many people having tea, and talking about home can charge a space, too!

MM **So, then, do the huts take on the narratives of their surroundings as well?**

JS There was one hut at Arts@Renaissance that was built in the basement of the former Greenpoint Hospital. It was a space with a lot of history—people's medical traumas, an abrupt hospital closing, the creation of a men's homeless shelter, a battle between the neighborhood and the city. The showers were still in place. The tiled morgue was still there. The neighborhood was dotted with waste transfer stations, and the garbage I collected was dirty and laced with a sense of toxicity. I ended up wrapping it into eighty-eight packages, sort of like medicine bundles, to contain the toxicity. This was a very physical process. When it came to dancing, all I felt I could do was circle around and around the hut, tilling the soil in some kind of kinesthetic way. My movements changed continually in response to how each part of the space felt from the bundles and the architecture. After an hour of circling, I moved out onto the adjacent abandoned

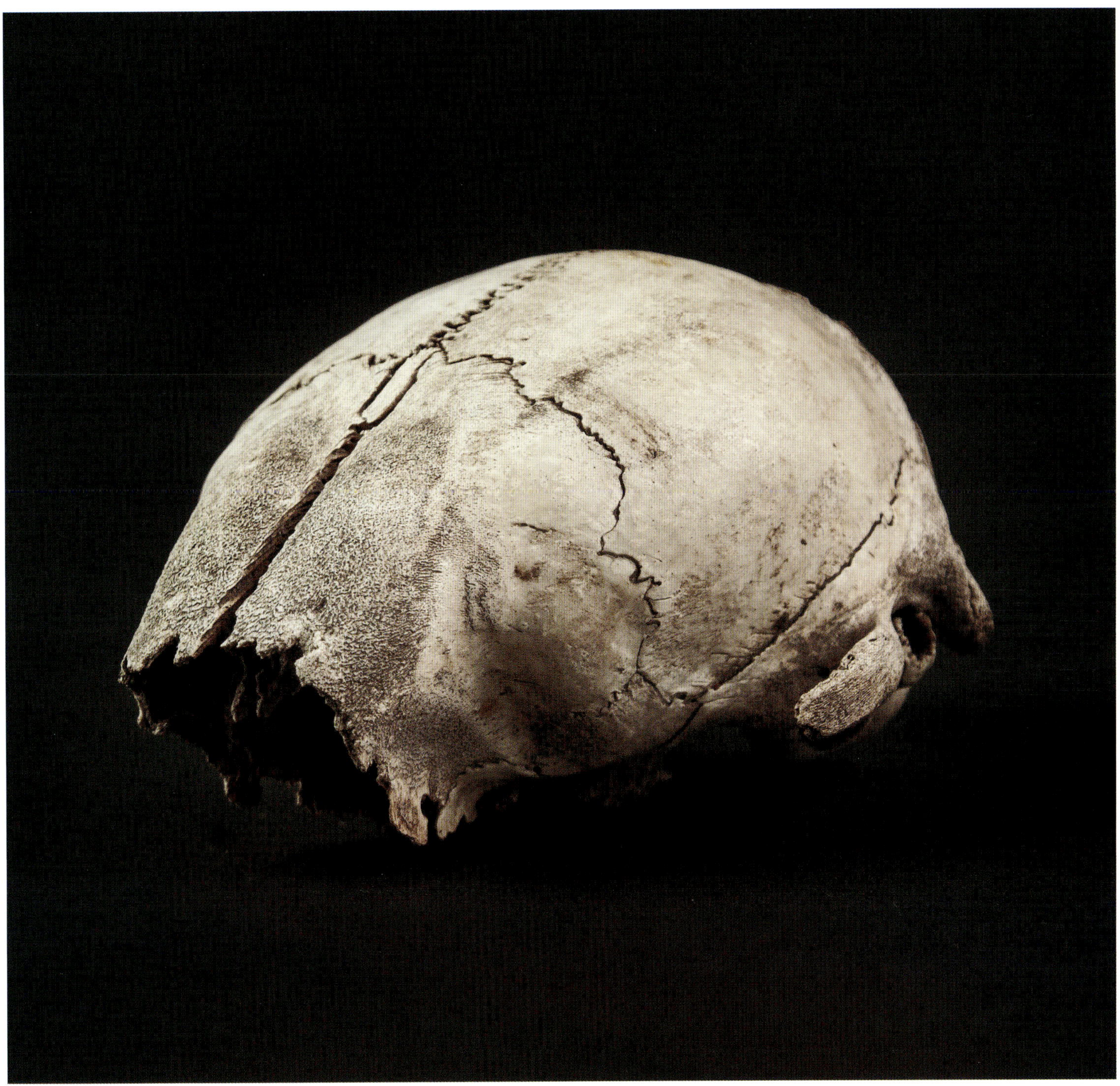

Animal skull collected by the artist as the first object for *Hut #10*, 2013

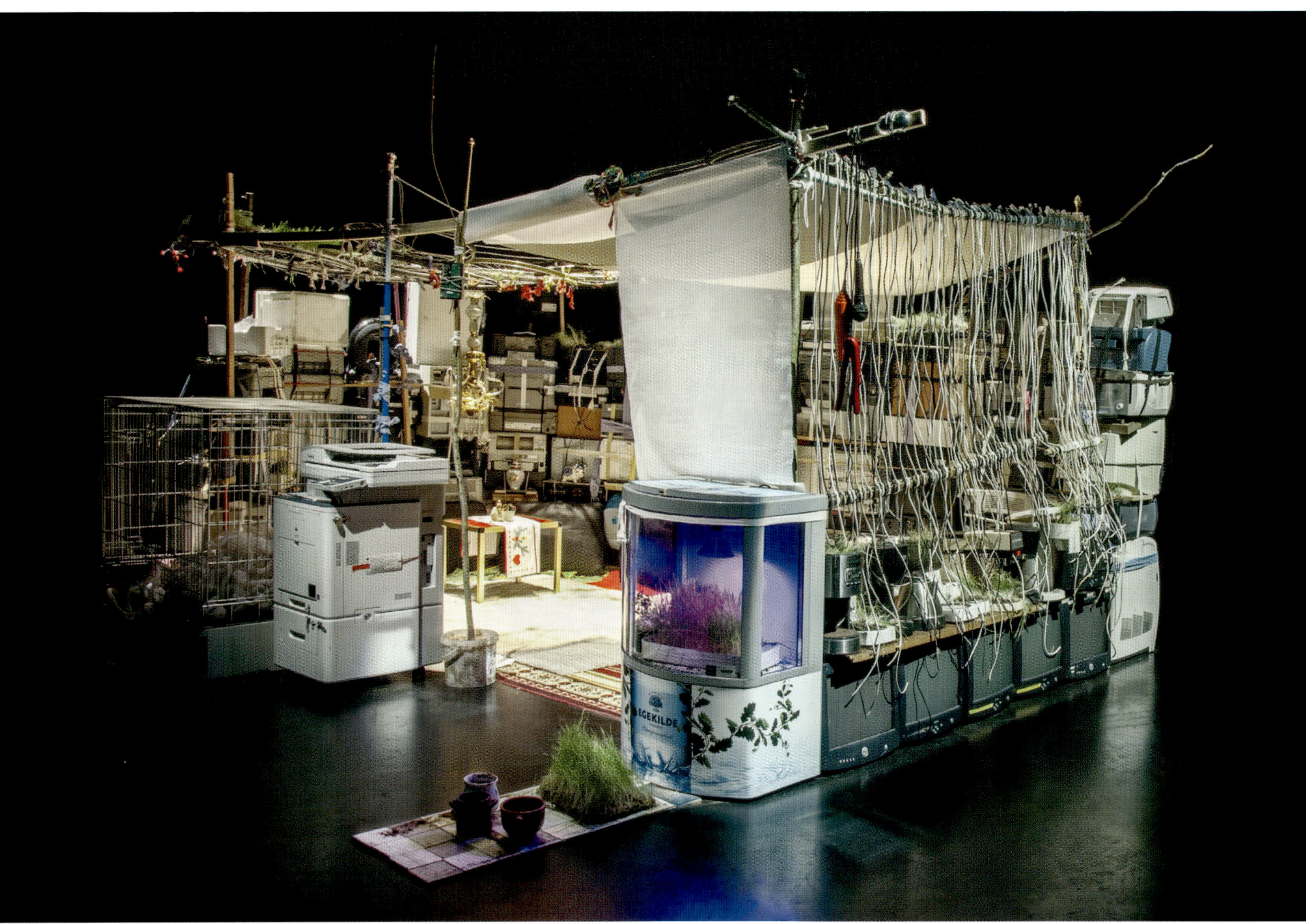

Hut #9, 2014

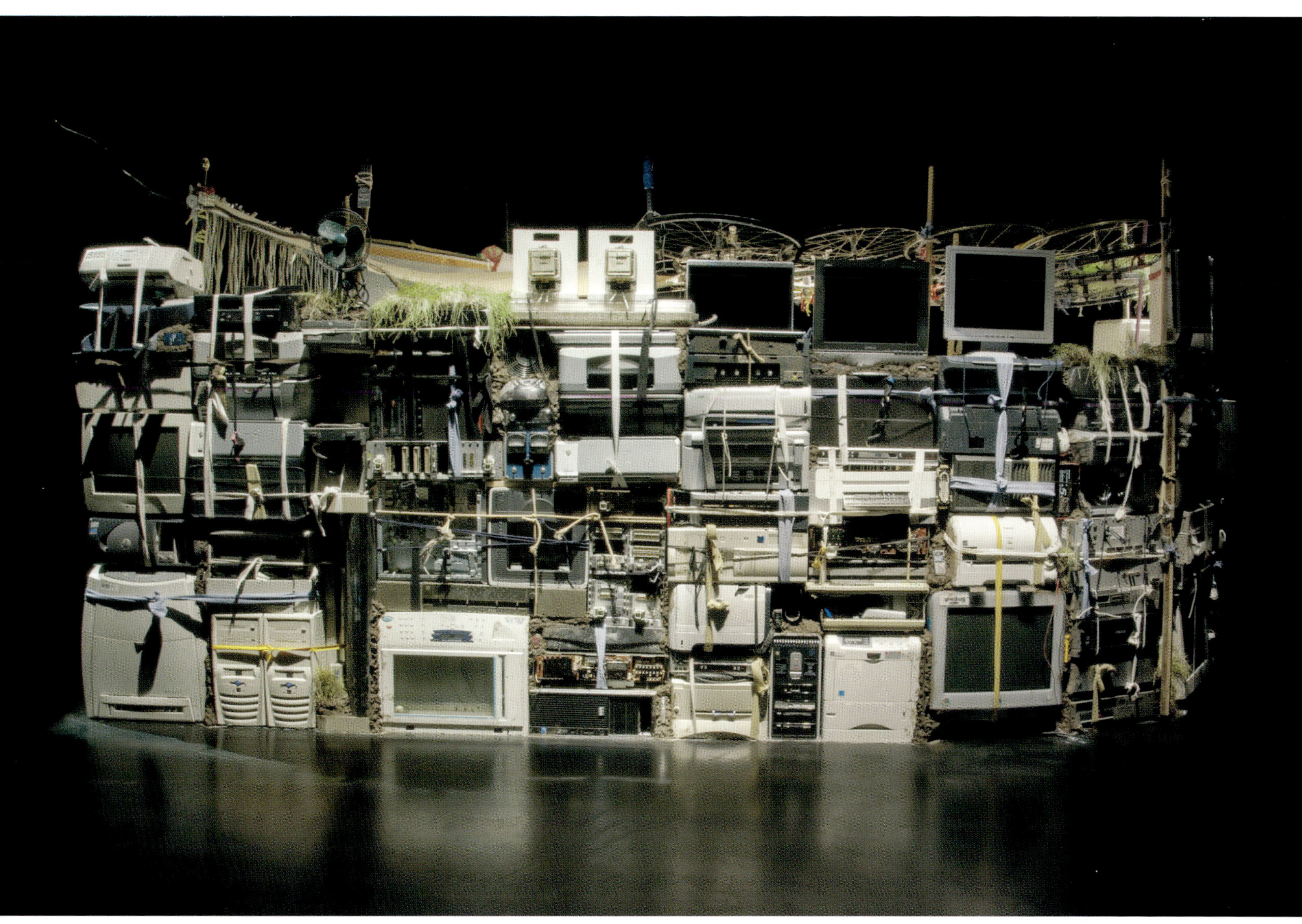

Hut #9, 2014

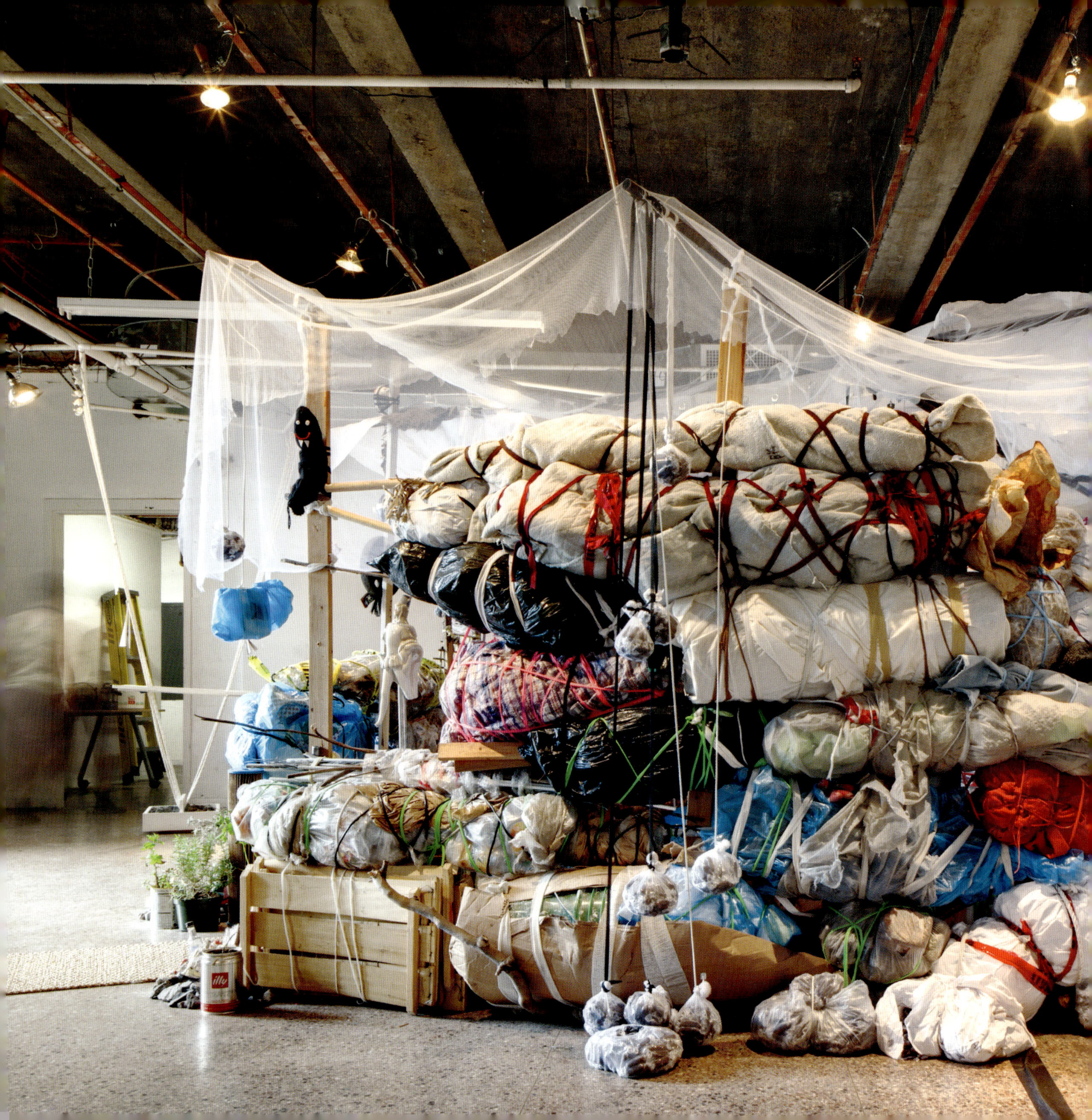
illy

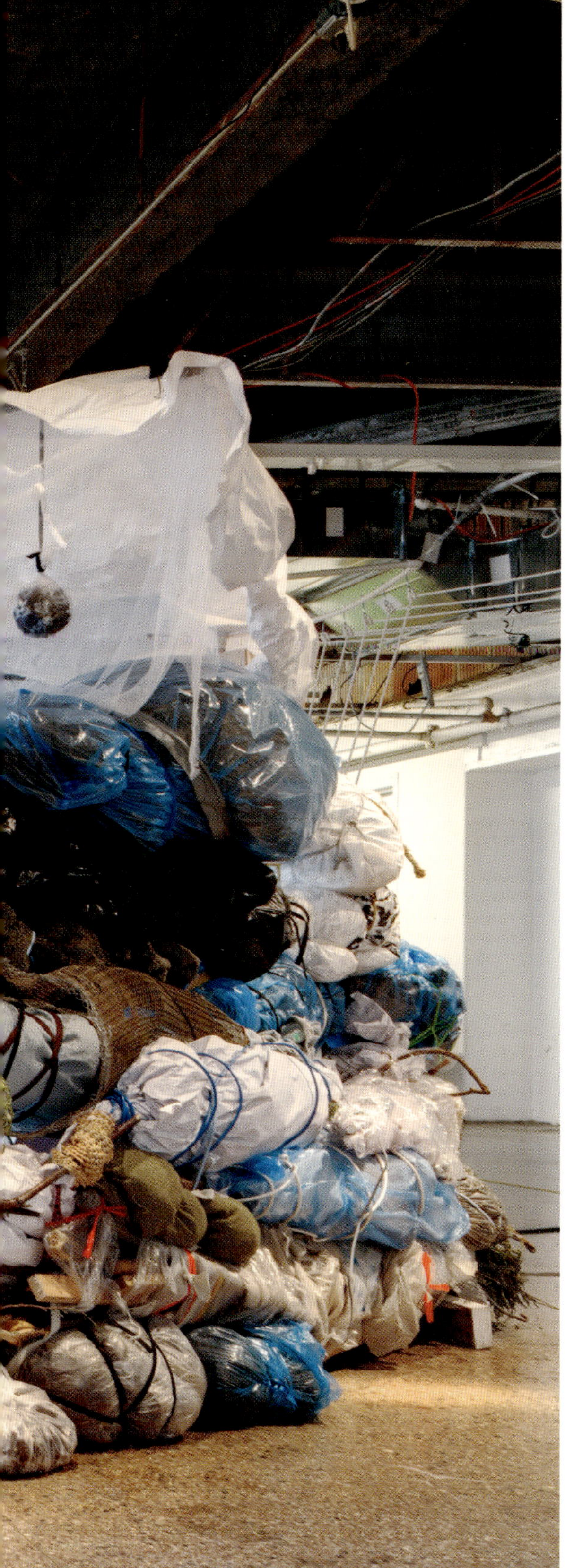

lot carrying a light on a pole and slowly, slowly walked the perimeter of the lot. To my surprise, the audience followed me all the way around! We were watched by men in the current homeless shelter on one side and people on the balconies of their luxury condos on the other. We had literally made a place, and a bridge, out of this "dead" space!

MM **The huts are made from "waste," "garbage," "detritus." First of all, is this how you think of the building materials?**

JS Well, I see them as resources. What is "garbage" or not of value in one context might be the perfect thing in another. It's about function and need. For example, in Norway I found many discarded skis. While their owners didn't want them, they made great tent poles for the lavvu structure I was starting to develop. At the end of each hut, I try to re-elevate the objects I've used back into the realm of value through "free stores" and underground economies. Usually I can give away at least 85 percent. I think art is about helping people to re-see the things around them, in this case quite literally!

MM **Not to be pedantic, but why are the huts created from cast-off objects? Why did you choose to use that material?**

JS Because there's a lot of it! No, seriously . . . waste is ubiquitous. I started finding all this waste near my studio in Bushwick, Brooklyn, and at first I thought, "Great, free materials" [*laughs*]. And then it just kept coming and I realized how that stream is always there, 24/7, in most parts of the world. And I started looking further and realized that my studio is on the border of a neighborhood that processes 40 percent of NYC's waste. And that I am right near a litter-clogged tributary of Newtown Creek, a hush-hush Superfund site polluted by years of oil seepage. So I started to realize the iconographic nature of this trash, the environmental nature of this trash, the cultural nature of this trash.

At one point I found about four hundred ACE bandages and I kept using them in hut after hut—because they are a great binding material and because the huts seem wounded in

Hut #7, 2012

some way, or maybe like manifestations of something larger that is wounded. Now I've finally run out of bandages and I usually tear up old clothes that I find, so the wrapping seems even more desperate in a way.

MM **So, is this also about environmental issues for you? Is it about consumption?**

JS Just because they use trash, the huts are not a commercial for recycling. I am also careful that they don't just become an apologia for our consumption—cute or pretty things you can do with the too many non-biodegradable products you throw away. At bottom, we need to think about where all this stuff comes from, why we have it in the first place. Maybe if we sit in a structure that's made of it and have some tea, maybe if we imagine the luxury condos of the future on the polderland of the Great Pacific Garbage Patch, we'll have a chance to take in the vastness of all our stuff. And how it never really goes away. This is also where the physicality comes in. If you really have a physical connection to something, if you are physically present to it, you don't just destroy it; you live in relation to it.

MM **We've been talking together about your huts for more than a year at this point. One thing you said when we were having coffee one day was that you viewed the huts as a poly-narrative as opposed to the mono-narrative stressed by dominant, commodity culture? Can you elaborate on that? I'm not sure I totally understood what you meant.**

JS Well, this is part of what's behind the low-tech, DIY aesthetic—using what is at hand is a way of resisting planned obsolescence on all fronts, unmaking a consumer culture. And it has a kind of illicit quality. Amazing that we have gotten to a point where things like noncomplicity in a mainstream culture of buying, or revealing our waste and stripping the gloss off of consumerism, somehow seem obscene or illicit. Something interesting to talk about is the connection between trash and technology. I built *Hut #9* out of e-waste in Aarhus, Denmark. Among the electronic artifacts that I found in less than two weeks were fifty discarded printers! Our infatuation with technology is a guarantee of a trash stream, given the practices of scheduled obsolescence and the current hungry markets (some not so well-regulated) for electronics recycling.

MM **When I look at them, I feel that there is a post-apocalyptic quality to the huts. Is this something you've thought of?**

JS Sure. The funniest thing someone said to me about one of the huts was, "When the shit goes down, I wanna be on your team. I'll kill and you build!" [*laughs*] I loved it. I sometimes joke that the huts are a dress rehearsal for the future, or a kind of emergency preparedness kit. But really, I think it has to do with this idea of re-seeing. Imagine a re-take on our culture, something that wipes the slate clean so we don't know what an Apple laptop box or a tampon applicator or an IV bag are. And we think that these things are so carefully made and so enduring that they must have been very important objects, like religious fetishes or icons.

I'm kind of obsessed with the question, how would a future without memory imagine us and our objects? And how would it re-invent them? What would a new "primitive" be? Weaving with red licorice strands? Growing micro-crops in soda bottles? Marking your house with a Macintosh mouse box? I make up practices like these to ask how things could evolve.

MM **By constructing a hut, it seems to me you are constructing something at the margins, something outside and, perhaps, uncomfortable. Has this been your experience? Are you comfortable with that?**

JS I guess if you work with trash you have to feel comfortable operating on a margin. You are dealing with a liminal zone, the cusp between people's personal possessions and dead objects, fossils, waste. When you collect trash, people see you differently. You have to be okay with feeling "other" . . . and

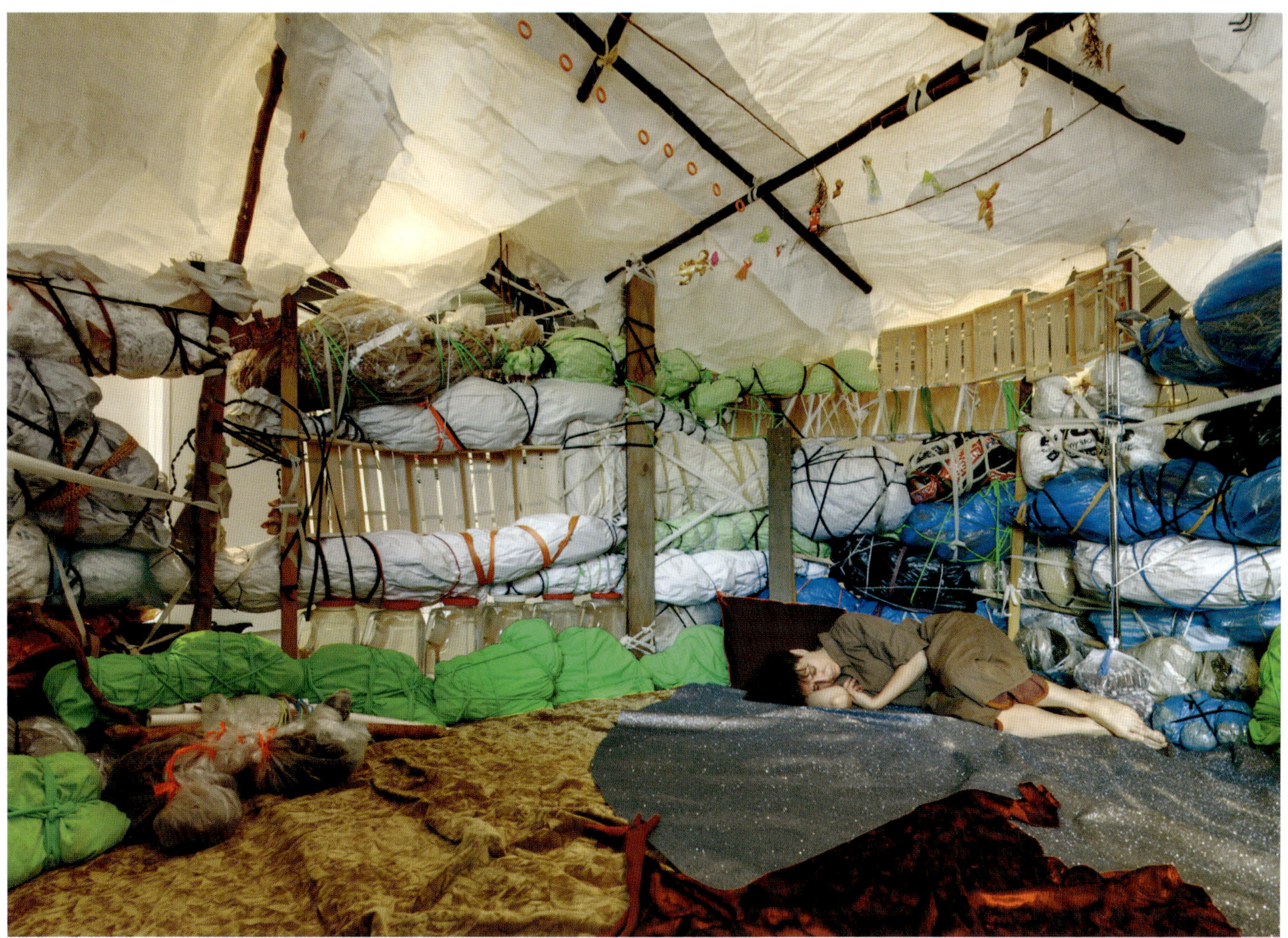

Hut #7, interior, 2012

then inviting the same people into the "home" that you've just built out of their waste and serving them tea!

You know, I think I'm pretty familiar with margins—although maybe not such visible ones. I grew up in Brooklyn in the '70s as a minority white person in a black neighborhood in a time that was racially and politically charged. I went to Princeton, but didn't come from an "Ivy" family. I grew up in a basement, mostly without walls and doors. And of Jewish heritage—from an immigrant culture that rushed to become "white" in this country, denying various histories of oppression and marginalization in exchange for mainstream membership.

So, invisible margins . . . I feel like my work is about revealing—making visible what isn't seen or doesn't make sense. And making it a place. *Making the margin a new place.* You know, I got so excited when I read something that Rirkrit Tiravanija said. He was talking about his place The Land and saying that it's not "a center" and that he is more interested in the multiplication of peripheries. And then he said, "Because the center lies on the outside." I totally get that!

MM **You've also referred to the huts as "outposts." Outposts of what?**

JS I do think of the huts as outposts. Outposts that concretize or make real what is unseen—an un-center. It reminds me of when I first saw Kabakov as a young person—it blew my mind. I had no idea such things could be art, that this kind of unacknowledged experience could be crystallized into something aesthetically valuable, into an artistic "place."

MM **The margin, the outpost, the repurposed discarded, surely there is something of a Queer discourse here, too.**

JS Sure. Art that works with trash as trash will inevitably be Queer art. Dealing in the revelation of invisible things, the breaking of accepted categories, the blurring of boundaries. I am not thinking about the glam, camp aspects of gay culture but about the unrecognizable, the invisible, and the ways representation of that is related to the choice of these nonslick, repurposed means.

In her book *The Queer Art of Failure*, Judith Halberstam keeps talking about failure—failure to reach the goals of amassing wealth and reproducing in a hetero-normative, self-reifying society. She sees failure as a utopian device, a way to imagine new goals for life and ways of being. Failure to "get it right." I think the huts are failures in this sense. They don't meet codes. They can poke you in the eye. They could fall down. They're held together by elastic bands. But they're just as precarious as all the sanctioned practices we take for granted in our own culture. So maybe instead of just being messy or awkward, they actually reveal something to us.

This also makes me think of what she says about collage—how she identifies collage as a mode of aesthetic production that denies the creative manufacture of self, the making of an active feminist subject, and by being about un-being embodies a kind of greater resistance. I feel like the work with trash is really related to this. First of all, it is collage. And second, like collage, trash blurs the boundaries between the object and the objet d'art, the original and its copies, and the self and the other. This un-being or un-becoming—Where is the "real thing?"—gives the lie to glitzy self-promotional ideas of agency and achievement, and acts as a deeper form of resistance to dominant structures that provide illusory rewards. So trash and collage—it's kind of a double whammy.

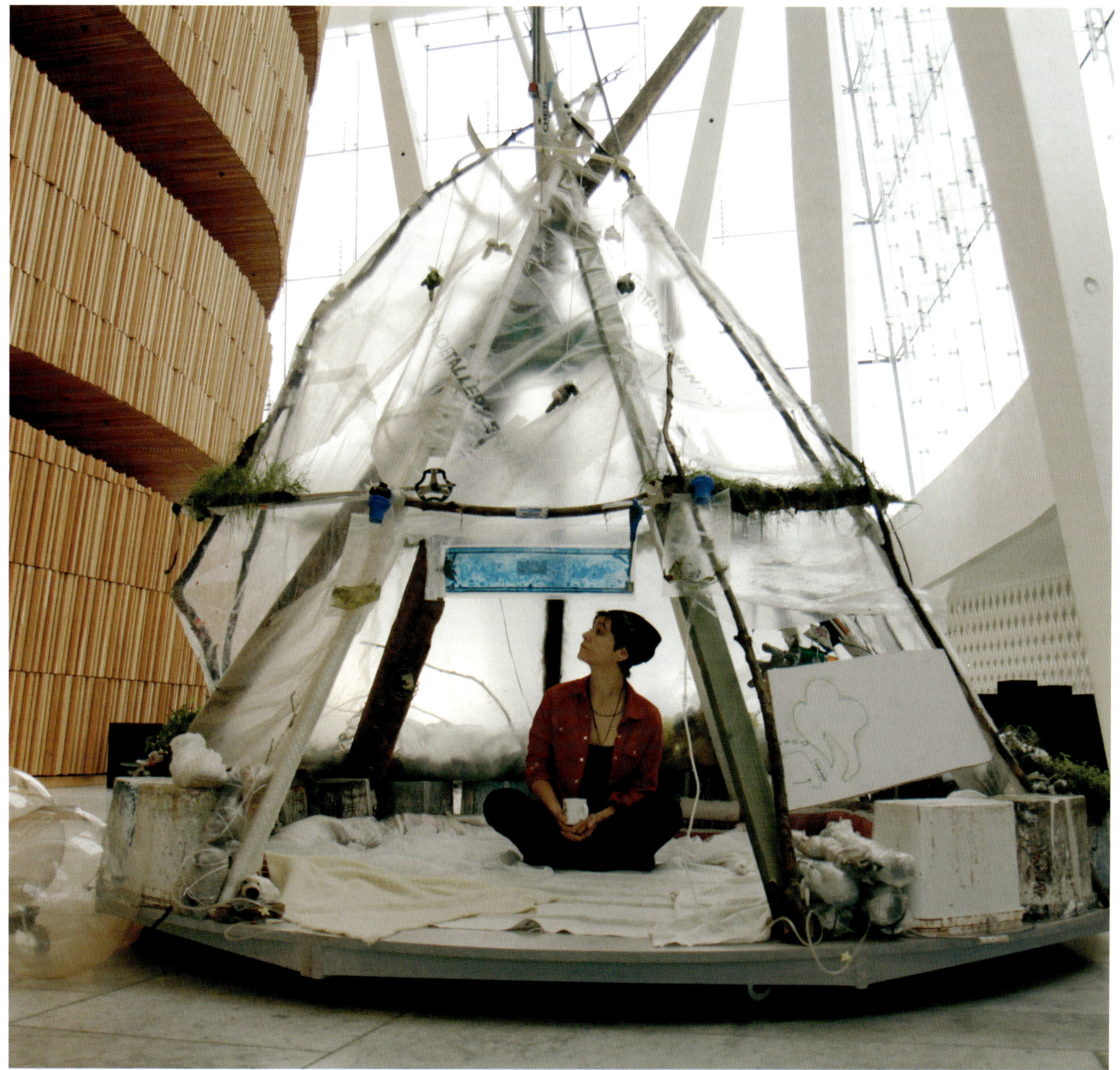

Hut #6, 2011

CAPTIONS

Pgs. 4–5: Aurora Robson, *Everything All At Once, Forever*, 2011, installation comprised of 16 sculptures, plastic debris (PET plastic), including approximately 3,000 bottles and 400 caps, rivets, tinted polycrylic, and mica powder; installed at the Figge Art Museum in Davenport, Iowa. Image courtesy of the artist

Pgs. 6–7: Jill Sigman, *Hut #9* (detail), 2014; Godsbanen, Aarhus, Denmark. Photograph by Elisabeth F. Lund, image courtesy of the artist

Pg. 10: Nick Cave, *Soundsuit*, 2010, dogwood twigs, wire, upholstery, basket and mannequin, 77 × 41 × 40 in., inventory #NC10.003. © Nick Cave. Photograph by James Prinz. Courtesy of the artist and Jack Shainman Gallery, New York

Pg. 12: Mac Premo, *The Dumpster Project*, 2011, mixed media assemblage; DeKalb Market. © Mac Premo. Courtesy of the artist and Pavel Zoubok Gallery, New York

Pg. 14: El Anatsui, *Alter Ego*, 2012, found aluminum and copper wire, 113 × 111 in., inventory #EA12.015. © El Anatsui. Courtesy of the artist and Jack Shainman Gallery, New York

Pg.17: El Anatsui, *Dusasa II*, 2007, found aluminum, copper wire, and plastic disks, 236 × 288 × 2 in. Metropolitan Museum of Art, The Raymond and Beverly Sackler 21st Century Art Fund; Stephen and Nan Swid and Roy R. and Marie S. Neuberger Foundation Inc. Gifts; and Arthur Lejwa Fund, in honor of Jean. © El Anatsui. Courtesy of the artist and Jack Shainman Gallery, New York

Pg. 18: El Anatsui, *Garden Wall*, 2011, aluminum bottle tops and copper wire, approximate installed dimensions: 205 × 209 in. (wall element), 209 × 295 in. (floor element), inventory #EA11.011. © El Anatsui. Courtesy of the artist and Jack Shainman Gallery, New York

Pgs. 20–21: El Anatsui, *Gravity and Grace*, 2010, aluminum bottle tops and copper wire, 145⅝ × 441 in., inventory #EA10.012. © El Anatsui. Courtesy of the artist and Jack Shainman Gallery, New York

Pg. 25: El Anatsui, *Waste Paper Bags*, 2004–10, printed plates (aluminum) and copper, individual measurements: 189 × 140 in., 189 × 136 in., 148 × 136 in., 141¼ × 98⅜ in., 139⅜ × 51⅛ in., 152⅞ × 75⅝ in., 146 × 108¼ in., inventory #EA04.001. © El Anatsui. Courtesy of the artist and Jack Shainman Gallery, New York

Pg. 26: El Anatsui, *Anonymous Creature*, 2009, found aluminum and copper wire, 95 × 240 in., inventory #EA09.002. © El Anatsui. Courtesy of the artist and Jack Shainman Gallery, New York

Pg. 30: Nick Cave, *Soundsuit* (detail), 2008, mixed media, 94 × 35 × 35 in., inventory #NC09.014. © Nick Cave. Photograph by James Prinz Photography. Courtesy of the artist and Jack Shainman Gallery, New York

Pg. 33: Nick Cave, *Soundsuit*, 1998, twig, wire, and metal armature, inventory #NC98.001. © Nick Cave. Photograph by James Prinz. Courtesy of the artist and Jack Shainman Gallery, New York

Pgs. 34–35: Nick Cave, *Soundsuit*, 2008, mixed media, 94 × 35 × 35 in., inventory #NC09.014. © Nick Cave. Photograph by James Prinz Photography. Courtesy of the artist and Jack Shainman Gallery, New York

Pgs. 37: Nick Cave, *Soundsuit*, 2012, dogwood twigs, wire, upholstery, and mannequin, 95 × 32 × 41 in., inventory #NC12.034. © Nick Cave. Photograph by James Prinz. Courtesy of the artist and Jack Shainman Gallery, New York

Pg. 38: Nick Cave, (left) *Soundsuit*, 2011, mixed media, 121 × 42 × 33 in., inventory #NC11.054; (right) *Soundsuit*, 2013, mixed media, including mannequin, fabric, ceramic birds, metal flowers, and antique gramophone, 134 × 58 × 35 in., inventory #NC13.003. © Nick Cave. Photograph by James Prinz. Courtesy of the artist and Jack Shainman Gallery, New York

Pg. 39: Nick Cave, *Soundsuit* (detail), 2010, dogwood twigs, wire, upholstery, basket, and mannequin, 77 × 41 × 40 in., inventory #NC10.003. © Nick Cave. Photograph by James Prinz. Courtesy of the artist and Jack Shainman Gallery, New York

Pg. 41: Nick Cave, *Soundsuit*, 2013, mixed media, including mannequin, metal and wooden chariot, fabric, ceramic birds, and metal flowers, 87 × 65 × 67 in., inventory #NC13.042. © Nick Cave. Photograph by James Prinz. Courtesy of the artist and Jack Shainman Gallery, New York

Pgs. 42–43, Nick Cave, *Soundsuit*, 2013, mixed media, including hats, bags, and rag rugs, 110 × 36 × 32 in., inventory #NC13.030. Photograph by James Prinz. Courtesy of the artist and Jack Shainman Gallery, New York

Pg. 44: Matt Eskuche, *Apocalyptic Permafrost*, 2012, flameworked and powder-coated glass, dimensions variable, © Matt Eskuche. Image courtesy of the artist

Pg. 47: Matt Eskuche, *Brittany Before Noon*, 2008, flameworked glass and oil paint, 17 × 74 × 10 in. © Matt Eskuche. Image courtesy of the artist

Pgs. 48–49: Matt Eskuche, *White Trash*, 2007, flameworked glass and oil paint, 13½ × 27½ × 10 in. Photograph by Ellie Bloom. Collection of Philip and Nancy Kotler

Pg. 50: Matt Eskuche, *There Goes the Neighbourhood*, 2012, flameworked glass, 12 × 12 × 12 in. Photograph by Nathan J Shaulis / Porter Loves Photography. © Matt Eskuche.

Pg. 52: Vanessa German, *Reality Check: To Call the Police Use this Phone*, 2013, mixed media souvenirs of Africa found at the thrift store, 46 × 24 × 14 in. Courtesy of the artist and Pavel Zoubok Gallery, New York

Pg. 55: Vanessa German, *Self Portrait of the Artist with Physicalized Soul*, 2013, mixed media assemblage, 59 × 18¾ × 13 in. Courtesy of the artist and Pavel Zoubok Gallery, New York

Pgs. 56–57: Vanessa German, detail studio photographs. Courtesy of the artist and Pavel Zoubok Gallery, New York

Pg. 58: Vanessa German, *The Story of America in Pictures*, 2013, mixed media assemblage, 43½ × 18 × 21½ in. Courtesy of the artist and Pavel Zoubok Gallery, New York

Pgs. 60–61: Vanessa German, detail studio photographs. Courtesy of the artist and Pavel Zoubok Gallery, New York

Pg. 62: Emily Noelle Lambert, *Curio Logic*, 2014, wood, plaster, steel, acrylic, plaster, and canvas, dimensions variable. Courtesy of the artist and Lu Magnus Gallery, New York

Pg. 65: Emily Noelle Lambert, *Road Path Way*, 2014, acrylic on panel with steel sculpture, 48 × 26 × 7½ in. Courtesy of the artist and Lu Magnus Gallery, New York

Pg. 66: Emily Noelle Lambert, *Triumph*, 2012, wood and acrylic paint, 9 × 24 × 32 in. Courtesy of the artist and Lu Magnus Gallery, New York

Pg. 69: Emily Noelle Lambert, *Fortress*, 2012, wood, plaster, and acrylic, dimensions variable. Courtesy of the artist and Lu Magnus Gallery, New York

Pg. 70: Emily Noelle Lambert, *Grand Whirl Stream*, 2014, acrylic on panel with wooden appendages, 91 × 91 in.; *Desire*, 2014, wood, buoys, acrylic, ceramic, and metal. Courtesy of the artist and Lu Magnus Gallery, New York

Pg. 72: Mac Premo, *The Dumpster Project*, 2011, mixed media assemblage. Photograph by Kacy Jahanbini © Mac Premo. Courtesy of the artist and Pavel Zoubok Gallery, New York

Pg. 75: Mac Premo, *The Dumpster Project* (detail)

Pg. 76: Mac Premo, *Smashbulb (Portrait)*, 2013, mixed media assemblage, 18½ × 8 × 4 in. Photograph by Kacy Jahanbini © Mac Premo. Courtesy of the artist and Pavel Zoubok Gallery, New York

Pgs. 78–79: Mac Premo, *The Dumpster Project* (detail)

Pg. 80: Mac Premo, *Smashbulb (Landscape)*, 2013, mixed media assemblage, 9½ × 18½ × 9 in. Photograph by Kacy Jahanbini © Mac Premo. Courtesy of the artist and Pavel Zoubok Gallery, New York

Pg. 83: Mac Premo, *The Dumpster Project* (detail)

Pg. 84: Aurora Robson, *Thundering Typhoons*, 2013, junk mail and acrylic on panel, 24 × 24 in. Courtesy of the artist.

Pg. 87: Aurora Robson, *Be Like Water*, 2010, approximately 80,000 plastic bottle caps and 9,000 discarded plastic bottles, approximately 25 × 120 × 14 ft. Courtesy of the artist

Pg. 88: Aurora Robson, *Fermi*, 2012, plastic debris (PET & HDPE), tinted polycrylic, rivets and crimping beads, 24 × 36 × 12 in. Courtesy of the artist.

Pg. 90–91: Aurora Robson, *The Great Indoors*, 2008, approximately 15,000 PET bottles, tinted polycrylic, and solar powered LEDs, approximately 16 × 40 × 40 ft. Rice Gallery, Houston, Texas. Courtesy of the artist

Pg. 92: Aurora Robson, *Thundering Typhoons*, 2009, 28 × 28 in., ink and junk mail on paper, Courtesy of the artist.

Pg. 94: Daniel Rozin, *Trash Mirror No. 3*, 2001–11, 500 discarded objects, including motors, video camera, wood, control electronics, and custom software, 76 × 76 × 6 in. Image courtesy bitforms gallery nyc

Pg. 99: Daniel Rozin, *Trash Mirror No. 3*

Pg. 100: Daniel Rozin, *Trash Mirror No. 3* (detail)

Pg. 102: Alyce Santoro, *Tell-Tail Thangkas (Sonic Sails, Musical Score Edition)*, 2007, 9 × 9 feet, sonic fabric, recorded with The Sounds of 1/2 Life sound collage, installation image. Installation Museum of Contemporary Art San Diego. Image courtesy of the artist and Klemens Gasser/Tanja Grunert Gallery

Pg. 104: Alyce Santoro, *Cowl-Necked Jacket*, designed by Koos Van Den Akker, 2003, sonic fabric; recorded with The Sounds of 1/2 Life sound collage. Image courtesy of the artist and Klemens Gasser/Tanja Grunert Gallery

Pg. 105: Alyce Santoro, *Voidness Dress*, 2007, sonic fabric; recorded with The Sounds of 1/2 Life sound collage. Photography by Erik Gould, courtesy of the Museum of Art, Rhode Island School of Design, Providence

Pg. 107: Alyce Santoro, *Jon Fishman's Sonic Fabric Rhythm Dress*, 2003, sonic fabric; recorded with samples from Phish percussionist Jon Fishman's personal cassette collection. Image courtesy of the artist and Klemens Gasser/Tanja Grunert Gallery

Pg. 108: Alyce Santoro, *Sonic Superhero Dress #1*, 2003, sonic fabric, 100 individual cassette tapes. Image courtesy of the artist and Klemens Gasser/Tanja Grunert Gallery

Pg. 110: Alyce Santoro, *Sonic Fedoras*, 2007, sonic fabric; inspired by Joseph Beuys, and constructed by Julio Cesar, recorded with Between Stations sound collage. Image courtesy of the artist and Klemens Gasser/Tanja Grunert Gallery

Pg 112: Jill Sigman, *Hut #8*, interior, 2012; discarded materials collected at or near the site; Sheila C. Johnson Design Center at Parsons The New School for Design, New York. Photograph by Rafael Gamo, courtesy of the artist

Pg. 114: Jill Sigman, *Hut #8*, 2012; Sheila C. Johnson Design Center at Parsons The New School for Design, New York. Photograph by Rafael Gamo, courtesy of the artist

Pg. 117: Animal skull found by the artist on the grounds of The John and Mable Ringling Museum of Art, October 2013; collected by the artist as the first object for *Hut #10*

Pg. 118: Jill Sigman, *Hut #9*, 2014; discarded materials collected at or near the site; Godsbanen, Aarhus, Denmark. Photograph by L2 Lab/Alejandra Ugarte, courtesy of the artist.

Pg 119: Jill Sigman, *Hut #9*, 2014; discarded materials collected at or near the site; Godsbanen, Aarhus, Denmark. Photograph by L2 Lab/Alejandra Ugarte, courtesy of the artist.

Pg. 120: Jill Sigman, *Hut #7*, 2012; discarded materials collected at or near the site; Arts@Renaissance (former Greenpoint Hospital building), Brooklyn, NY. Photograph by Rafael Gamo, courtesy of the artist

Pg 123: Jill Sigman, *Hut #7*, interior, 2012; Arts@Renaissance (former Greenpoint Hospital building), Brooklyn, NY. Photograph by Rafael Gamo, courtesy of the artist

Pg. 125: Jill Sigman, *Hut #6*, 2011; discarded materials collected at or near the site; CODA Oslo International Dance Festival at the Oslo Opera House, Oslo, Norway. Photograph by Elisabeth F. Lund, courtesy of the artist